Published by Human Resource Development Press, Inc.
       22 Amherst Road
       Amherst, Massachusetts 01002
       1-800-822-2801
       413-253-3488

Copyright © 1991

Printed in the United States of America

ISBN 0-87425-157-5

First Printing, April 1991

Production services provided by Susan Kotzin
Editorial services provided by Lisa Wood
Cover Design by Old Mill Graphics

D1126544

TOTAL QUALITY TRANSFORMATIONS:

Optimizing Missions, Methods, and Management

by Dr. Marlene Caroselli

Interviews with

Philip B. Crosby, Founder, Chairman, *Philip Crosby Associates, Inc.*

Kent Kresa, President, CEO, *Northrop Corporation*

William E. Conway, President, *Conway Quality, Inc.*

Colonel Dale A. Misner, Commander, *Department of Defense, Defense Contract Management Area Operations, El Segundo*

Dr. A. Blanton Godfrey, Chairman, CEO, *Juran Institute*

Sharon Sarris, Manager—Community Relations/General Affairs, *New United Motor Manufacturing, Inc. (NUMMI)*

Shirley L. Powell, Quality Assurance—Total Quality Management (TQM) Coordinator, *AiResearch-Los Angeles Division of Allied-Signal*

Mark E. Crumly, Chairman, *American Society for Quality Control*

William B. Bullock, Vice President, Operations, *Lockheed Aeronautical Systems Company*

Carl G. Thor, President, *American Productivity and Quality Center*

Mark A. Apicella, Chairman, CEO, *United Security Industries*

Dr. David Nadler, President, *Delta Consulting Group*

To Dr. W. Edwards Deming,
with appreciation for the transformations
you have wrought in my interior landscapes

ACKNOWLEDGMENTS

When busy people try to contact busier people, the result is often "telephone circuitousness." I thank the following individiuals for their efficiency in helping me arrange interviews and/or providing me the information I needed for this book.

Laura Sutherland, Administrative Assistant to Dr. Juran

Jenny Edwards, Administrative Assistant to Dr. Godfrey

Sharon Conway-Hall, Private Seminar Coordinator for Conway Quality, Inc.

Deborah Eifert, Research Assistant for Philip Crosby

Alice Fernandez, Associate in the Office of the Chairman/President of the American Productivity and Quality Center

Ceil Kilian, Secretary to Dr. Deming

Irene Drootin, Research Associate for Charles Bernstein, Vice President, Total Quality Management (TQM) at the Northrop Corporation

Gwen Brock, Executive Secretary, Northrop Corporation

Special thanks are due Ahren Misha Edison for his proofreading assistance.

ACKNOWLEDGMENTS

TABLE OF CONTENTS

What Do You Mean by Quality?

Foreword by Dr. Ronald L. Heidke
Vice-President and Director, Corporate Quality
Eastman Kodak Company

Joe Juran once asked a group of managers: "Does Quality cost more or cost less?"

The managers were certain that as a Quality guru, Joe was going to convince us that Quality costs less, and so we answered: "Less!"

"Wrong," he answered. "The answer is both." Joe went on to explain that the quality of a Cadillac costs more than the quality of a Chevrolet, so the answer is more. But quality within an organization can substantially reduce waste, so the answer then is less.

This story helps to demonstrate the communication problem associated with the word **quality**. Often what is meant by quality is product features and performance. However, quality within a manufacturing organization is often used to describe the reliability of manufacturing processes and the purity of material.

To an organization's employees, quality has an additional meaning—it relates to how they are rewarded for a job. To a planner, quality can mean highly accurate and precise sales and delivery estimates. Quality thus becomes a magic word which can mean almost whatever one wants it to mean. Such ambiguity about defining quality can be very counterproductive, so it is imperative for organizations to be much more specific about gaining understanding of quality in terms that meet customer expectations.

What the customer wants is **Value**—that combination of features, reliability, cost, delivery and service that meets or exceeds their expectations. What the organization wants for improved quality is reduced cycle time and fewer defects per opportunity, as so well-described by Motorola.

There are still other perspectives on quality. What the shareowner wants in a quality stock is value maximization. And what employees want is a quality company that acknowledges their intelligence and contribution, as is so evident at Florida Power & Light.

Any treatise on quality must deal with these differences and the associated ambiguity. When I was asked by a newspaper reporter about my new job as Director of Corporate Quality for Kodak, I told him that the concept of quality has become too broad—almost to the point that the word itself is obsolete.

I feel it is necessary for us to more narrowly look at quality as encompassing the way things are done. We need to focus on our processes through a structured means of assessment, planning and execution. Then we must objectively measure how well we have fulfilled our customer service objectives. Only then will we come to a common understanding of Quality.

In this perspective, I commend Dr. Caroselli for bringing together perspectives from some leaders in the Quality movement. Their views will help provide this focus on a common understanding of Quality.

Introduction

Background

"Even a thought, even a possibility, can shatter us and transform us," Nietzsche wrote in *Eternal Recurrence*. It is my hope that the thoughts and possibilities in this book will shatter paradigms and "congealed selves." Only then can transformations—of individuals and groups and cultures—occur within corporations. Only then can the Quality Revolution gain universal participation. Only then can quality envelop an organization and become the common language, the common perspective from which decisions are made and behavioral patterns are formed.

Some of the leaders I contacted for this book led, and continue to lead, the Quality Revolution.* Others, such as Philip Crosby, William Conway and David Nadler, have advanced the initial work through their writing and consulting efforts in large companies. Still others, such as Carl Thor and Mark Crumly, hold positions within professional Quality organizations. A final group, consisting of Kent Kresa, Colonel Misner, Mark Apicella, Shirley Powell, Sharon Sarris, William Bullock and consultant Don Ford have helped to make Quality a central theme in the operation of large corporations.

While each of these individuals has made a unique imprint upon the corpus of Total Quality Management (TQM) knowledge, there are distinct similarities in the methods they have chosen to transform cultures and advance the Quality mission. They may differ on the means selected to achieve the end, but they are unanimous in believing that the end is always a quality product or service.

---

*To eliminate possible confusion, "quality" will be capitalized when it refers to the Quality Movement and left lower case when it retains its usual meaning.

The leaders selected for inclusion in this book were all willing to share—their time, their ideas and their enthusiasm—so that others might become similarly infected with the desire to bring about change by way of an insistence on excellence. For example, despite being 90-years-old and delivering full-day seminars all over the world, Dr. Deming wrote, "I will do whatever I can to help you with the book." It is this spirit of cooperation that penetrates the pages of this work. It is the same cooperative force behind the book's purpose: to help the reader transform internal and external conditions into Quality cultures.

Years ago, when I taught literature classes, I would tell students that we come to know fictional characters through what they say, what they do, and what others say about them. With this book, I have come to understand these real-life characters by what they say (in their interviews, their writing, their seminars, their videotapes), what others say about them, and also by what they are doing to advance their ideas so that others might learn about Quality.

This is a book designed to bring about awareness, to help prepare the reader for Quality transformations or—if the transformation has already been made—to help him* continuously refine the process by exploring other perspectives on the Quality movement. "The future enters into us, in order to transform itself in us, long before it happens." Rainer Maria Rilke's words capture the intent of these interviews exactly: to have the future internalized before it happens.

The Quality transformation process really begins with communication. As Philip Crosby notes, such Quality dialogue is "essential to ongoing quality improvement." The book communicates interviewees' responses (written in italics) to questions in the following broad areas:

---

*For the sake of writing and reading convenience, the masculine pronoun is used throughout, with the full understanding that the references apply to both women and men.

- barriers
- challenges
- change
- culture
- customers
- implementation
- leadership

• optimization/improvement
• planning
• statistical tools
• suppliers
• teamwork
• training
• quality control circles/work teams

Originally, the book was designed for use in human resource/training departments in their efforts to make employees aware of basic tenets on which the Quality movement is founded. However, I found many people interested in learning the views of these quality leaders—people who were not part of the human resource or training departments. Therefore, the interviews are presented, with discussion questions at the end, as a series of informational pieces about Quality for any reader interested in learning more about this movement that has finally begun to affect the way we do business. (An accompanying resource guide has been designed specifically for trainers and consultants. It transforms the interviews into exercises, graphics, handouts, and surveys.)

The overarching framework presented in this book provides a means for formulating one's own theory about Quality. I have tried to facilitate that formulation by telling how the word is defined by recognized Quality advocates, how it is achieved, how it can transform individuals and corporations alike. Ideally, the reader will acquire new perspectives and insights that will enable him to formulate his own Quality-consciousness.

The importance of having such a theoretical base cannot be minimized. Five years ago, an advertisement such as the following would seldom have appeared in the *Wall Street Journal*. Today, such ads are fairly common sights.

VICE PRESIDENT QUALITY

E-Mu Systems, Inc. is a growing company in the electronic music synthesizer business. Our goal is to implement a Total Quality Program which will establish E-Mu as a world class competitor in its chosen markets.

The candidate will establish a plan to implement and conduct company-wide training, facilitate processes, establish statistics, customer satisfaction measurement, benchmarking, cost-of-quality metrics, and be the caretaker of the total quality theology. It is our desire to qualify for the Malcolm Baldrige Award in three years.

(reprinted with permission of E-Mu Systems, Inc., 1600 Green Hills Road, Scotts Valley, California 95066)

The Malcolm Baldrige National Quality Award

Such ads reflect our growing national concern with quality, a concern that has been translated into federal action. In 1982, Congress passed legislation for the formation of a national conference to address the concern about declining productivity and quality. The conference participants were government and business leaders. One significant result was the Malcolm Baldrige National Quality Improvement Act, signed on August 20, 1987, by President Ronald Reagan. Another important result was the recommendation for the establishment of the Malcolm Baldridge National Quality Award to recognize companies that excel in quality achievement.

The Award focuses on seven areas:

Leadership The senior executives' success in creating and sustaining a quality culture.

Information and Analysis The effectiveness of the company's collection and analysis of information for quality improvement and planning.

Strategic Quality Planning The effectiveness of integration of quality requirements into the company's business plan.

Human Resource Utilization The success of the company's efforts to realize the full potential of the work force for quality.

Quality Assurance The effectiveness of the company's systems for assuring quality control of all operations.

Quality Assurance Results The company's results in quality achievement and quality improvement, demonstrated through quantitative measures.

Customer Satisfaction The effectiveness of the company's systems to determine customer requirements and demonstrated success in meeting them.

Our Quality Tradition

The Award is one attempt to restore pride to the "Made in America" label. That manufacturing pride began in the first wave of the Industrial Revolution, set into motion with Eli Whitney's invention of the cotton gin. Henry Ford, with his introduction of mass production, started the second wave of the Industrial Revolution. And, according to William Conway, the third wave began about 40 years ago when American statisticians went to Japan to help them rebuild their war-devastated economy.

While our collective concern for quality is relatively new, individual voices have been proclaiming the Quality message for several decades. Unfortunately, as a nation, America turned deaf ears to that message. Dr. W. Edwards Deming is the acknowledged pioneer, the American statistician who was invited by the Japanese Union of Scientists and Engineers (JUSE) to give quality control lectures to researchers, managers, and engineers. Dr. Deming's response to their invitation reflects the quintessential educator's eagerness to share ideas. It also reflects his ineffable generosity: "As for remuneration I shall not desire any. It will be only a great pleasure to assist you." The Japanese have been employing his statistical process control efforts and his Fourteen Points ever since.

Dr. Joseph M. Juran went to Japan shortly afterwards and worked to make his definition of quality—"fitness for use"—a widely accepted one. Dr. Juran was equally well-received in Japan, as evinced by his award of The Order of the Sacred Treasure by Emperor Hirohito "for the development of quality control in Japan and the facilitation of U.S. and Japanese friendship."

The third of those individual voices belongs to Philip B. Crosby, whose quality concepts have been expressed in easily remembered phrases: "Do it right the first time," "zero defects," and "Quality is free" (which is also the title of his book, published in 1979, the year in which he formed the Crosby Quality College).

Differing Similarities

These three Quality proponents began the revolution that so many others have joined. While their viewpoints and battle cries may differ (or their opinions about whether to even have battle cries), Dr. Deming, Dr. Juran and Philip Crosby have a parallel faith in the power of Quality concepts to transform American business. Their basic position is the same: start from the top of the organization (or near the top) and move down to make quality something that everyone works to produce, every day. Management must remove barriers that may be in the way of improving systems/processes, but everyone can participate in the improvement if teamwork is encouraged. The final result is both customer and employee satisfaction.

Yes, you will hear differences in the syntaxes with which they explain their position; in fact, you may even hear contradictions. Purists will align themselves with one particular Quality camp and will subscribe to the philosophy of that camp. Generalists will create an amalgam of concepts or practices from each of these three leaders, thus fashioning their own interpretation of Total Quality Management (TQM). For example, at Boeing, they call their version of TQM "Continuous Process Improvement (CPI)." At the Hughes Corporation, it is "CMI: Continuous Measurable Improvement." At Rolls-Royce, it is "Total Quality," and at New United Motor Manufacturing, it is "kaizen."

The definitions of quality are changing, as are the extents to which statistical process control is included. No matter what particular phrases are associated with a particular figurehead, the common emphasis on high-quality products and services transcends the diversity. And, as world-class quality products become part of a global economy, it will be increasingly important for us to create a unified belief system. As a nation, we have moved from self-resourcefulness and economic in-sularity to become a cooperative partner among world traders. As Quality-advocates, we must find what works best in our environment—a singular philosophy or an eclectic one—and transform that environment, making it receptive to, and reflective of, the Quality philosophy.

> Dr. Marlene Caroselli, Director
> CENTER FOR PROFESSIONAL DEVELOPMENT
> 10305 Summertime Lane
> Culver City, California 90230

A Note to Trainers and Consultants

There has been a great deal written about the Quality movement. But words, after all, are just black marks on white paper. And words are easily forgotten. What makes the words memorable? What emblazons an idea upon cerebral neurons? What brings to life a workable philosophy? As all instructors know, there must be exercises aligned with the concept. There must be actual physical engagement that takes ideas from the cerebral cortex where they are formed and transforms those ideas into behaviors that are relevant to work and life situations. There must be exercises to move us beyond roteness and into reality. Such exercises can be found in the accompanying resource guide.

As Confucius said, "I hear and I forget. I see and I remember. I do and I learn." It will be discussions and thinking, combined with related actions, that will make the ideas presented here applicable to real-world circumstances. New Quality-oriented ways of thinking and behaving and interacting should result from the training that is provided. If nothing changes, the training has failed.

This collection of essays is an overview, a series of informational interviews with outstanding figures in the Quality field. You can view this collection as the first layer of exposure to employees, the first step in making them aware of Quality. If you are responsible for training employees on the basic principles that constitute Quality improvement, you will find in these pages discussions of those principles by some of the best minds in the field.

The book need not only be used as a prelude for launching a Quality program, however. It can also be used as a periodic review of training that has already been presented. It can easily supplement Quality training already in place. Various sections can be correlated to specific training that has been instituted. It is beyond the scope of this book to give in-depth, intensive training, particularly in the field of statistical quality control. For such, we suggest managers participate in programs such as those offered by the very individuals who are featured in the book.

As a trainer or consultant, you are in a unique position to influence others. Whether you work alone or in concert with others, you can have an impact on thought, you can facilitate receptivity to change, you can soften the sharp edges that are often associated with transformations. Can one person truly make a difference? For the answer to that question, you need only consider the individuals who have contributed to this book.

Philip B. Crosby, Founder, Chairman
Philip Crosby Associates, Inc.

"Always assume that people are
vitally interested in the quality
improvement process. They will act
to fulfill your conviction. No one knows
for sure what is going on in other people's
heads. Assume the best and that is
usually what happens."

Background

So closely is Philip Crosby identified as a leader in the Quality revolution that he was once spotted in an airport and asked to "say something in guru." He has been a Quality advocate for nearly 40 years and has taught thousands of people through his teaching, speaking, and writing that "Quality means conformance to requirements." His books include *Quality Is Free; Quality Without Tears; The Art of Getting Your Own Sweet Way; Running Things; The Eternally Successful Organization; Let's Talk Quality;* and *Leading: The Art of Becoming an Executive.* In Lee Iacocca's opinion, "Nobody talks quality better than Phil Crosby."

In 1979, Crosby held his first Quality College class in Winter Park, Florida; 47 students were graduated. In the same years, he published *Quality Is Free,* which he dedicated to Harold Geneen, his mentor at ITT. Today, the Quality College has over 17,000 graduates and Philip Crosby is a name that is synonymous with Quality. This high-powered, highly productive man has devoted more than 35 years of his life to asking Quality questions and ensuring not only that answers were given but also that those answers would be shared with as wide an audience as possible.

A former vice president at ITT, Crosby currently heads Philip Crosby Associates, Inc. (PCA), writes extensively, and lectures internationally. His company, with headquarters in Winter Park, Florida, has annual revenues of $100 million and not a single salesperson. PCA's clientele includes thousands of worldwide organizations in which more than a dozen languages are spoken.

Training

"You are a master of metaphor," I observed during the course of the interview. I had as evidence the following comparisons from *Let's Talk Quality*:

> "When management encourages procedural Band-Aids, employees lose confidence in them and in the process." (page 6)

"Change should be a friend. It should happen by plan, not by accident." (page 7)

"A quality improvement team is not a SWAT squad that has to go solve problems. Quality improvement training is education of the team members, coordination between operations, and leadership of the process. It is a living entity that survives its members. It is not a ritual, it is leadership." (page 109)

And these from *Leading: The Art of Becoming an Executive*:

"The business desert is layered with the bones of those who felt they understood completely and stopped learning." (page 9)

"The ecology of an organization is as delicate and vulnerable as that of a forest." (page 27)

And these gems from *Quality Is Free*:

"Quality is ballet, not hockey." (page 13)

"Hockey is detection; ballet is prevention." (page 135)

"Quality has much in common with sex." (page 13)

"Audit is the Bat Masterson of business." (page 67)

With such rich analogies as a backdrop, I asked Crosby to what he would compare training programs, such as those offered by his Quality College. His reply:

Training programs are very much like grade school. The thing we all get in grade school is the basics, an understanding of reading, writing, arithmetic. After that, we get off into the specialty items.

You could also say quality is the basic fabric of an organization. The business of getting things done right the first time is routine if quality is built in. Then all the rest of it gets built in.

Crosby believes Quality must be something more than the work the Quality Assurance (QA) people do; it must be the coin of the realm if the organization is to thrive and remain competitive. There are estimates that only 50 percent of the employees in a manufacturing concern actually touch the product. Clearly, then, if Quality is to become the basic fabric, an understanding of it must go beyond the reaches of the QA department. Quality must be understood and committed to all layers, all levels of the company, whether or not they touch the product. Crosby says,

When we talk about communication up front, we must have a common understanding. We need to get clear requirements of what work is and what we are going to do. We need to get the performance standard clear and we need to educate people around that. The performance standard must be a product that is defect-free.

Once people understand the standard, then we need to train them on how to do the job. We need a means of communicating how the work is progressing. Finally, we need to support our people in their efforts to meet the standard.

In *Vanguard Management,* James O'Toole substantiates the need for continuous training by noting that brainpower becomes obsolete more quickly than does equipment.

At Levi [Strauss], a significant part of the annual merit evaluation of managers is based on how well they train people. The typical manager is expected to cross-train at least two people per year and to take responsibility for mentoring one younger person. The company even creates "training jobs"—lateral "promotions" for managers in which they may broaden their skills while waiting for the opportunity for a true, vertical promotion.[1]

A number of corporations that have undertaken Quality training are providing that training to every employee, not merely to the uppermost levels of management. For Quality to be discussed on a daily basis, the communication of it must be top-down as well as bottom-up. One thing Crosby recommends to ensure the ongoing attention to Quality is "show-and-tell" programs. These events allow individuals at every level to take pride in, and be recognized for, their contributions to Quality. As Crosby asserts, "Every action taken by every employee involves Quality."

Statistical Tools

Continuing along training lines, I asked Crosby what tools or concepts he thought every employee should be aware of. Specifically, I asked about the Pareto Chart, a bar graph depiction of a problem based on prioritized causes. With typically Crosbian candor, he gives this response:

The Pareto Chart is pretty much useless. As far as Statistical Quality Control is concerned, the real thing we are after is prevention. Yes, employees should learn about such things, but the idea behind prevention is to think things out in advance and plan them out to get agreement about what the requirements are. People then have to be trained to meet those requirements.

Statistical Quality Control has been around for 50 years and has been used for 40 years. Those were the same 40 years in which we have produced so much junk, the years when America earned a bad reputation.

Statistical Quality Control is like an accounting procedure. This is like saying we are going to try to manage our financial resources by having a really good accounting procedure. The procedure is certainly part of it, but it does not really make a great deal of difference. For example, you can have the best procedure in the world for investing your money, but if your money is in the wrong places, the procedure will not do you very much good at all.

Statistical measurement has been around since after the War, but it is only a tool.

Expanding on the idea of Quality and profit being dependent on prevention, he continues:

Statistical tools do not make much difference. That is quality control. Quality control is something you need to do in different areas, but quality control catches and fixes things. It does not prevent them.

This viewpoint is echoed in the words of Bertha Davis:

"Churn out work as fast as you can and reject the worst 5 percent of what emerges." Such a directive falls far short of a formula for quality production, but industry critics deem it typical of standards that prevailed for far too long in far too many American industries. Quality control under that standard meant simply inspection plus rejection of the worst.[2]

She acknowledges the importance of product quality in gaining or retaining market share, but laments, as does Crosby, inappropriate reactions to the drive toward Quality.

The drive to increase American manufacturing competitiveness has produced a wave of interest in quality, but unfortunately, many quality campaigns have been ill conceived. Instead of initiating programs to get work right in the first place, efforts have focused on more rigorous inspection of finished work. For some companies the results have been disastrous. More defects are found, and the costs of fixing them have raised costs of production to a degree that threatens the basic purpose of the whole enterprise, becoming more competitive.[3]

Changing Mindsets

Crosby feels it is possible for a company to turn around within six or eight months of working with a firm such as his own, Philip Crosby Associates, Inc. But both the changer and the change must be intent upon transforming the corporate culture, says Crosby, and making Quality as frequently spoken a term as "profits" or "bottom line."

In *Quality Is Free*, he tells us that

There is a theory of human behavior that says people subconsciously retard their own intellectual growth. They come to rely on clichés and habits. Once they reach the age of their own personal comfort with the world, they stop learning and their mind runs on idle for the rest of their days.

They may progress organizationally, they may be ambitious and eager, and they may even work night and day. But they learn no more. The bigoted, the narrow-minded, the stubborn, and the perpetually optimistic have all stopped learning.[4]

Crosby's description of the stultified mind is akin to Gail Godwin's comment in *A Mother and Two Daughters* about the two different kinds of people in the world:

One kind, you can just tell by looking at them at what point they congealed into their final selves. It might be a very *nice* self, but you know you can expect no more surprises from it. Whereas, the other kind keep moving, changing...They are *fluid*. They keep moving forward and making new trysts with life, and the motion of it keeps them young. In my opinion, they are the only people who are still alive.[5]

Special attempts have to be made to reach the congealed selves in the organization, the individuals who have stopped learning. Crosby says these specific questions about Quality education have to be asked of those employees who tend to be "don't-rock-the-boaters."

- What is Quality?

- What is your system?

- What is the performance standard?

- How do you measure it?

- Why should you worry about it?

- How does it evolve in relationships with people?

Crosby has faith that turnarounds can occur:

Everyone should understand Quality the same way. They all have or should have the same tools. The employees can change the culture of the company and do just fine in their efforts.

Of course, you never really get done.

It is this attitude of continually determining what the process is and then working to improve it that disturbs the ground in which the managerial ostriches have buried their heads. Even in retail businesses such as the much-acclaimed Stew Leonard's grocery market, the continuous improvement of process can be made part of the firm's operating policy. Each Friday, Stew Leonard fills up a van with store employees and drops them off at various competitors' stores. The employees do benchmark comparisons and then report back at a group meeting about the things they saw and liked and believe could work in the Leonard store. It is by learning about the best practices that we can adapt those practices to our own special circumstances. In time, we ourselves become exemplars because of whom others refine their processes.

Preparing the Work Force

The American work ethic has often been compared, with unfavorable results, to the work ethic of European or Oriental countries. Many believe that American workers make a poor showing, but not because of disinterest or laziness or lack of intelligence. It is felt by many that the decline in our productivity growth rate is directly related to the lack of preparation workers bring to the workplace.

The $40+ billion that corporate America is spending each year on "remedial education" represents time and money that could be directed toward producing the product. Training, of course, is critical, but the training should be to acquire skills that could not have been acquired prior to workplace entry. Instead, we are exerting considerable sums to retrain, or reteach what should have been taught in our schools.

Recognizing the importance of such skill deficiencies, numerous efforts are underway through both formal and informal networks to encourage young people to learn about their fields of interest before they actually enter them. The Demos Project, for example, has Yale undergraduates going in to elementary classrooms to give children hands-on opportunities with science experiments.

Matilda Cuomo, wife of New York State's governor, chairs a mentoring program, which forms partnerships among students, businesses, organizations, and individuals. Adult mentors talk with students about workplace realities. It is this kind of collaboration that could make the difference between a well-prepared work force for the new century and one that is woefully unaware.

Many foreign countries have specific programs for young people who will not attend college. In America, vocational education is not generally regarded as a source of the best workers. In fact, some firms are reluctant to hire young people who have gone through such a program, believing that their "voc ed" training implies they were not capable of handling a regular, more rigorous academic program.

The interview at this point touched upon the similarities between high school classrooms and corporate training rooms. I mentioned my own communications workshops in corporations and cited the problem so many employees have shared with me: having a report or letter, covered with red marks indicating errors, returned by the boss to the writer. The subordinate is often embarrassed, perhaps even insulted, by the boss' seemingly harsh reaction. Employees often tell me they feel they are being singled out for humiliation, made to feel like children.

I try to point out that the boss probably wishes he did not have to take time to correct errors of this nature. Such defect-detection is a waste of his time, but the boss probably feels a poorly written document is a poor reflection on the department or on the company. In all likelihood, the boss has other, more valuable jobs he could be doing.

Scenarios like this are wastes, and, they are microcosmic reflections of the macrocosmic corporate misuse of time and talent. Not only is the boss taking time away from more important matters, but the employee has to take time to write the document over. Often, such subordinates are channeled into writing classes, which are certainly valuable, but which represent another duplication of effort: the information the employee acquires in such classes has been presented in junior high, in senior high, and often again in college.

The corporation takes over because earlier learning did not occur. There are numerous possible reasons why learning does not occur, but an exploration of them is beyond the scope of this chapter. We shall limit our consideration to the suboptimization situation just described and depicted in Figure 1.

FIGURE 1

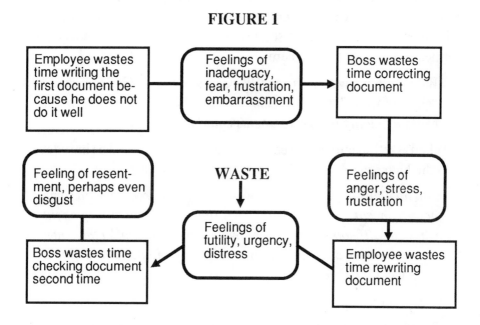

As Crosby says in *Let's Talk Quality,*

> When the corporations in this country tell the schools that they are not satisfied with the way quality and other things are being taught, things will change. It is silly to hire college graduates who can't write a decent letter.... If only things were being done right the first time....[6]

Ask Crosby what can be done to bring about change. He will give you no-nonsense answers:

The basic problem is the teachers not the students. [His words echo Dr. Deming's in a telephone conversation: "The workers are not the problem."] *I do not see any reason why we couldn't put Quality awareness information into the training teachers have to undergo to keep abreast of developments in the field.*

The use of the conditional tense and of first-person pronouns in the following reflects Crosby's enthusiasm—his belief that where there is a will, there is also a way. He sounds as if a committee has already been formed to work on the problem.

Why couldn't we use a tape like the one the BBC made called "Quality Man?" If nothing else, something as simple as that would explain Quality in terms students could understand.

When asked specifically if certain Quality precepts could be introduced into the high school curriculum, Crosby gives this response:

I do not think high school kids would have any problem with some of the concepts. My books are pretty simple. You are talking about work ethic. If nobody ever tells anybody about the work ethic, then they will just make it up as they go along or will perhaps define it from what they see on T.V.

He elaborates,

Teachers pretty much assume you are not going to get it right because one of the things that screws up the school system is the grading system of A, B, C's. Theoretically, a doctor could go all the way through medical school with C's.

Of course, none of us would choose that type of doctor if we knew we could select another doctor who had received all A's. But what if, in the academic Utopia Crosby and others envision, there was no grading, no comparisons between students, but rather an examination that every medical student had to pass before being allowed to practice medicine? What if, instead of grades that are so often arbitrary, there were the highest possible standards—not minimal competencies, but the highest possible standards—reflected on that examination? And one either passed and became an excellent physician or failed and went on to some other career.

Could such a system be translated into the schools? Of course it could! Imagine study teams as they have in law school, with each student helping another student to pass, rather than each student competing with other students to achieve the highest class rank.

Education

"Educate" is derived from the Latin *ducere* meaning "to lead" and the prefix *ex* meaning "out of." The educator leads others out of the darkness or ignorance surrounding a particular sphere of facts. In a sense, he heads the march from a comfortable old world of information to a new situation requiring new cognitive abilities. Crosby alludes to this unique opportunity, of which any single agent can partake, when he encourages,

> This is an opportunity to be a hero. Someone has to begin every march. As you and your team deal with the other people in the company, they will begin to realize that your department is different. When they discover that it is simpler to get requirements straight up front, they will begin to ask how you learned all this. It is a wonderful opportunity to influence and lead the corporation.[7]

Quality depends, one might say, not so much on the methods as on the movers. And the movers must be educated and must in turn educate others. It is not difficult to become a Quality convert if you have done your homework—the reading and thinking and discussing and seminar-attending that will immerse you into a philosophy that works.

Quality is common sense, a striving toward perfection that will leave you convinced there is no other way to approach your work. When you regard your output as a product with your personal hallmark (visible or not) imprinted upon it, you will fully understand Quality and its potential impact upon an organization. It has often been said that the best investment you can make is in yourself. And we "invest" in ourselves by acquiring knowledge that leads to team success/corporate profits, which ultimately enable us to invest in real estate or junk bonds in a much greater way.

Some of the deepest insights about Quality will come from reading beyond your given field. Problems are solved so often by learning about other disciplines and drawing parallels. For example, Jean Henri Fabré was a nineteenth-century French entomologist who studied procession-ary caterpillars, so called because they follow the leader in a procession. Fabré conducted an experiment in which he arranged the caterpillars in a circle, and was not surprised to find them following their leader in a continuous, circular path. Fabré then placed food in the center of the circle, just inches away from the caterpillars. To his amazement, he found not a single caterpillar was willing to deviate from the circle in order to reach the food. In little time, the caterpillars all died, even though their means of survival was easily within their grasp.

Such knowledge often enables employees to realize they must some-times assume a leadership role and make suggestions or initiate improve-ments that may run contrary to the way things have always been done. A Quality environment encourages such open communications so that improvements can indeed be continuously made to the process of work.

Quality and education are inseparable. Without sufficient knowledge, there cannot be sufficient productivity. "Assure that everyone is edu-cated," Crosby advises, "so they can perform."[8] There should be no shame in not knowing; the only shame is in refusing to learn. Crosby affirms the centrality of learning to participation in the Quality revolution when he asserts that

> It is necessary to devote time and energy to learning ahead of everything else. When you don't want to do that anymore, it's time to negotiate early retirement while they still love you.[9]

Quality also means refining skills, becoming as expert as possible on the job you are being paid to do. Just as processes can continuously be improved, so too can the body of knowledge always be amplified. "Nobody knows everything about everything,"[10] Crosby tells us. It should be apparent that the "know-everything" executive is obsolete, if indeed such a person ever really did exist.

Changing the Culture

Someone once asked Andrew Carnegie which was the most important aspect of industrial success: labor, capital or brains. Carnegie's reply was quick and incisive. "Which," he asked in return, "is the most important leg of a three-legged stool?" Similarly, the important aspects of any business must be woven into the fabric of the organization so there is a seamless blending of thought and purpose and resources. Quality may be first among equals, as its proponents assert, but it is still one of the equals.

Quality has to become a work style, not just a word if it is to thrive in an integrated environment. Quality precepts must be so ingrained that employees will do what is right almost intuitively, without having to ask themselves or others if a particular action is an appropriate one.

No matter what product or service the organization provides, Quality improvement has to move beyond the quality control or quality assurance departments. The culture must be changed from a narrow focus holding one department responsible, to an attitude of universality, with totally shared responsibility for excellence. Production departments and quality departments have often been viewed adversarially. The "problem" of quality was usually left for Quality departments to wrestle with. But, as Crosby points out, since only about half the employees in a manufacturing firm actually come in contact with the product, the other half must also be made aware of Quality requirements, no matter what their jobs.

To change the culture, we must first believe it can be changed. If we have that belief, the next step is to define the culture. As part of the definition process, we ask questions such as these:

- What is the culture?

- Who defines it?

- Is it receptive to change?

- What are the barriers to change?

- Who refines the culture?

- What weaknesses exist in the culture?

- What are the values of this culture?

- To what extent is the culture accepted by the people who work in it?

Defining the culture is the stepping stone, of course. Extensive research into the various types of cultures has been done by Jeffrey Sonnenfield, who directs the center for Leadership and Career Change at Emory University. As reported in the *Wall Street Journal*,[11] there are four types of cultures:

ACADEMY

International Business Machines Corporation (IBM) is cited as possessing the prototypical Academy culture, in part because of the extensive training (at least 40 hours a year) managers are expected to engage in. IBM has long been known for priming its most promising employees. It identifies early those who are destined for the fast track and then offers them multiple opportunities to become, in time, quasi-experts on each of a dozen different topics in the same sphere of specialized knowledge. Individualism, achievement, and visibility are rewarded; these traits usually lead to promotions.

CLUB

Club cultures encourage rapport, teamwork, the merger of individual efforts into the overall company objective. Moving up the career ladder takes longer than it does for the Academy employee, who has probably been trained and rewarded for his own success. In the club environment, by contrast, promotions do not come as readily. Success is determined by measuring the extent to which the group has advanced the mission of the company. While IBM may be cited as promoting "vertical" knowledge (an individual ascends the ladder of knowledge from the bottom to the top and becomes quite expert about the rungs of *that* ladder but not the many other ladders that support the uppermost level of corporate policy), Club companies promote "horizontal" knowledge, more generalist than specialist in nature. Clubbers might jump from one ladder to another several times during the course of their careers.

BASEBALL TEAM

These cultures differ markedly from the other types of cultures. They are characterized by an entrepreneurial spirit, by an encouragement of, and rewarding for, quick results. Competition and succeeding in the marketplace are gods to whom obeisance is paid. There is a lot of free agenting in Baseball cultures—it is understood that if a firm cannot provide what the individual finds rewarding, the individual will leave, perhaps to start a company of his own. While loyalty and womb-to-tomb thinking permeate other cultures, the Baseball culture fosters independence. Although it does not encourage employees to leave, it fully understands when they do. In such a culture, security is not a valued condition; risk-taking is. Creativity and innovation are two of the distinct values of this culture.

FORTRESS

Companies that have known lean times, or that have experienced feast-or-famine histories, or that are beginning to recognize the wisdom of diversification, are known as Fortresses, more concerned with survival than anything else. Reorganization is inevitable with such firms, and consequently, the environment shows less concern for the welfare of the whole than for the welfare of the individual parts. Unlike Academies that groom employees for the long-term, Fortresses are unable to offer security or to provide rewards for team or individual success. They are often in turmoil, and so a champion or victor who provides solutions or a turnaround will surely be hailed as chief. But for those who thrive in constant-flux situations, such a culture may be exciting. Certainly, one's chances to be visible are greater when a company is undergoing dramatic upheaval. There is very little to lose and so an employee may find upper management most willing to listen to suggestions for streamlining or lowering the bottom line.

Once the culture has been defined, there are deliberate steps to be followed if the culture is to be transformed. Those steps are depicted in Figure 2.

FIGURE 2

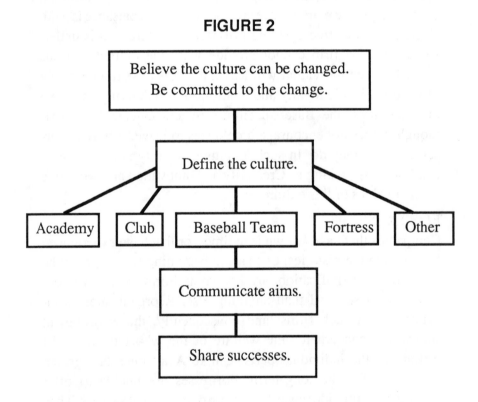

Bringing Quality to an organization can be facilitated if an identification has been made of the organization's culture. Or, it may be one, or any combination of, the above. It may be a culture best described in broad, general strokes of the management-definition brush. Nonetheless, the culture must be defined before the strategy for changing it can be effectively implemented.

The next step in this lengthy, multistage undertaking is to communicate what you are doing to anyone and everyone. The communication of the Quality aims (elimination of defects, reduction of waste, continuous improvement of the process, doing it right the first time, conformance to requirements) should be ongoing and should penetrate every stratum of the organization. Everyone should be familiar with these aims and should understand them fully. Clear definitions of expectations—the internal customers', the external customers', and the suppliers'—must be established and periodic measurement undertaken to ensure those expectations are being met.

Changing the culture to make it conducive to Quality is never a facile task, despite the logic of the steps presented in Figure 2. However, it is a task that, seriously undertaken, will bring powerful results to an organization.

In *Let's Talk Quality*, Crosby encourages managers to "teach your people, explain things to them. Put them through the quality education they need to change their culture."[12] He elaborated upon this advice during the interview:

> *You have to talk about Quality for the executive and for management. You have to educate the people. You have to get people to routinely do things right the first time.*

That change need not be expensive or painful, Crosby feels. But it does need to be ubiquitous and it does depend on the communication of shared experiences inside and outside the organization. Crosby endorses the sole-source supplier relationship and even likens it to the longevity of a sole-spouse marriage, an arrangement that has worked well for millions. Additionally, he supports holding meetings with suppliers so they can discuss problems they may be experiencing, and so solutions favorable to both sides can be reached.

The more pervasive the communication, the more likely the formation of a Quality culture.

Discontent with the Present

"One who is contented with what he has done will never become famous for what he will do." Christian Bovee's words, while directed toward self-acclaim, nonetheless capture the subterranean force that causes culture plates to shift and slide. Quality-driven employees are not content with what they have done. They are ever seeking to improve, to integrate their plans for Quality with the overall mission of the organization.

Quality-driven employees accumulate data from all possible sources, in order to compare or "benchmark" what they are doing with what the best are doing. "We do not hide things in this country," says John A. Heberling, president of Anaheim-based PJ Communications.

He shares the true story of an internal employee publication, which—as an April Fool's joke for their April issue—ran the fabricated story of a new piece of complex machinery that had been purchased by a large manufacturing firm. In total jest, the article described the robotic arms of this equipment, with a 6000-tool capacity. "The tools do not have to leave the system," the article declared, "because they sharpen themselves."

The machinery was further described as a 14-axis, 10-pallet, state-of-the-art machining marvel. The article's author made up a name for the equipment and declared it to be like no other ever built. "It can assemble and serve an actuator in 24 hours," continued the hyperbole, "and can load and unload parts." Training was offered for anyone interested in learning how to operate this latest mechanical wonder, supposedly just purchased by this manufacturer of aerospace products. Within a week of the publication, two representatives from a Japanese firm were sent from Washington to make benchmarking inquires...for a product that did not exist.

Benchmarking data on *real* products and services are assessed with the aim of developing standards and improving processes. One simple way to acquire basic benchmark data would be to request a copy of the company's annual report, from several different companies, including your own. Take notes on each call to see how you, a potential customer or employee or stockholder, were treated in terms of professionalism, efficiency, manner, etc.

If your own company did not fare well by comparison, analyze where it failed. Then try to ensure that your team, or your subordinates, treat others in the same manner as did the company representative who gave the most outstanding service in the experiment you conducted. As Crosby affirms in *Leading,* "Quality is the result of a carefully constructed culture; it has to be the fabric of the organization—not part of the fabric, but the actual fabric."[13]

One of the stories making the management rounds is of a young man who was working on a piece of machinery when the boss happened to stroll onto the shop floor. The boss observed that the machinery needed oiling and informed the young man of what should be done. Politely, but with firmness, the employee replied, "I am sorry, sir, but that's not in my job description."

The boss thought a moment, and then invited the employee into his office. He asked the young man to be seated while he went through his files. When he came upon the employee's job description, he ripped it up and then informed the young man, "I am rewriting your job description. From now on, you will only have to abide by these three words." He wrote on a new job description form, "Use your head!"

The executive attitude that is Quality-focused will encourage cooperation and interdependency. It will help to create a permeating sense of "We are doing this together. We take pride in what we do." And those distinguishing traits by which the corporate culture is described must be fostered and extended from the uppermost echelons. Says Crosby,

We learn more and more that the quality of an organization is very much a layout of the executive attitudes and direction, as opposed to the amount of tools that you put in.

Quality has to be continuous, invasive, pervasive. It will not work unless employees believe in it and believe in their extensions of it. Crosby believes in people being fanatics about their work and about satisfying the customer. Fanatics, who he claims "leave footprints instead of just dust," can be defined this way:

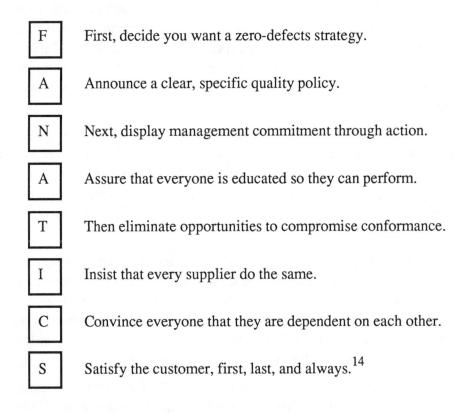

F	First, decide you want a zero-defects strategy.
A	Announce a clear, specific quality policy.
N	Next, display management commitment through action.
A	Assure that everyone is educated so they can perform.
T	Then eliminate opportunities to compromise conformance.
I	Insist that every supplier do the same.
C	Convince everyone that they are dependent on each other.
S	Satisfy the customer, first, last, and always.[14]

The continuous improvement aspect of Total Quality Management is captured in the words of Charles Roth: "Analyze yourself periodically, and mentally resolve ways to improve your effectiveness." This recommendation can be applied equally well to an individual, a team, a department, a whole organization. Fanatics make such applications.

Summary

Asked to supply a metaphor for training, Philip Crosby likens it to grade school, where we are given the basics that we need. For specialized knowledge, however, we need to go beyond the confines of the initial education.

In another metaphor, Crosby calls quality the fabric of an organization and points out that in a typical manufacturing environment, only 50 percent of the employees actually touch the product. So, it is especially important to spread the quality message to those who have no contact with quality assurance or quality control departments. People have to be educated about the performance standard—namely, a product that is defect-free.

Communications is a critical link in the training chain, and Crosby encourages "show and tell" meetings at which individuals can share their Quality success. We can prevent defects, he insists, if we train people to meet requirements and recognize them when they do.

Changing the corporate culture is a matter of reaching individuals who may have stagnated or congealed, as far as their openness to new ideas is concerned. Benchmarking is a way of learning about the successes of others and working to incorporate such successes into the situation at hand.

Training is another way to make employees aware of Quality. Such awareness could be introduced in high school, thereby lessening the corporate financial responsibility. Many organizations have begun to form liaisons between the worlds of school and work. Waste can be eliminated when employees take advantage of learning possibilities the first time they are presented.

Anyone can be a leader of others, assuming he is committed to Quality and committed to learning—sometimes from other fields. In changing to a Quality culture, it is necessary to define the kind of culture that currently exists. Jeffrey Sonnenfield proposes that cultures fall into one of four categories: Academy, Club, Baseball Team or Fortress.

Finally, Crosby recommends an eight-step, FANATIC approach to instilling Quality in an organization.

For Further Consideration

1. If you had been asked to "say something in guru" about the Quality movement, what would your message be?

2. What metaphor would you use to describe quality or Quality training?

3. What is the performance standard for the product your firm makes or the service you deliver?

4. Can (or Do) Quality "show-and-tell" programs work in your business environment? Explain.

5. Think about some of the "congealed selves" in your organization. How do you think they could be turned around?

6. Assume that you were responsible for the kind of benchmarking Stew Leonard does. How would you accumulate your data?

7. What specifically do you think the corporations in this country should be telling our schools?

8. From what you know about Quality, how much of it could be understood by high school students?

9. How can we bring Quality into the nation's schools?

10. What are your thoughts about the value of cooperation versus competition in the school system?

11. What "marches" have you begun lately? What march would you *like* to begin?

12. What parallels can you draw between some field (history, science, music, etc.) and Quality?

13. If you had been assigned the responsibility for ensuring universal participation, what measures would you undertake?

14. How would you describe your company's culture: Academy, Club, Baseball, Fortress or something else?

15. Describe the steps you have taken to ensure you fully understand your suppliers' expectations.

16. What benchmarking measures have been taken (or should be taken) in your company?

17. How would you like your job description to read? Your business card? How could you streamline a subordinate's job description?

18. How committed are you to SPC? Are you satisfied with the extent of that commitment?

References

[1] O'Toole, James. *Vanguard Management: Redesigning the Corporate Future* (Garden City: Doubleday & Company, 1985), p. 115.

[2] Davis, Bertha. *Crisis in Industry: Can America Compete?* (New York: Franklin Watts, Inc., 1989), p. 92.

[3] *Ibid.*, p. 92.

[4] Crosby, Philip B. *Quality Is Free* (New York: The New American Library, Inc., 1979), p. 68.

[5] Godwin, Gail. *A Mother and Two Daughters* (New York: Penguin Books USA, Inc., 1982), p. 43. Reproduced with permission of McGraw-Hill, Inc.

[6] Crosby, Philip B. *Let's Talk Quality* (New York: McGraw-Hill Publishing Company, 1989), p. 32. Reproduced with permission of McGraw-Hill, Inc.

[7] *Ibid.*, p. 107.

[8] *Ibid.*, p. 102.

[9] Crosby, Philip B. *Leading: The Art of Becoming an Executive* (New York: McGraw Hill Publishing Company, 1990), p. 151. Reproduced with permission of McGraw-Hill, Inc.

[10] *Ibid.*, p. viii.

[11] Sonnenfield, Jeffrey. "Which Corporate Culture Fits You?" *The Wall Street Journal* (July 17, 1989), p. B1. Reprinted with permission of *The Wall Street Journal* © 1989, Dow Jones & Company, Inc. All rights reserved.

[12] Crosby. *Let's Talk Quality, op.cit.*, p. 121.

[13] Crosby. *Leading, op. cit.*, pp. 39–40.

[14] Crosby. *Let's Talk Quality, op. cit.*, p. 104.

Kent Kresa, President, CEO
Northrop Corporation

"It is important to pursue specific, high leverage, advanced technologies that hold promise of changing the very nature of defense systems and, indeed, of dramatically increasing the military value of America's strategic and tactical forces. But the real emphasis today has to be on improving our management skills and the quality and influence of our business management people in order to get the maximum leverage out of our technical skills."

Background

"We intend to insure that this company is a strong organization—technically, managerially, and fiscally. We intend to be technologically versatile; a world leader in certain leverage technologies that will be important for our future; a company with a sound ethical structure of business systems and management that will make us profitable, make us a sought-after investment and a center of opportunity and challenge for our employees and future employees."

With these words, Northrop Corporation's Kent Kresa addressed the annual Shareholder's Meeting. He also, indirectly, addressed the Northrop work force, for a synopsis of that meeting was shared with Northrop employees via the company newsletter.

Kresa has been president of Northrop since 1987 and CEO since the beginning of 1990. The titles are a natural culmination of academic and professional careers centering on aeronautical systems. He attended the Massachusetts Institute of Technology, where he earned his bachelor's and master's degrees, as well as an engineering degree, in aeronautics and astronautics. Following a senior scientist position with AVCO Research and Advanced Development Division and MIT's Lincoln Laboratory, he served as deputy director of the Strategic Technology Office of the Defense Advanced Research Projects Agency (DARPA). In 1973, he assumed directorship of DARPA's tactical technology and, while serving in that capacity, was awarded the Secretary of Defense Meritorious Civilian Service Medal for "exceptionally meritorious service...in the development of new concepts with potentially major influence on the future capability of our military services."

His preeminence in the field has been recognized repeatedly. In 1975, he received the Navy's Meritorious Public Service Citation for his "invaluable assistance to the United States Naval service." He also was cited, via the Arthur D. Flemming award, as one of the top ten individuals in the United States government. In the same year, he was selected to the Chief of Naval Operations Executive Panel and chaired the Science and

Technology subpanel. Kresa began at Northrop in 1975 as vice president and manager of the Research and Technology Center.

Northrop, founded in 1939, defines itself as an advanced technology company whose primary commercial focus includes aircraft and military electronics design, development and manufacturing. Net sales of this Los Angeles-based company exceed $5 billion; it employs more than 38,000 people and has several divisions: Aircraft, B-2, Electronics Systems, Defense Systems and Precision Products, and a subsidiary, Northrop Worldwide Aircraft Services, Inc., in Lawton, Oklahoma. (This subsidiary provides helicopter and aircraft maintenance to a number of military installations.)

In a recent survey by *Computerworld* magazine, Northrop was ranked first among aerospace, automotive, and industrial manufacturing companies for its effective employment of information systems. Despite such recognition, Northrop is not inclined to develop a business from its clear superiority (the company was ranked third among all American companies) in the computer domain of information management. Its interest in information systems lies in having these systems as ancillary tools for achieving a closer fit between engineering and manufacturing capabilities. The company aims to achieve quality in all its operations, not just its information resource management.

As its press kit asserts, "Northrop plays a major role in some of the nation's most advanced weapons systems. It is prime contractor for the U.S. Air Force B-2 Advanced Technology Bomber and is a prime contractor to the Air Force for the Advanced Tactical Fighter (ATF)."

Communication

Kresa was asked what specific steps managers could take to ensure that information about Total Quality Management (TQM) flows from the bottom up as well as from the top down. He responds by calling communication "the essence of TQM," and then elaborates upon that definition:

We will have TQM only to the extent that it is understood and practiced at all levels. While TQM is being started up, communication in both directions is achieved by explicitly structuring events on the job. The interpersonal, teamwork, and leadership skills necessary for TQM are gradually acquired through use and practice. Emphasis on open communications, and efforts to eliminate barriers, need to be continuously maintained until the TQM style of behavior becomes ingrained in everyone. Later, when open and effective communication is a natural result of the TQM culture, the specially introduced mechanisms can be eliminated.

As Figure 1 shows, the tripartite spheres of practiced interpersonal skills, team skills, and leadership skills form the bases on which the TQM structure must be placed. Without the integration of these elements, TQM will be merely a nostrum—a recommended cure for an ailing industrial economy—but one which has no empirical record of effectiveness.

FIGURE 1

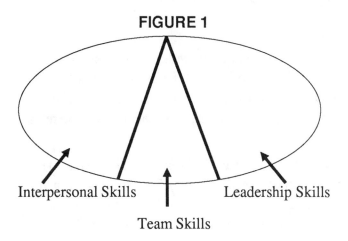

Interpersonal Skills   Leadership Skills

Team Skills

Kresa's actions validate his words. In each issue of the company newsletter, *Northrop News,* is a lengthy column titled "The President's Message," which Kresa uses to share with employees the emerging forces on both the Northrop and the national horizons. His words are without guile or obliqueness; they address thorny issues but leave the reader believing that all is not lost. Here is an excerpt from a recent column.

> Last week the Air Force announced they had awarded the contract to produce the remaining 50 Inertial Measurement units [IMU's] for the MX Peacekeeper missile to Rockwell International and not us. The problem wasn't that the Air Force thought we couldn't produce—they know we can—or that they thought we weren't dedicated to quality—they know we are, or that we hadn't worked hard to reduce our cost of doing business. Simply put, we lost this contract because our price was higher than our competitor's price.[1]

Kresa's stance is a balanced one. He speaks of the need for us as citizens to understand the federal government's mandates to get "more bang for the buck," and the subsequent need for Northrop employees to respond to budget cutting. His motivational messages, expressed in the first person—both singular and plural—offer hope: "It's up to you and me to make it happen."

Efficiency, he stresses, will enable the company to continue successfully in the military products industry. So will employee support and the deployment of TQM techniques. In simple terms, Kresa advises employees to eliminate steps or procedures that do not add value; he endorses continuous improvement of work processes. A strong, team-oriented inspiration concludes Kresa's message. "If you will work with me to improve efficiency," he tells his readers, "we can remain competitive."

The coach persona of the leadership psyche is evident in his concluding words: "I have confidence in each of you. Let's learn from the IMU contract. Let's not let anyone take another of our products away from us. As a team, we're too good to let that happen again."

Implementing TQM

Paralleling Kresa's views are those of management consultant Donald J. Ford, who lists several concepts as fundamental to successful implementation of TQM. Communication is the recurrent theme in Ford's identification of essential elements. He cites the following TQM concepts as ones with which every employee should be familiar:

- *continuous improvement (or "kaizen" in the Japanese language, also compared to "achievement motivation" in the United States)*
- *customer expectations and satisfaction as the basis of all business*
- *taking a long-term strategic view*
- *team building*
- *problem-solving*
- *measurement and analysis of work processes*

Ford proposes an implementation strategy (shown on page 46), a strategy that will require considerable investments of time, money and effort on the company's and individual leaders' parts. The company must, of course, first have a clearly articulated vision, must seek to share that vision with all employees, and must exemplify consistency in all its efforts to support that vision. The rudimentary tenets of TQM must be incorporated into that vision. Carefully and correctly promoted, the vision should result in greater employee participation in the corporate goals. The greater the participation, the greater the ultimate end products of quality and profits.

New Relationships

Quality, then, must be viewed as the glue that binds organizational aims. Leadership must help internalize Quality in daily operations; it must ensure that a Quality vision is shared by all employees. In a Quality environment, the old "us-versus-them" way of thinking must be replaced by a shared drive toward excellence, attained through cooperation. We are beginning to see that sense of togetherness emerge in labor/management contracts. A recent article in the *Total Quality Newsletter*[2] cites the "dramatic restructuring" of union/management relationships in numerous American businesses. Of particular importance are some of the joint governance agreements between the company and the union shop regarding what happens on the shop floor.

COMMITMENT

Gain the commitment and active support of top management to the concepts of continuous improvement, customer satisfaction, strategic thinking, etc.

PLANNING

Build commitment to these concepts throughout the organization by setting goals, establishing pilot projects and action plans, and providing an overview of TQM philosophy.

DATA-GATHERING

Focus on the customer, both internal and external. Clarify customer expectations and explore the reasons for customer dissatisfaction.

ACTION

Teach the specific tools and techniques of TQM, starting with team building and problem-solving and then moving to the analysis and measurement of work processes with an eye toward identifying opportunities for improvement.

MONITORING

Evaluate results, identify new problems, and recycle through the process again.

Another example of cooperation can be found in teams composed of engineers, union representatives, salespeople and management—teams that have valuable contributions to make to decisions about the design of products and the ways to handle customer-service problems.

Acknowledging the inherent risks for both sides in such agreements, the article points out that these joint efforts "to create empowered employee operating teams, participatory management structures and other total quality initiatives are becoming more the rule than the exception." Larry Bankowski, national president of the American Flint Glass Workers Union of the AFL-CIO concedes that union leaders are often asked by their membership why they support so many TQM programs. Bankowski invariably gives them his one-word answer: "Survival."

Asked what Human Resources departments should be emphasizing to cultivate a TQM environment, Kresa replies:

There needs to be an effective partnership between human resources and management at all levels. Only in such an environment can Human Resources support management in implementing TQM. Naturally, the Human Resources Department is a critical supplier of services in such areas as communication, coaching, and training.

Transitions

Communication, coaching, training—companies must invest in all three if the transition from usual to unusual productivity via TQM is to be achieved. Such investment can lessen the potential severity of a shock to the corporate system. The shock can also be mitigated through the introduction of TQM pilot programs, which are gaining more and more support from management and labor alike. William B. Scott, reporting in *Aviation Week & Space Technology,*[3] tells of the introduction of TQM into numerous factory floors via pilot programs. In other companies, the pilot projects have been extended and results are beginning to show. While it will no doubt be several years before serious gains in productivity levels can be seen, some improvement, nonetheless, can definitely be seen.

Many of these restructuring efforts (pilot and otherwise) were discussed in the first National TQM Symposium, held in Denver in November, 1989. Two of the aerospace leaders—McDonnell Douglas and Martin Marietta reported on their efforts:

- McDonnell Douglas (which underwent major organizational restructuring in early 1989 to accommodate its company-wide incorporation of TQM practices) flattened its pyramid and developed product teams. The restructure was necessary, in view of the company's history of losses. (For the preceding 30 years, Douglas produced 2,442 commercial aircraft at a loss of over $1 billion.)

While McDonnell Douglas' financial problems are far from over and while some industry analysts feel the revitalization may have come too late, the company is nevertheless attempting to analyze the past in order to improve the future.

Robert H. Hood, Jr., president of Douglas Aircraft Company (which handles the commercial transport business of the parent company) spoke of the transition the company underwent as a difficult one. He acknowledged that not enough attention had been paid to communication and training.

We embarked on a communication plan that we thought would cover everything possible. But...if we had doubled it, we would still have come up short. Any time you embark on an organizational change of this magnitude, people are starved for communication. You have to talk to them—not through newsletters and videos, [but] eyeball-to-eyeball. That's the only way they understand your commitment, and that's what they're looking for.[4]

Hood also spoke of underestimating the amount of training needed. (In an effort to erode communication barriers, Douglas' training classes are conducted informally; participants wear jeans and open shirts.)

- Martin Marietta has trained 12,000 people in TQM philosophies but admits they are still in the beginning stages of their training program. They cite as an example a savings of $27 million to an Army customer and an additional $10 million back to the company as a result of one process action team's TQM-related efforts. They also cite improved inventory accuracy, improved accuracy of parts kit composition, increased first-time product yields, and decreases in scrap and in equipment returned from field due to latent defects.

- A different project team worked to reduce the number of vendors from 5,000 to 30, produced $10 million savings in 1989, and ensured that over 90 percent of orders are received within 24 hours.

Leaders are responsible for orchestrating such changes and for helping to shape the destiny of the companies they manage. Sometimes that destiny-shaping means bold ventures into new arenas. Peter Drucker has observed that "every new product, process or service begins to become obsolete on the day it first breaks even." The way to prevent a competitor from making a process, product, or service obsolete, he maintains, is to be the one who makes it so.

Strategic Planning

In view of that paradoxical motivation, I asked Kresa what trends he foresaw for Northrop in the decade ahead. His response embodies the leader's ability to move from what was to what is and to take followers to what should be, can be, and ideally will be:

In the 1970's, Northrop embarked on a strategy of investing the earnings from our very successful F-5 and international services businesses into high technology programs. These investments were being made while these programs were "in the prime of life." That strategy paid off in excellent growth through the 1980's, substantially in excess of the industry average.

Today, Northrop has a range of programs that span the typical life cycle for aerospace products, with most of the programs we won in the 1980's now in the developmental or early growth stage. The B-2 is transitioning into initial product, Tacit Rainbow and others are still in full-scale development, and ATF is in demonstration-validation and won't reach full-scale development for another year. Even our older products such as the 747 and F-18 fuselage sections are periodically improved to extend their life cycles. For example, a new surge of orders has been created by the improvements to the 747, which resulted in the 747-400.

As our development programs make the transition into production, we will see significantly increased sales. Our clear-cut path to growth—as well as earnings improvement—in the 1990's is continuously improving our performance on what we have already signed up to do, rather than the acquisition of new programs.

This strategy has important ramifications because every dimension of our business must be scrutinized for possible improvement—using TQM. In the effort to achieve customer satisfaction, we are intensifying Total Quality Management. TQM in design; in manufacturing; in product support functions; and in contract management, will keep costs down, margins up, customers satisfied, and will significantly contribute to our competitive posture.

Teamwork

When speaking of the future, Kresa inevitably emphasizes the importance of teamwork. In a recent address to Northrop's management clubs, he elaborated upon the company's commitment to TQM principles and to the defense industry itself.

I just want to let all of you know that my strategy, and the corporate strategy, is that Northrop is in the defense business to stay. I think that we have built a team of highly skilled men and women who have the technical skills to carry out this very sophisticated business.[5]

When asked about preparing the incoming work force to assume TQM responsibilities, Kresa again mentions teamwork.

There are some very significant differences between the focus and rewards of the educational system as compared with the environment in which today's students will later spend their work lives. In school, students are rewarded for their individual task perfor-

mance. A TQM oriented work force tends to be process *team focused.*

We must learn to work in groups as our interactions with others become as important as our individual performance on specific tasks. We must develop interpersonal and team skills. The earlier in life these capabilities are acquired, the better for the individual, the company in which that person works, and our nation.

The shift from individual problem-solving to group problem-solving is discussed in an article by Tennant Company employees Roger L. Hale, Douglas R. Hoelscher, and Ronald E. Kowal.[6] The authors speak of the pronoun "we" as the operative word and attribute the most significant quality improvements to small groups that seek not to find fault in individuals but rather to solve problems with strategies that cut across department lines. Two out of three Tennant employees work in these small groups, which have a "champion" in the upper echelons who will fight to implement the solutions the groups have found.

Psychologists have told us for years that the behavior that is rewarded is the behavior that is repeated. Similarly, the authors acknowledge that the rapidity with which group commitment dies is directly proportional to the lack of upper management response to group efforts. Barrier-elimination, then, is a major responsibility of the managers who head the vertically integrated teams.

Remedial Education

Kresa commented that the earlier a person is exposed to the rudiments of a discipline—whether that discipline be a sport or a foreign language or a TQM philosophy—the more easily he can gain comfort and fluency in its use. The schools, then, are an ideal breeding ground for the propagation of mindsets receptive to TQM philosophies.

Unfortunately, a number of experts are lamenting the lack of fluency exhibited by American students as far as technological and communication skills are concerned. Business leaders are noting with alarm the trend in the United States toward general illiteracy as well as scientific illiteracy. An article by Stanley W. Kandebo in *Aviation Week & Space Technology*[7] specifies the combination of the illiteracy trend, the increasing dependence of our populace on technology, and the politicians' avoidance of these two concerns as placing the United States in jeopardy, as far as both national security and the ability to remain globally competitive are concerned.

Citing Mikhail Gorbachev's regret at his own country's failure to understand the impact of scientific and technological changes, Kandebo opines that the United States is close to making the same mistake. As American companies strive to produce quality products at lower prices, they are hampered by the billions of dollars having to be spent on providing employees with basic skills. Another factor that affects individuals and corporations alike is the dropout rate, which translates into more than $240 billion in lost wages, lost taxes and welfare programs. The figures related to our educational crisis are staggering:

- 25 percent of American high school students do not graduate. The figure is even higher for minority students.

- Half of those who do graduate do not take mathematics courses past the tenth grade.

- Only 16 percent of the students have had a year of chemistry.

- Fewer than 10 percent have taken a course in physics.

- The average Japanese student does better in mathematics than the top 5 percent of American students.

- 25 percent of our 13-year-olds cannot handle elementary school arithmetic.

- Only 6 percent of our 17-year-olds can handle algebra.

- 27 million Americans are functionally illiterate.

- 45 million are marginally literate.

- Only one-third of American high schools offer enough math courses to enable a student to enter an accredited engineering college.

Corporations are concerned and so are making inroads into territory once thought to be the sacrosanct domain of academicians. Conferences are being sponsored to examine these very problems. One such amalgam of education, business, political, and labor leaders was recently held in Rochester, New York. Its purpose was to find solutions for traditional illiteracy and also for "workplace illiteracy."

According to Phil Ebersole of the *Democrat and Chronicle*,

An estimated one in five U.S. workers lacks the ability to read basic materials required to hold a job, recent research indicates. But employers, particularly in high technology manufacturing industries, require even more than just the ability to read. They want workers who not only know how to read and do math, but also know teamwork, decision-making, listening and speaking.

With fewer young adults entering the work force, employers are waking up to the need to educate those who do, said David Mathes, an organizer of the conference. The Center for Public Resources found that three out of four of the biggest U.S. companies provide some kind of basic skills training for their employees.[8]

The New York State Department of Education saw the need for such a conference and selected Rochester because of the strong support its school system receives from Eastman Kodak Company and the Xerox Corporation (both of which were founded in Rochester), as well as from Delco Products and AC Rochester divisions of General Motors. These firms and several labor unions are all sponsors of skills training programs and so were ideal representatives.

In response to a question about what corporations could and should be doing to aid education, Peter M. Palermo, vice president and general manager of the Consumer Imaging Division of Eastman Kodak Company, discusses the Rochester Brainpower Program, of which Kodak is a leader.

*We are starting with the assumption that without a quality educa-
tion, you do not have any choices. The degree to which everyone
on the faculty of the institution has a sense of pride and a feeling
of quality in what they do, is the degree to which Quality will
permeate an entire organization.*

*The Rochester Brainpower program is a community-wide effort
to involve all sectors of the community in the improvement of
education. It is predicated on this notion: educaton is everyone's
business. One element of the program encourages business people
to go into the schools (preferably those schools from which they
have graduated) and share some visions, some thoughts about
Quality.*

*Nationally, we have joined Alan Page, the National Football
League Hall of Famer in the Kodak/Alan Page Challenge to
encourage young people to think about the value of education
through an essay competition. With him as our spokesperson, we
are committed to that notion. With it, young people can build a
quality education and ultimately a quality life.*

Anthony Carnevale, vice president for the American Society for Training and Development, lauded the effort—not a widespread one in our
country—that brought together educators and employers to face an
urgent issue that affects us all. Conceding that the goals of education go
beyond preparing students for the work force, he nonetheless expressed
hopes for deeper commitments to learning on the part of both educators
and employers.

In *The Technology Edge,* Gerard O'Neil discusses the difficulty many
corporations are experiencing in finding well-educated people in the pool
of college students.[9] He cites an IBM executive for whom the quality of
education in America is a "chief concern." Lew Branscomb laments the
fact that only one in five high school students in this country takes a
science class during his junior or senior year. Further, only half the
students take math courses during their last two years of secondary
education. Chemistry is studied by only one out of seven high school
students, while physics is studied by only one in fourteen.

In a similar vein, David T. Kearns, Chairman of the Board of the Xerox Corporation, 1989 winner of the Baldrige National Quality Award, responded this way to the question of what Quality concepts should be introduced to the high school curriculum.

I believe the single most important thing we can introduce to the curriculum to improve quality is statistics. This is one area where the Japanese excel and we are very weak. The entire concept of quality improvement demands that we use statistical tools to identify problems, measure performance, and so on. Most American high school graduates are totally unfamiliar with this.

The results of this limited academic pursuit are destructive, O'Neill asserts, both for the students and for the nation itself. One unfortunate consequence is the decline in the amount of patent activity. Another regrettable consequence is the paucity of engineers for our business: only one third as many as they have in Japan and only one sixth as many as they have in Germany.

Human Resource Development

Since so few well-trained workers are coming into the work force, the corporation must assume educational responsibilities. And within the corporate context, the training role often falls on the shoulders of Human Resource (HR) developers. In an article titled "Join Forces for Total Quality Control or Take a Trainer to Lunch," Roland A. Dumas[10] explores the expanded role HR trainers can play within companies.

Dumas expresses regret that in some places, HR departments are still viewed as performing the traditional and restricted personnel duties. Just as macrocosmic partnerships are being formed between the leaders of industry and education, Dumas recognizes a need for partnerships between "organizational development and training functions."

He likens the metamorphosis HR professionals are undergoing to the metamorphosis that Quality Control professionals have had to undergo to escape the "inspection" image. There are three aspects (depicted in Figure 2) that he views as paramount to Quality efforts.

FIGURE 2

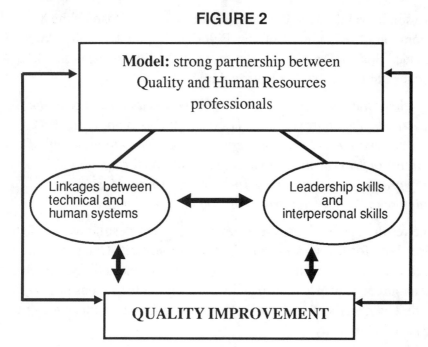

He decries the extant void in Quality training programs, a void which he asserts could be filled by HR departments, which are strong in the very areas that Quality programs call for. That most HR departments are relegated to minor supporting roles and are not included in critical decisions is a situation Dumas finds unfortunate. A greater involvement by HR professionals, Dumas asserts, could "dramatically accelerate acceptance and implementation of advanced quality systems."

After mentioning a number of firms that have merged their training and their organizational development functions to better implement Quality programs, Dumas concludes,

> We saw a wide variety of approaches, and a wide range of successes. The common denominator among the more successful efforts is that they consider technical and human systems to be inextricably linked, and that a true partnership between quality and human resources professionals is one of the best ways to model this belief.[11]

His final thought echoes Kresa's position:

> We have repeatedly found that there are foundation skills, general leadership and interpersonal management skills, that consistently make or break a quality effort. Without these skills in place, the role of quality management will likely include rolling stones back up Sisyphus' hill.[12]

Optimism

Despite the knells being sounded about the lack of skills possessed by both future and current employees, many corporate spokespersons, Kresa among them, have cause for optimism. They feel that TQM can and will ensure a better quality in our labor force and thereby, a better quality in our products and services. Kresa advises his managers:

> As a world power, this country will require a strong defense. It's going to continue to be a very big and important business. And the sophistication of our business, both in the technology that we need to run it and in the way the whole process is carried out, say that there will be unique opportunities for companies who are willing to dedicate themselves to that business.[13]

Kresa repeatedly talks of meeting the challenge to deliver quality products on time and within budget; the way to do this, he insists, is by employing TQM processes. He solicits employees' ideas to help the company become more efficient, to make every employee recognize the importance of his or her contribution. He speaks of exciting results that can ensue when cooperation and innovation become guidelines for everyday behavior, and encourages communications across disciplines. Of special importance is his appeal to employees to realize that their future will be determined by their own efforts, not by someone else's decisions.

Small Successes

Efforts to make improvements without increasing costs can be found in large as well as small examples. What is important is that employees are always seeking ways to improve the processes of their work. Ford speaks of one such improvement at a large company where he has worked. He describes it as a "very small success that illustrates the way TQM can make incremental improvements in an office environment."

When I came on board, we began to talk about TQM in staff meetings and started by identifying areas of our work where problems were occurring.

One that the librarian mentioned was her daily distribution to key managers of a computer database search of the Commerce Business Daily. *At the time, she had computerized the database search and download, but was manually cutting and pasting the various items requested by each manager, and then photocopying them by hand for distribution in the morning mail.*

As we began to flowchart the process, we found that it took about 15 minutes to do the computer search, and nearly an hour to cut and paste the requested items, and photocopy and distribute them in the mail. This was consuming the librarian's time, preventing her from serving the reference needs of walk-in patrons.

Our analysis led us to focus on the manual cut and paste process as the one that could most benefit from improvement. Accordingly, I set my staff the task of coming up with alternatives. After investigation, one of my staff discovered that he could use our word processing package, WordPerfect, to automate this manual process. The way he did it was to write several macros to instruct WordPerfect to automatically load the text of the database search, scan it for key terms, paginate the document and print out those sections that matched the key search terms.

After automation, the entire process was cut from an hour and 15 minutes to less than 30 minutes, a time savings of 60 percent. With the extra time, the librarian was better able to serve the needs of walk-in patrons, resulting in higher customer satisfaction.

Summary

A number of important ideas are advanced by the TQM philosophy proponents quoted in this chapter. Kent Kresa, in his role at the helm of the Northrop Corporation, talks of the need for open communications, teamwork, and barrier-elimination. As more companies seek to reduce their budgets and yet produce higher quality products at lower prices, the TQM emphases on efficiency and waste reduction assume first-magnitude roles. By continually enhancing work processes, by making TQM universally understood and applied, and by planning strategically for the long term, we can help to ensure customer satisfaction.

Donald Ford presents a five-step TQM-implementation strategy and endorses the need to view TQM as an incremental process of small successes leading to ultimate accomplishment of corporate goals. He, too, discusses the importance of relationships that will make multiplicative the efforts toward problem-solving.

The possible alliance of human resources and organizational development groups is another possible fount for increased productivity. According to Roland Dumas, Quality improvement efforts are maximized when the Quality professionals and the human resources professionals form partnerships that can serve as models for other connections between the technical systems and the human systems. The formation of such linkages, however, calls for leadership, interpersonal, and management skills.

If the productivity and growth of American industries is to continue, if we are to achieve world-class status once again, we must pay more attention to the products of our school systems. Until our academic results reach international levels of excellence, we must continue relying on the corporations to provide the training that is necessary. And so, the efforts of human resource departments to train and to forge cooperative relationships are vitally important. When they work with companies like the Xerox Corporation and Eastman Kodak Company, the crucial partnerships that evolve represent the best way to tackle America's "toughest assignment."

The relationships, however, need not be restricted to internal teams: a number of organizations are pooling their resources to help us make the work force better qualified. And the earlier that work force is introduced to TQM concepts such as team problem-solving, as opposed to individual task-accomplishment, the more cause we have for optimism that America can indeed be a key player in the international trade contests.

For Further Consideration

1. What do you think your company should "intend to ensure" for the decades ahead?

2. Other than the company newsletter and the annual report to shareholders, how can leaders communicate a Quality message? Think of some innovative ways.

3. Define leadership. To whom should leadership training be given? What should it emphasize?

4. What is the "TQM style of leadership"?

5. Do you agree with Kent Kresa that interpersonal, team, and leadership skills are the bases for the TQM structure? If you do not agree, what bases would you list?

6. Within the parameters of your own job, identify steps or procedures that do not add value.

7. In some companies, Quality training is provided by the CEO, in an effort to have top-down communication. How would such training be received in your company?

8. Devise a strategic plan for your company, as if you were the CEO intent upon having Quality cascade throughout the organization.

9. How are problems typically solved in your organization?

10. Of the various elements that constitute a description of your job, what is being measured?

11. Are there some barriers that can be viewed as good things to have?

12. Unless your organization has 100 percent of the market share, your external customer probably has some dissatisfaction with your company's product or service. What might be the source of that dissatisfaction?

References

[1] Kent Kresa. "We Must Remain Competitive," *Northrop News,* Vol. 48, No. 6 (March 23, 1990), p.3.

[2] "Restructuring Union Relations Profoundly Impacts Quality," *Total Quality Newsletter,* Vol. 1, No. 3 (June 1990), pp. 1–3. Reprinted with permission from Lakewood Publications, 50 South Ninth St., Minneapolis, MN 55402. All rights reserved.

[3] William B. Scott. "Aerospace/Defense Firms" see "Preliminary Results from Application of TQM Concepts," *Aviation Week & Space Technology,* Vol. 132, #12 (January 8, 1990), pp. 61–62.

[4] *Ibid.,* p. 62.

[5] Kresa. *op. cit.,* pp. 1, 4.

[6] Hale, Roger L. *et al,* "Tools for the Manager," *Total Quality Handbook* (Minneapolis: Lakewood Books, 1990), pp. 193–194. Reprinted with permission from Lakewood Publications, 50 South Ninth St., Minneapolis, MN 55402. All rights reserved.

[7] Kandebo, Stanley W. "Performance of U.S. Educational System Threatens Defense Base, Economic Position," *Aviation Week & Space Technology,* Vol. 131, #25 (December 18, 1989), pp. 34–35.

[8] Ebersole, Phil. "Conference Tackles 'Workplace' Illiteracy," *Rochester Democrat & Chronicle* (November 2, 1989), p. 1A.

[9] O'Neil, Gerard K. *The Technology Edge* (New York: Simon and Schuster, 1983), pp. 270–271.

[10] Dumas, Roland A. "Join Forces for Total Quality Control, Or: Take a Trainer to Lunch," *Total Quality Handbook* (Minneapolis: Lakewood Books, 1990), pp. 89–92. Reprinted with permission from Lakewood Publications, 50 South Ninth St., Minneapolis, MN 55402. All rights reserved.

[11] *Ibid.,* p. 92.

[12] *Ibid.*

[13] Kresa, *op. cit.,* pp. 1, 4.

William E. Conway, President
Conway Quality, Inc.

"A great majority of our companies, I'm afraid, will not learn to compete, or they will be too late. We will continue on what I now see as a downhill trend.

"It does not have to be this way. There is still plenty of time and opportunity to continue to be at the top."

Background

William E. Conway has associated himself with Quality long before the word became popular. A graduate of "quality" schools—Harvard University and the United States Naval Academy—Conway is the former president and CEO of Nashua Corporation. The packaging for Nashua's magnetic media products contains this information about quality:

> *Quality* is a word that's rather easily tossed around today. Every manufacturer of diskettes is quick to promise you the highest quality available. But, at Nashua, quality has a much tougher definition. It not only means high performance and reliability; it also means *consistency*.

> Nashua can promise you quality with unequaled consistency because we manufacture our diskettes using a totally unique philosophy. It's called the "Statistical Control of Quality." And it's the same concept that revolutionized the Japanese economy, replacing a shoddy image with a reputation for product excellence.

> Simply put, the idea is this: You can't inspect quality into a product. Inspection can only separate good from bad after the fact. That's not only very expensive but unreliable as well. The way to attain consistent quality is to make every product right *in the first place*.

> What makes that possible? Nashua's dedication to statistical control, as an integral part of the manufacturing process, makes that possible. Literally hundreds of charts, like the one shown here, control the enemy of any manufacturing process—variation.

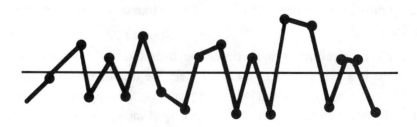

These charts visually ensure that each step of the manufacturing process is under statistical control. Finally, every single diskette is certified to make sure it meets or exceeds system requirements. The result is that our product is the same today, tomorrow, and thereafter. You can trust our diskettes to store and preserve your most important information.[1]

The Nashua message parallels the Conway message, a message that has been delivered to more than 60,000 executives in more than 1000 companies, both nationally and internationally. These companies have engaged Conway Quality, Inc. (located in Nashua, New Hampshire) to bring Quality to their firms via the new management system. William Conway, who began his career as an industrial engineer for Eastman Kodak, has presided over Conway Quality since 1983. His new management system is based on the precepts developed in the "Right Way to Manage," a management system that targets continuous improvement.

Quality Control Circles/Work Teams

One method of developing teams of people to improve quality is the Quality Control (QC) circle. These circles, often called quality circles, are primarily used at the lower levels while project or process improvement teams are used at higher levels.

Quality Control circles were a natural outgrowth of an insistence by Dr. Deming that the root cause of a quality problem is most likely a default or defect with some aspect of the process being used for manufacturing the product. Quality control is a process. And, the workers involved with it are in the best position to determine problems with that process. The quality circle enables them to discuss ways of solving problems. Management, of course, must be receptive to the circle's ideas, since only management can change the system of which the process is a part.

If it is the equipment that is defective, it should be repaired or replaced. If there is a problem with an employee, the employee probably needs further training. If training is not the problem, the employee may simply have to be reassigned or perhaps replaced. If the system or process itself is the source of error, then the system must be assessed and changes must be implemented.

To determine root causes, QC circles are formed by a small group of individuals closely associated with a specific process. They establish a regular meeting time in order to evaluate the current process and to suggest ways of improving the process and thereby improving the quality of their product. The product, of course, is what is being delivered to their customer, and their customer will either be internal or external.

The small-group format has several distinct advantages:

- It allows a sense of camaraderie to develop.

- It fosters the kind of pride that can only be derived when a cohesive group works together toward specific achievements.

- It kindles a sense of commitment and responsibility to the process.

- It melts the fear that often governs large, official meetings by encouraging each employee in this informal setting to make suggestions and contribute insights. Even if their comments are critical of the process, employees need not fear being ridiculed or penalized by a superior.

Quality circles work best where employees voluntarily agree to meetings related to the product they are responsible for delivering to a customer. The focus of the circle's convening is always to produce a better product, whether that means improving morale, or improving the process, the machinery, or the workplace. All these considerations and others impact upon the efficiency and cost with which a product is created or manufactured.

The concept of QC circles is an American one, although it was popularized in Japan and then returned to America, once businesses here began to understand how these QC circles promoted productivity in Japanese industry. The Japanese Union of Scientists and Engineers

(JUSE) formally endorsed the formation of QC circles in the early 1960's, not to increase productivity so much as to make the workplace a more pleasant and significant environment.

Millions of Japanese workers are now involved in QC circles. So indigenous are the circles to the workplace, that there are QC circle chapters established in the eight regions of Japan. All kinds of meetings are held each year, including an annual conference of QC leaders. It is not uncommon in Japanese firms to find expanded quality circles, which include a company's employees and employees at the subcontracting company as well. According to Masaaki Imai, more than half the companies in Japan have introduced QC circle activities. Imai supplies the JUSE definition of such circles:

> a small group that voluntarily performs quality control activities within the shop where its members work, the small group carrying out its work continuously as a part of a company-wide program of quality control, self-development, mutual development, and flow-control and improvement within the workshop. By engaging in QC circle activities, the circle members gain valuable experience in communicating with colleagues, working together to solve problems, and sharing their findings not only among themselves but with other circles at other companies.[2]

Quality circles are not designed as forums for employee complaints. Instead, the meetings are conducted in rooms where discussions and analyses can take place. Since the goal of the QC circle is to take action when justified and empowered to do so, and to make recommendations to management when not empowered by management, the process of arriving at those recommendations is dependent on correct data.

No other organizational development program has caught hold in America with quite the degree of success QC circles have. Considering that stress is identified with feelings of loss of control, it is not surprising that these meetings are well-received by employees, for they return some of the control to the individuals who are closest to the actual production.

The circles succeed when the climate encourages their growth. That climate begins with management receptivity to employee suggestions. When management does not listen, or does not follow through on what has been said, employee initiatives, and morale as well, plummet. When employees feel management "allows" the circles to exist but does not really recognize their value, circles will either cease to exist or will become a source of possible negativity or even subversion. So, while employees may express willingness to engage in Quality circles of their own volition, it is important that management first be sold on the idea. Of course, if management is the source of the circle's creation, it is necessary for top levels of management to work slowly and carefully to encourage employees' participation.

As with all change, management-driven Quality circles have the best chance for success when they are introduced gradually and when the education and training emphases are continuous. Outside speakers can be invited to address small groups of employees who have been invited to participate. Exposure to other people and other companies that have experienced QC success almost always guarantees involvement by targeted parties.

An individual should be appointed to regulate the QC program so that it is not construed to be overlapping the Quality Assurance (QA) or QC shores. This individual should publicize the successes various groups are having. He should also ensure that participating groups are provided with all the training tools they need. Special care must be given to the selection of the circle leader. If an influential but negative individual is chosen, the Quality circle will not succeed. The leader or facilitator must be a positive force in translating problems into performance.

Similarly, team leaders are instrumental in helping work groups to improve processes, including the processes that determine what problems will be addressed. Teams bring multiperspective thinking to the task or problem at hand; they work to gather data, which provides the information needed to improve the process or solve the problem.

Teams maximize output through collaborative and cooperative efforts. They begin by examining the system—a logical sequence of steps that are expected to lead to a specific function being performed so that a specific product or result is produced. Systems are characterized by organization—employees know what is expected of them, they know how to do the jobs that keep the system running. The various processes that make up the system are clearly delineated. Systems are flexible enough to be changed and teams that communicate and work well together can bring about the needed change. The modifications developed by teams lead to continuous improvement of the process.

In their consideration of processes to be improved, teams consider questions such as these:

- What management-defined aspect of the process adds value?

- What management-defined aspect of the process does not add value?

- What employee-altered aspect of the process adds value?

- What employee-altered aspect of the process does not add value?

Preparing flowcharts helps teams to answer these questions, which usually lead to modifications.

Before the modifications are implemented, however, the team leader will ask additional questions of his team:

1. What is the goal of this modification?

2. Is there a better way to accomplish the same end?

3. How extensive need the modification be?

4. Have we utilized the expertise of everyone who works with the current procedure?

5. Are there precedents for our modification? If so, with whom could we talk to see if the proposed modification is working?

6. How will the next customer—internal or external—react to the modification?

7. Who else—including upper management—may be affected by the modification?

8. Does the cost of the modification warrant its incorporation into the process?

9. How long should we test the proposed modification before implementing it?

As project/work teams (often described as self-managed, semi-autonomous or cross-functional) acquire more control over their own work processes, their satisfaction with their work increases and so ultimately does the quality of their output.

When employees have some ownership in decisions being made about the work being done, when their contributions are actively sought, they inevitably feel greater commitment toward the work processes and the final product of those processes. On the other hand, when employees' potential is not tapped, they may become apathetic, giving only what is asked of them and little more.

As Joan Smith, manager of Federal Systems Division Pricing at TRW observes, "People like to be part of the fix, not part of the problem." Regarding team meetings she notes, "The meetings succeed because people want them to. People are making it happen." She attributes the success of such teamwork to positive attitudes: "The process and product are improved because of these attitudes." This kind of receptivity toward change has a further advantage: it lessens the training time required to introduce the change, since employees have already been exposed to, and have accepted, the new procedure.

Data Collection

Conway warns, however, that work groups will only "scratch the surface" of improvement unless they follow certain steps. It is not enough to simply work toward improving systems or processes: work must be founded in careful analyses of the processes. And data collection is imperative if comparisons are to be made between pre-change and post-change effects.

Some employees cringe at the phrase "statistical control of quality," believing that without formal training in statistics or higher mathematics, they will not be capable of collecting or analyzing data. And yet, we deal—all of us—with statistics every day of our lives. The advertisements we read, the news we hear, the articles we read, the reports we prepare—all deal with numbers that provide information.

"Statistics" simply refers to a number of tools or methods with which we gather, assess, interpret and then reveal information by using numbers. We need the data provided by statistics to help us make decisions about our jobs and about our lives as well. H.G. Wells has noted that "statistical thinking will one day be as necessary for efficient citizenship as the ability to read and write." And Dr. Deming has asserted that statistical studies are designed to "provide a basis for action."

Work groups begin the data collection process by asking questions. The information acquired may either be internal or external, primary (original information acquired for the problem being studied) or secondary (acquired from some other source). We need to bear in mind, too, the differences between the two kinds of studies. The **enumerative** study is a count or an evaluation of something, whereas the **analytic** study seeks causes.

A clear example of the aim behind each study is cited by William W. Scherkenbach:

> When there is an earthquake or a flood, a vital question is how many people, adults, infants, and infirm are there in need of the necessities of life. The aim is not to try to find out why so many people lived there, nor how to foretell the coming of an earthquake.[3]

The enumerative study involves counting for the purposes of knowing how many relief supplies will be needed. The analytic study has a different aim: it collects data so that a future situation can be improved.

Scherkenbach relates this story that Conway shared with Ford management on the importance of having the right tools:

Let's suppose we are going to have a little contest. And so I take Bill and Charlie to my office and tell each of them that if he wins the contest he will have a big pension, take his family on an around-the-world cruise, and otherwise be set for the rest of his life. Each of them is motivated and enthused about doing the job. They couldn't have better attitudes. I now explain that the contest consists of putting five wood screws into a pine board. I give each the screws and a board. But before the contest begins, I give Charlie a little technical tool. I give him a screwdriver. Bill will just have to do the best he can. Well, the contest begins and Charlie obviously wins and Bill is still saying that Charlie wasn't playing by the same rules. Of course he wasn't. He was using everything he had at his disposal. He would be dumb if he didn't.[4]

Scherkenbach declares we would be dumb not to use statistical tools. They are available; they are at our disposal. I asked Conway how a company begins the process, how it goes about collecting worthwhile data:

What it requires is this: active leadership at whatever level we are going to start. Of course, it is best if the leadership starts with the CEO and cascades down throughout the organization, but in many cases, that leadership might start with a first-line supervisor in a given department. The leadership could also come from any place in-between the first-line supervisor and the CEO.

The supervisor meets with the people working with him. They discuss the troubles or problems they may be having in the operation. They consider the ways of doing things right—emphasizing not what is wrong but what can be right. Their discussion centers on the question, "What do you think the trouble is here?"

People give various answers and express their opinions. The boss then says, "Instead of opinions that may be right, why don't we get the facts? We cannot really proceed until we get the facts." How do you do that? The boss makes an announcement, sets up the check sheets.

Decisions are made about who is going to collect the data and how they will measure it. How are they going to record it? Where are they going to record it? What are they going to do with the check sheets? Correlate it? Put it together?

Then after we have put together all the data, we use simple charts to convert the data to information. Then we are on our way.

Graphically, the Conway Data Collection/Presentation process would look like this chart.

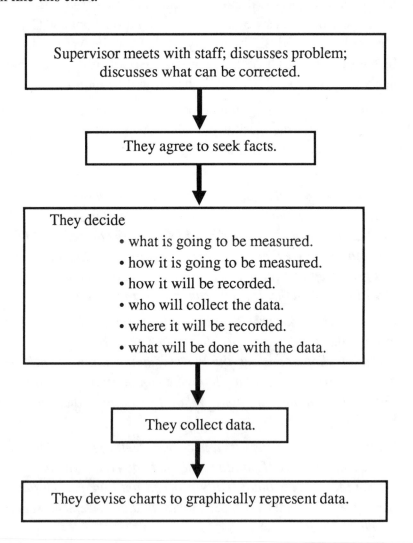

Supervisor meets with staff; discusses problem; discusses what can be corrected.

They agree to seek facts.

They decide
- what is going to be measured.
- how it is going to be measured.
- how it will be recorded.
- who will collect the data.
- where it will be recorded.
- what will be done with the data.

They collect data.

They devise charts to graphically represent data.

Gathering the data and then preparing the charts were the first two steps in a five-point plan that Conway presented in an address to the Board of Directors meeting of the National Association of Manufacturers. According to Conway, if work teams are truly serious about improving processes, they must engage in a formalized process of data collection.

The charts that result are summarizations and interpretations of all the data that were compiled. Merely reporting the raw data is useless, says Conway. You must make sense of the data; you must convert it to information. Imagine, for example, that you were interested in opening an ice cream parlor in New Orleans. Your researchers have studied the ice cream eating habits of the residents of that city. Imagine if they had just presented you with the dates, locations, prices being charged, and purchaser characteristics for every single cone that was sold over a three-month period.

These enumerative data would be of little use to you in and of themselves. What you would need, in order to make decisions about the profitability of your enterprise, would be analytic data. Such data would interpret the enumerative figures and would be able to present you with a clearer picture of the type of consumer you should design your advertising for, the price you should charge, the best place to locate your store, etc.

Causes

The third step in the Conway method, as applied to manufacturing processes, is to determine both the special causes and the common causes for variation. The fault or defect is not always attributable to a person. In fact, Dr. Deming has repeatedly asserted that the worker, in all likelihood, is not the problem. And yet, it is the worker who is usually blamed as being careless or lazy or incapable. The majority of the problems or errors that arise in the production of a product or delivery of a service lie with the system, according to Dr. Deming. A minimal percent can be attributed to workers.

I should estimate that in my experience most troubles and most possibilities for improvement add up to proportions something like this:

94 percent belong to the system (responsibility of management)

6 percent special.[5]

Since management has established the system and subsequently maintained it, the responsibility for changing the system must lie with management, most of the time. Workers simply do not have the authority to change the system. And yet, they are held in the system's thrall and then are blamed when the system does not function as it should. The common (environmental) causes are germane to that system and to any other system operating in the same way.

The special causes can be specific worker deficiencies. They can also be unusual or temporary circumstances that account for the variation. Whatever the special causes are, they have to be fixed, as Conway asserts in his fourth step. These special causes are not part of the usual process but rather of some external force or unusual conditions.

The five-step Conway Plan for improving manufacturing processes looks like this:

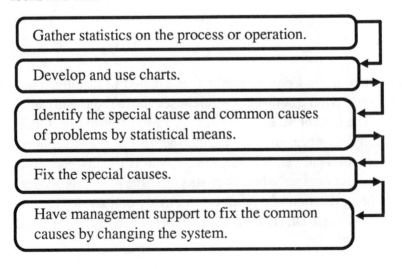

Gather statistics on the process or operation.

Develop and use charts.

Identify the special cause and common causes of problems by statistical means.

Fix the special causes.

Have management support to fix the common causes by changing the system.

The New Management System

Conway is convinced that America has all the tools it needs to regain and then sustain the competitive position in world markets that began eroding in the second half of the 20th century. The problem is not the tools necessary for our emergent cognizance of Quality principles. Nor is the problem our ability to apply the tools we have. Rather, maintains Conway, America needs a new management system, one that will loosen the rigidity of existing paradigms, one that will help us better manage technology. He observes,

> *What we have in the new management system is a revolution in work. It is very important to understand that there is a revolution in work. We have to make certain we are working on the right things and to improve the way we do that work. Whether it is working with people, machines, energy, chemical processes...let's consider the work and work process.*

> *Webster's Dictionary will tell you that a revolution is a "drastic change" and that is exactly what we have.*

Drastic Change

The change Conway tirelessly endorses is a total change in both cognitive and physical processes, which will bring about the change in work processes. Understanding the new management system will require launching an invasive attack upon the old way of doing things. So compelling will this new mindset be that employees will think and act and communicate and view their work with a new perspective. When this happens, management knows that paradigms have shifted and Quality has become the fabric of the organization as well as the natural way of doing things. Upon attainment of this Quality-dense culture, the organization can rest assured that Quality is here to stay. Here is Conway's prediction:

> *What is going to happen is that there will be a continuation of work going on here in the Western world. Company after company is starting to see it. Improvements are being made.*

The question really is whether senior management of our organizations, of our government, is going to recognize the true significance of this. Will they see the change we are talking about? And if they do, are they going to act as leaders to convert it from something a few people do, to something all the people in their organizations are going to do all of the time?

Unfortunately, so far, the progress being made in the Western world on an overall basis, particularly here in the United States and Canada, is at a relatively modest level.

Dr. Deming cites Conway's inveterate belief in the need of top management to begin the process of bringing the Quality mindset to their companies.

It is not enough that top management commit themselves for life to quality and productivity. They must know what it is that they are committed to—that is, what they must do. These obligations can not be delegated. Support is not enough: action is required.

"...and if you can't come, send nobody."

These are the words in a letter that William E. Conway [then president and CEO of the Nashua Corporation] wrote to a vice president in response to the latter's request for an invitation to visit the Nashua Corporation.

In other words, Mr. Conway told him, if you don't have time to do your job, there is not much that I can do for you.[6]

The advice from our Quality masters is direct, unadorned, definite. Words are not minced, because survival is what is at stake. Conway acknowledges that some companies are taking direct steps in the right direction, although he laments the failure of others to listen to the clarion call to action:

That does not mean I could not give you examples of some companies that have done extraordinarily well and continue to do so. But when you put that in the perspective of our entire economy, when you consider all of the large corporations, unfortunately, the few that are succeeding pale by comparison.

"Drastic change" is what we need in the way things are going to go. I would say we are going to see it continued working in a new way, more and more people doing it, some organizations being effective at it.

Those companies that are effective will gradually become world class companies at what they do, here in our own country or around the world. Unfortunately, a great many of the others will not.

Remaining Competitive

Conway has reduced the new management system to a simply-phrased, easily understood definition: "the continuous improvement of all work processes forever through quality to please the external customer." Improvement means detecting and then rejecting waste, constantly working toward a waste-free environment—one that does not permit waste to creep back in. It is self-driven actions that will make us competitive, he believes, not government-driven actions that make us "competitive" by eliminating competition.

As competitive pressures build up, there will be more and more requests—just as there are now—from individuals and companies wanting protection or wanting protection extended. Of course, we do not call it that. We have to buy American, have marketing agreements and all those other things. It is nothing, of course, but pure protectionism.

We will never really be protected unless we learn how to compete. The more protections we have, the less pressure will be put upon people to change the way they do things.

Peter Drucker concurs with the potentially damaging effects of protectionism on initiative, in his examination of the growth of multi-nationalism:

Even less valid than the common beliefs about the nature of multi-nationalism are the popular explanations of its causes. One sees in it a response to protectionism. Companies build factories abroad, it is being argued, because they can no longer export. But this explanation, while plausible, simply does not fit the facts.

The period of most rapid growth of multinationalism—the fifties and sixties—was the period of the most rapid growth of international trade. Indeed, during this period the world trading economy grew faster—at an annual rate of 15 percent or so in most years—than even the fastest growing domestic economy, i.e., that of Japan. And the Japanese clearly could not have grown at the rate they did if protectionism had made impossible economic expansion based on exports abroad. It is not in the most heavily protected industries where multinationalism has forged ahead the fastest.

Multinationalism and expanding world trade are two sides of the same coin. And far from being a cause of multinationalism, protectionism is incompatible with it. Indeed, an emergence of protectionism would be the greatest threat to the multinational corporation.[7]

It is John Naisbitt's contention that since we are no longer an industrial economy, we can no longer hope, should no longer hope, to regain our position as the world's primary industrial power. Instead, he asserts, we should regard ourselves as part of an interdependent global economy and as one of several economically strong nations, instead of regarding ourselves as a self-sufficient national economy and as the world's strongest economy. "It is too late to recapture our industrial supremacy because we are no longer an industrial economy,"[8] he insists.

There is no point in rehashing the *why's* here. The point is that our recent failures are real. And after a period of blaming everyone but ourselves, many of America's business people finally accept the unhappy reality behind the statistics of the past decade. To its credit, American business has started experimenting with various strategies designed to build a better economic future—for example, creating American versions of quality circles and shifting from short-term to long-term strategies.[9]

Conway feels that America *can* regain its competitive edge, despite the transition from an industrial to an information-oriented economy. There is optimism in his voice and hope in his words as he discusses a return, or at least a partial return, to what once was.

A great majority of our companies, I'm afraid, will not learn to compete, or they will be too late. Gradually, the economic role will change: we will be continuing on what I now see as a downhill trend.

It does not have to be that way. If a way could be found to get top management (owners, directors, senior managers) of the leading organizations in the United States to work this new management system way, they could fight being way behind. Some industries we may never get back, but there are loads of others where there is still plenty of time and opportunity to continue to be at the top.

I hope I will see this change. As yet, we have not had enough chance to bring this eventuality about.

Training the Work Force

The cushioning of America's fall from first-ranked economic grace will depend, in part, on having a skilled work force. Unfortunately, radical measures will have to be taken to reform the national educational curriculum, in much the same way that corporate mindsets are being made receptive to the new management system.

Despite the 1980 prediction (made in a joint report of the U.S. Department of Education and the National Science Foundation) that most Americans are headed toward "virtual scientific and technological illiteracy," little improvement has been seen in the years since the report was published. Educational experts forecast Third World wages for American workers unless the educational system is restructured to provide as much attention to vocational training as it does to college preparation.

Just as Conway urges "drastic" change in the study and improvement of work, the Commission on the Skills of the American Workforce recommends "radical" redesign to help the United States match the educational emphases of other countries. Just as Dr. Deming decries the use of traditional performance appraisals, the Commission proposes eliminating the traditional high school diploma. In its place would be a Certificate of Initial Mastery, to be earned by age 16. This certificate would be based on world educational criteria, not the minimums that most states now have mandated. The Commission also advocates guaranteeing all students four additional years of education, either in trade programs or college degree programs.

If the recommendations are adopted, employers would be required to devote one percent of their payroll funds for training the adult work force. In an interview with *USA Today's* Dennis Kelly, Ray Marshall, former Secretary of Labor states, "We have the worst system of any major industrial country for non-college-bound students." The conviction in his words: "We've got to find ways to get people moving on this agenda and we will,"[10] is not unlike Conway's certainty that TQM principles can be introduced to teenagers.

I see ways the Quality movement could be brought in to the high school curriculum, but if they understood the true effect of this drastic change in the way people work, then Quality concepts would be taught in the schools relatively quickly.

Unfortunately, since the realization is not there in most of our areas of top government officials (be they state or federal), since it is not there with most of our top officials of industry, that is going to be a hard thing to do, to bring about.

A seven-step plan for creating the new management system is espoused by Conway. Directly or indirectly, each of the steps deals with education.

1. Educate the people.

2. Lead the people at all levels of the organization.

3. Identify and quantify the waste at all levels.

4. Enable people to work in this new way by changing the organizational behavior. (Remove the barriers to working in the new way.)

5. Give the people the appropriate training on the technical tools to make continued improvement.

6. Start projects at all levels so that everyone knows, understands and works in the same way.

7. We are now well on the way to creating the new system.[11]

Conway has engaged in this kind of education, this spreading of the Quality word, in places other than the seminars put on by Conway Quality, Inc.

I have done some work in Phoenix, Arizona, as part of some efforts there with the McDonnell Douglas Helicopter Company. And, I have addressed school boards and various superintendents of schools. I have done the same things with Dow Chemical Company in their Texas operations along the Gulf Coast. Too, I have spoken with local universities and community colleges there as well as the members of school systems all over the South Texas area. I have talked to 354 teachers and all the top people in Russellville, Arkansas, because of the great interest of their governor, Bill Clinton, who led a Quality conference there.

On September 25, 1985, Conway addressed the annual meeting of the Society of Automotive Engineers' Quality and Productivity Conference in Dearborn, Michigan. He spoke of using the tools of industrial engineering with all employees, all the time. The three concepts and four simple tools for everyone to study and analyze work are as follows:

1. Work — Full time, necessary and required work provided by management.

2. Pace — Everyone working at a reasonable pace.

3. Time — Use on all parts of work.

4. Flowchart — Steps in any process.

5. Work Sampling Techniques — Everyone trained in use.

6. Work Simplification — Everyone trained and using every day.

7. Methods Analysis — Everyone trained and using every day.[12]

Conway insists these tools are so understandable that every worker can use them on a regular basis. In fact, he asserts, "They can all be taught effectively in the seventh grade." It is not difficult to see why Conway refers to education as the "key" to making the new management system work in an organization. He has stated repeatedly that "training in statistics should be carried out at all levels starting in high school. For most people," he declares, "this statistical education can be basic and simple."

Dr. Deming champions the status of workers by specifying that most of the problems in the work environment can be traced to management and the systems they have in place. A parallel might be drawn with expecting young people and entry-level workers to have some knowledge of Quality techniques. Their jobs would be facilitated if that knowledge were, in fact, introduced in seventh grade. But we cannot fault the student when the educational system is to blame.

If school administrators are not aware of Quality concepts, certainly the students will not be. In fact, when I called the Deputy Commissioner of Education in a large western state, and explained that I sought an interview (subsequently denied) on the topic of Total Quality Management, I was asked, "What is it?"

Quality Sharing

Clearly, there are a number of areas that bring personal satisfaction to Conway, but he cites as his greatest source of accomplishment the help he has given to those sincerely interested in bringing Quality to their organizations.

I am most proud of having been part of a group of people that were some of the first in a substantial company to work this way. This group also learned how to apply the teachings of Dr. Deming in the American and Western environment. We not only learned how to apply those teachings, we learned them well enough to be able to put together a system, to be able to help others to do it as well.

My satisfaction comes from my company. I, and the people who work with me, are now able to say these things. We are now able to get it across so that many of the senior management and top management people in the country believe and understand and are willing to take action. That is my major satisfaction.

Conway speaks with noticeable pride about his work at Boeing Company, where more than 15,000 people have attended his seminars. Boeing hired Conway in 1986 to assist in educating employees about quality. (To dramatize the extent of losses in that company, William Selby, Director of Operations, assembled 6,000 employees and had garbage trucks dump $15 million work of defective metal and paper scrap in front of the workers. In 1986, Boeing's wastage was up 50 percent from the previous year and totaled $1.4 billion.[13])

Thousands of employees at the Portsmouth, New Hampshire, Naval Shipyard have also benefitted from Conway's teachings. Regarding exposure to Quality concepts, Conway has this to say:

It is going on and on around the world. We do have contact through mass seminars as well as through videos with great numbers of people in some of the major organizations. It does spread down. Of course, it will never spread down unless you get the top people committed, get them on board.

Corporate training departments can assist in spreading the word, but Conway feels they must be thoroughly trained themselves and must know and understand the new management system. Further, they must support the line organization to help in teaching everyone in the use of the system.

It is very important that they [corporate trainers] understand that this training is not training for training's sake. I see millions of dollars being wasted in the United States by people training and being trained before they are "educated," educated as to what the system is and why the changes to this system are required. Money is wasted, too, if training is provided before the leaders (senior and middle managers) down through the organization are ready to be active leaders in the change.

When we train in those cases, we are just wasting the training. The goal of training people should be to train them when they are ready and when they are ready to utilize this data because they have the leadership around them to put it into practice.

Training, he contends, without receptivity equals waste.

It will not do the company or the country any good to train people if leaders are not ready to put their training into action. Otherwise, we are just wasting our resources.

Quality Indices

When asked to identify the key phrases that he associates with the world "Quality," Conway replied,

The external customer is very important. So is the "new system" as opposed to the old system. Major changes are implied with the new system. The old one involved comparing things to the budget, to last year, to last month. We compared ourselves to the competitor.

All those things are important and we should compare to things like that. But the key thing in the new management system that makes for the drastic change is that we compare everything to Utopia or getting to Utopia. We measure where we are versus perfection, rather than just comparing to the budget or to where we were last week, last month.

The new management system is continuous improvement in all the work and all the work processes through Quality, forever, to

please the external customer. We are going to do it by way of Quality. What do we mean when we say "Quality"? We mean we are going to find all the waste and convert it into opportunities for improvement. We are going to track the waste down and get rid of it and keep it gone.

How do we do this?

We do it through the technical tools of variation, seeing the differences between things, all the time, doing it to please that external customer who uses our product or our service, or who pays our bills.

In his seminars, his writings, his appearances, Conway inevitably acknowledges the work of Dr. Deming, whose teachings helped the Nashua Corporation turn around its productivity and quality problems. It is not surprising then that he would end this interview with a similar tribute:

I want to always say thank you to Dr. Deming for having been for four years my teacher and for having worked with me on a regular basis. It is difficult to tell you how much this has meant to me.

Summary

William Conway's mission is to find waste and eliminate it forever. One of the ways employees can ferret out waste is to work in teams, groups of people working together. Use of Quality Control circles to find ways of improving the system or the workplace is one way to do that. But, Conway cautions, Quality circles will only do a superficial job unless they employ statistical tools for measuring processes. He encourages using all the tools at one's disposal.

In efforts to control processes, a distinction must be made between enumerative studies (which acquire data for immediate action) and analytic studies (which acquire data for making predictions about future eventualities).

It is also important to think about the causes of variation in processes— Dr. Deming maintains that 94 percent of the causes are common causes,

causes that are part of the system and therefore problems that only management can take care of. The remaining 6 percent are special causes. They must be investigated and fixed.

Conway has a five-step plan for improving manufacturing processes. It involves gathering statistics on the process in operation; developing and using charts; identifying both the special and common causes of problems by statistical means; fixing the special causes; and having management support to fix the common causes by changing the system.

Conway's new management system is a revolution in the work process and is bringing about drastic change. But if top management is not committed to bearing arms for this revolution, the revolution will fail. He defines his system, quite simply, as "the continuous improvement of all work processes forever through quality to please the external customer."

Unlike John Naisbitt, who feels America will never regain its dominant position in the world's industrial economy, Conway feels we can. But self-driven actions are required, he maintains, not government-driven actions. Peter Drucker's views on multinationals' growth without protectionism parallel Conway's belief.

One way we can recapture our preeminent position is to have a skilled work force. Many feel that a refined vocational training system is what is needed. The Commission on the Skills of the American Workforce has put forth some ideas as radical as those proposed by Conway. The Commission is working toward eliminating the high school diploma and creating a Certificate of Initial Mastery by age 16. The requirements for this certificate will be world requirements and not minimum standards imposed by state education departments. If adopted, this plan would call for employers to make 1 percent of their payroll funds available for training the adult work force.

If students are to be trained, particularly for Quality skills, then teachers and administrators will have to do some learning as well. But training will be wasted if, as Conway says, people have not first been "educated."

For Further Consideration

1. What can customers of *your* product or service trust it to do or to be?

2. What are your thoughts about Quality Control circles?

3. Do you agree with H.G. Wells that "statistical thinking will one day be as necessary for efficient citizenship as the ability to read and write"? Why?

4. What enumerative studies would be beneficial to you in the work that you do? What analytical studies would be useful?

5. In what ways could management in your company enhance a system (or systems)?

6. What are some of the rigid paradigms with which you have to live (or have chosen to live)?

7. What company would you cite as an example of a firm with a Quality-dense culture? What indices led you to that selection?

8. Do you agree with William Conway's assertion that "we will never really be protected unless we learn how to compete"?

9. How do you react to John Naisbitt's contention that it is too late for America to recapture its industrial supremacy?

10. Discuss the idea of Certificate of Initial Mastery, based on world educational criteria, to replace the traditional high school diploma.

11. Have you ever received training before you were "educated"? Explain.

References

[1] Nashua Corporation, *The Nashua Quality Story* (Nashua Corporation, 44 Franklin Street, Nashua, NH 03061). Printed material on diskette packaging. Reprinted with permission.

[2] Imai, Masaaki. *Kaizen: The Key to Japan's Competitive Success* (New York: Random House, 1986), pp. 101–102.

[3] Scherkenbach, William W. *The Deming Route to Quality and Productivity: Road Maps and Roadblocks* (Washington: CEEPress Books, 1990), p. 97.

[4] *Ibid.*, pp. 95–96.

[5] Deming, W. Edwards. *Out of the Crisis* (Cambridge: Massachusetts Institute of Technology, Center for Advanced Engineering Study, 1986), p. 315. Reprinted from *Out of the Crisis* by W. Edwards Deming by permission of MIT and W. Edwards Deming. Published by MIT, Center for Advanced Engineering Study, Cambridge, MA 02139. Copyright © 1986 by W. Edwards Deming.

[6] Deming. *op. cit.*, p. 21.

[7] Drucker, Peter. *Management: Tasks, Responsibilities, Practices* (New York: Harper & Row, Publishers: 1974), pp. 732–733.

[8] Naisbitt, John. *Megatrends: Ten New Directions Transforming Our Lives* (New York: Warner Books, Inc., 1982), p. 56.

[9] *Ibid.*, pp. 57–58.

[10] Kelly, Dennis. "U.S. Must Train Its Workers Better," *USA Today* (June 19, 1990), p. 1D.

[11] Conway, William E. "The Right Way to Manage," *Quality Progress* (January 1988), pp. 14–15.

[12] Conway, William E. "The World Competition Secret," Remarks delivered at the annual meeting of the Society of Automotive Engineers' Quality and Productivity Conference in Dearborn, Michigan, September 25, 1985.

[13] McCluskey, Robert. "Boeing Develops a New Design to Cut Down on Corporate Drag," *International Management* (April 1987), p. 57.

Colonel Dale A. Misner, Commander
Department of Defense, Defense Contract Management Area Operations — El Segundo

"TQM gives us permission to deviate from formalities, from fixed ways of doing business. With TQM, we have a greater ability to figure out what is the best way to fit the system."

Background

Executive Order #12637, signed by President Reagan in 1988, implemented a quality improvement program, based on Total Quality Management (TQM) principles, throughout the levels of the federal government. Aimed at involving all employees by giving each one some responsibility to carryout TQM initiatives, the goal of this executive order is error-free, cost-effective goods and services for both internal and external customers. There are well over 2 million federal employees and a civil service payroll of $60 billion. When the world's largest employer mandates the inculcation of TQM behaviors, it is no surprise that other organizations are following suit.

Colonel Dale A. Misner, U.S. Army, is a graduate of Purdue University; he entered the U.S. Army immediately upon receiving his commission from ROTC at Purdue. He was then commissioned in the Army's Ordnance Corps, with a specialty in guided missile material and maintenance.

His overseas assignments include Viet Nam, Alaska and Korea. A number of honors have been awarded him, among them the Defense Superior Service Medal, the Bronze Star, three Army Meritorious Service Medals, the Vietnamese Honor Medal First Class, and the Boston Federal Executive Board's Distinguished Federal Executive Award.

Misner has since served in a variety of material acquisition positions, including training with industry, principal contracting officer for the Patriot missile system, battalion level commander of the Defense Contract Administration Service Plant representative at Raytheon, and finally brigade-level commander of the El Segundo (California) agency.

The Defense Contract Management Area Operations (DCMAO) in El Segundo has 6 military and 430 civilian specialists overseeing the administration of 20,000 contracts with a face value of more than $9 billion. The agency is responsible for surveillance of approximately 1,200 contractors. Their mission specialties include contract management, quality assurance, installation services and small business. TQM, a Department of Defense (DOD) priority is being implemented, along with In-Plant Quality Evaluation programs. Part of the implementation of these Quality programs is the concurrent training of personnel.

The contract management area is involved with engineering services, financial services, production surveillance, transportation and packaging guidance, property administration and other functions. Quality assurance personnel evaluate contractors' quality systems to ascertain their conformance to government standards.

TQM Philosophy

Misner was asked how DCMAO is moving TQM from an abstract concept to a set of practices actually used in interactions with internal and external customers.

We feel strongly that we should always be looking for new ways to do business, better ways to do business. TQM gets us out of some rigid rules, which—if followed too closely—might not fit a specific situation. It gets employees more involved in their own jobs and in decision-making, and gives flexibility to do a job according to a situation.

Misner's words echo those of Michael J. Pepe, Brigadier General and Executive Director of Quality Assurance for the Defense Logistics Agency (DLA). Pepe has established the following as TQM initiatives:

TQM

- recognizes that *everyone* has a customer for the product of their work efforts.
- necessitates close *involvement* with each customer's needs.
- relies on *people* and involves everyone.
- involves people using a *process*.
- demands a *profound knowledge* of each process with which one is involved.

- dictates a thorough *analysis* of each process.
- requires development of *disciplined systems* for making process improvements.
- requires *measurement* of the effectiveness of each process.
- demands *continual process improvement* at every level.[1]

Misner endorses the DLA interpretation of the continual process improvement principles of TQM, i.e., that employees evaluate their individual work process in order to make changes that may be needed. He reveals that

TQM gives us permission to deviate from formalities, from fixed ways of doing business. The Los Angeles Quality Assurance program requires us to deal directly with contractors and Quality Assurance people, and not necessarily the people who make the product.

With TQM, by contrast, we have the opportunity to deal with anyone we need to deal with in order to get the job done right. We have a lot of paperwork that our people have to do under the regular system. Under TQM, we have a greater ability to figure out what is the best way to fit the system.

Reduction of Waste

There are many who believe the military procurement system may be dying of its own weight. The obesity stemming from legal waivers, engineering analyses, regulations, military standards, pre-award surveys, deficiency reports, etc. are enough to bloat any system. While most taxpayers would applaud the government's efforts to reduce waste and minimize the possibility of fraud, the supervision and overseeing of such efforts requires extensive paperwork that can, ironically, inflate costs further. There are estimates that over-regulation can raise the cost of defense procurement by 30 percent.

Misner feels that TQM affords some shortcuts out of the paper maze:

Reduction in paperwork is a possible way to improve productivity, a way to be more current, to get people involved in what is the best way to do things and not necessarily by following a cookbook solution.

Misner cites other ways to improve productivity:

We really stress doing it right the first time. We never get to the point where we are too good. "Good enough" is a phrase that is difficult for me to accept. We use anything we can here to encourage a drive toward excellence—charts, books, briefings, classes, guest lecturers—to raise awareness, to make certain managers and management are visible.

Figure 1 depicts the TQM emphases at Misner's agency.

FIGURE 1

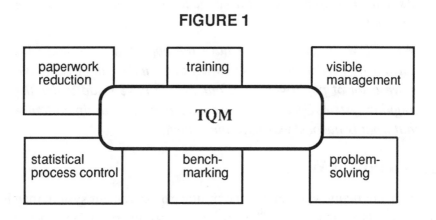

Misner speaks of the advantages of honestly-conducted visible management:

Visible management provides opportunities for subordinates and superiors to share in the analyzing and processes that constitute the essence of the organization. When conducted properly, visible management allows an open exchange of problems and possible solutions.

In terms of making personnel aware, here is the message from the top as stated in "A Pocket Guide of Tools for Continuous Improvement," a copy of which was distributed to all DLA employees. The words belong to Charles McCausland, Lieutenant General, United States Air Force.

> Rest assured, Total Quality Management has my fullest attention and commitment. I expect it to have yours too. As you become familiar with the Total Quality Management "life style," I trust that you will share my enthusiasm and lead DLA along the path of Total Quality Management.[2]

Misner mirrors the Director's words:

> *It is important for employees to see that I and the region and all of DLA are committed. We offer proof that we really mean to do things the TQM way. We want our entire work force to be aware of what TQM is and what we are trying to accomplish with it.*

> *But the awareness must come first. After that, we then get into more detail with teams. We analyze process, we conduct studies.*

Statistical process control is strongly endorsed by DLA. The pocket guide presents information on graphic problem-solving techniques, including flowcharts, check sheets, brainstorming, nominal group techniques, Pareto charts, cause and effect, run charts, stratification, histograms, scatter diagrams, control charts, process capability and force field analysis.

In referring to the agency's intent to train employees in problem-solving methods, Misner declares, "I do not see how people can perform their jobs without knowledge of statistical tools." As shown in Figure 2, the discrepancy between what is and what should be represents the problem. Problem-solving techniques are the bridge between the problem and the solution or the achievement of the idealized state. Organizations that are not quality-driven are satisfied with what is. They do not assess the status quo or question it or benchmark it. They may have problems and do not realize that they do, simply because there is no thrust to continually evaluate and subsequently improve the delivery of their product or service.

FIGURE 2

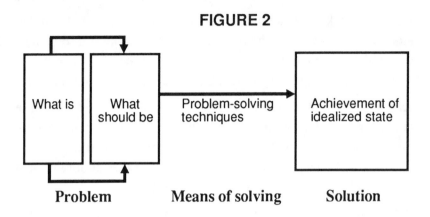

| Problem | Means of solving | Solution |

While some organizations may simply be unaware of their lack of quality, others may be aware they are less than they can be in terms of productivity of profits or Quality, but they do not care enough to reverse the trend or perhaps do not believe such a reversal is possible.

TQM allows organizations to not only solve problems but even to create them, so to speak. By anticipating how a future eventuality may impact negatively upon current situations, some firms proactively seek solutions before the problems have become entrenched. In Misner's words,

We were doing TQM here before TQM had a name. The reason is that we had certain problems that were not textbook problems. We had to figure out a way to solve them since solutions were not in the book.

For example, we had a contractor with a backlog of deliveries to the government and this delivery problem had been going on for years. Ordinarily, we had been doing a policing action or compliance review, issuing report cards saying you are not doing well enough. We would identify his problem but not help him to solve it.

We began taking an unconventional but successful approach at about the same time that Quality principles were gaining wide

acceptance. Our way of turning around a contractor with such a history of long-term problems was to work with him, not against him.

Today, with TQM principles behind us, we help solve instead of simply identifying and then walking away, leaving the contractor to solve his own problems. We stay, in fact, until the problem is solved. We roll up our sleeves and get dirty right along with the contractor if need be. We now view ourselves as being part of the solution.

The first step in problem-solution must always be problem-definition. As Dr. Nancy Mann points out,

It is important to get to the root of problems and to eliminate their causes. The philosophy is not one of crisis intervention, i.e., attempting to deal with symptoms when they become too severe. And allowing the workers to be part of the observing team and to participate in problem solving minimizes the costs of these activities. When problems have been identified and solved, then innovation can emerge. And when results of such innovation bring new problems, statistical techniques can be used to bring the system back under control at new, higher levels of productivity. It is a never ending process.[3]

Here are some considerations to be used as preliminary steps in eliminating the causes of problems in a given system.

QUALITY ARENA

- Could the materials we are using be improved?

- Could the machines we are using be improved?

- Could our processes be improved?

- If the customer could see what we are doing right now, would he be willing to pay for it?

- Do we systematically meet with customers, both internal and external to learn the extent of their satisfaction with our product?

- Could our drive toward Quality be made more apparent? If so, how?

- Are we working with our suppliers to solve problems?

- How much benchmarking do we do?

- Are we using sole-source suppliers?

- Do our employees need more training? better training?

MANAGEMENT ARENA

- Can everyone define the organization's mission?

- Are our efforts paralleling that mission?

- Are our managers visible?

- Are we aware of our "vital few" and our "trivial many" efforts?

- What is the source of conflict in our department?

- Is the conflict being handled? If so, how?

- Do we have departmental objectives?

- If so, are all employees aware of them?

- Do team members manage time as well as they can?

- Are regular planning meetings held?

- Are we anticipating the future and adjusting accordingly?

- What can be done to encourage peak performance from each employee?

TQM ARENA

- How is the effectiveness of processes being measured?

- How often is it measured?

- What was the last improvement we made to our process? When?

- What measurement techniques are in place?

- What training have we given and been given on Quality concepts?

- Do we have Quality Control circles? Work teams?

- If so, how well do they work? If not, why not?

- Are our processes in control?

- If not, what are the causes of the variation?

- Have we implemented Dr. Deming's Fourteen Points?

- Can we reduce the number of our suppliers?

- Do we possess "profound knowledge"?

- Are we employing the "Plan-Do-Check-Act" cycle?

Ishikawa or Fishbone Diagram

Identifying problems is a necessary first step in improving quality *and* productivity. When Dr. Deming was asked how the improvements could be made simultaneously, he responded,

> Let me give it to you in two words: "Less rework." As you improve the quality, you have less rework and less waste, so the customer gets more for his money. My friend, Dr. Feigenbaum, a consultant in Quality, made a little study. It showed that the cost of most American products include from 10 to 40 percent waste. What does that do? It can slowly put American products out of business.[4]

One way to look at problems—general problems of how to improve productivity and quality, or more specific problems having to do with systems—is through the Ishikawa or fishbone or cause-and-effect diagram. It is one of the tools DLA employees—many of whom enter the agency immediately upon high school graduation—are expected to use.

It stands to reason that the problem-solving training such employees receive on-the-job could, conceivably, have been introduced in their senior year. I asked the Colonel to discuss the prospect.

The math area, especially statistics, is most important. So, when they are involved in a process, they can understand how to control it. They have to know when it is in control, when it is behaving normally. Statistical control itself is probably not being taught in schools and yet I think young people could handle it.

I also think fishbone diagrams could be applied to any number of situations.

The fishbone diagram is so-called because of the skeletal shape the diagram assumes. It is a useful tool in problem identification as it helps determine the multiple possible causes for a given effect. A graphic, bare-bones means of examining a potentially complex situation, the fishbone process begins with the definition of the problem, written in a box at the right of the skeletal drawing. An example is provided in Figure 3.

FIGURE 3

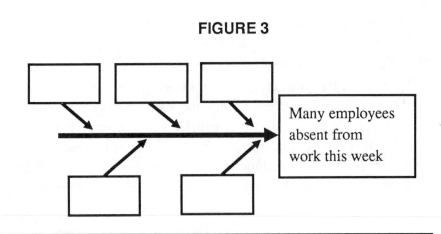

Many employees absent from work this week

Management consultant William Scherkenbach points out the advantages of the cause-and-effect diagram:

> Management and others whose work is more art than science often say that they don't need to use a cause and effect diagram, that it is a waste of time as they use their experience in their jobs. But when we force the issue and sit down with them to construct one, they usually say that it was worthwhile because they hadn't thought of a specific source of variation. They also readily recognize the meaning of the phrase "Pay me now, or pay me later." Downtime costs a lot of money, and a large part of downtime can be troubleshooting time. Construction of cause and effect diagrams in advance can save a lot of trouble-shooting time.[5]

The next step in constructing the diagram is to list (in the boxes beside the primary bone-lines) the major categories under which the possible causes of the problem could be subsumed. In the days before gender-sensitivity, the alliterative 5 M's were used: Materials, Machines, Measurements, Methods, and Manpower. Today, we consider the 4 M's and 1 P. In a slight alteration of the traditional fishbone diagram, some problem-solvers add additional M's—Milieu, Mission, and Money. These additional considerations are listed not so much as sources of problems but rather as additional perspectives from which to view the situation.

FIGURE 4

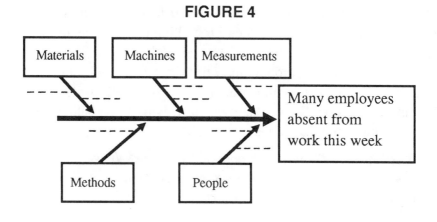

Subcauses are next added in intersecting lines, as shown by the dotted lines in the preceding diagram. After discussion of the most likely subcause (some groups will vote so consensus can be brought about), the group will focus on the cause and learn more about it. To verify whether the identified cause is really the source of the problem, additional data may have to be gathered. If a given cause is not having the suspected effect on the situation or is determined not to be causing the problem, the next most likely cause will be scrutinized in the same way until the problem is solved. Note that the fishbone diagram can also be used to analyze the causes of positive changes that have been introduced into the work environment.

This kind of refined, as opposed to haphazard, analysis can be encouraged in virtually any environment, Misner asserts, but it is up to management to make expectations clear via communications that are clear. Employees can commit to an "I'll-do-it-right-the-first-time" attitude, but bosses must offer sufficient encouragement and then recognition so the attitudes are translated into standard operating procedures. Misner says,

If a supervisor gives an assignment but is not clear in his directions, employees may go off and do a lot of work and it may not result in what was expected. So, team building focused around a common intent should cut down on mistakes.

A word of caution is in order here. While the common mindset to which Misner alludes results in group cohesion, that cohesion is not to be equated with "groupthink." When groupthink operates, team members often voice concurrence publicly, but privately express either reservations or rebellion. Or, groupthink will bring about such uniformity in thought and action that members are unable to critically assess the worth of courses of action. When Quality is the driving force behind a team's behavior, then, as Misner avers,

A common understanding dominates actions. If we do not all understand the problem in the same way, then we will come up with solutions that are inappropriate.

Changing Mindsets

"Learning to love change," Tom Peters insists, "is the only survival course." And in this era of rapid technological advances and immediate information access, organizations that adapt readily—not frantically to every wind of change, but readily to the winds that affect their survival— are the organizations that will flourish.

When organizations plan for change, as DLA is doing to comply with the mandates of the TQM Executive Order, they assess the critical elements in their basic way of doing business. They decide which elements need restructuring. Often, those elements are integrated, so the change process may involve several of them simultaneously.

What are those critical elements that comprise the organizational essence? Again, they fall into the broad alliterative divisions we cited in the fishbone diagram: Materials, Machines, Methods, Measurement and People, with the additional considerations of Mission, Milieu and Money.

But alterations in any one of these areas will be upsetting if not handled well. People are not quick to change. Consequently—since people impact all the critical areas—functions and operations are also slow to change or be changed if the alterations are not fully embraced by employees. Misner has encountered the inertia with which change is usually met.

I have to be honest with you and tell you that at this point the results of our TQM efforts are mixed. We are not very far into our plan yet. Some people will always be hesitant to leave their comfort zone.

Over one hundred years ago, Ralph Waldo Emerson stated, "A foolish consistency is the hobgoblin of little minds." Little-minded or big-minded, most people act habitually; they take solace if not delight in established patterns. Even when events dictate that change is inevitable or imminent, some people will still cling to their familiar routines. For example, the math phobic is often also computer-phobic. But computers are here to stay and those who wish to survive in today's competitive business environment must add computer skills to their repertoire of expertise domains. Studies show that successful business leaders are more willing to adapt, more likely to be restless with the status quo, more receptive to new ideas than are other people.

Encouraging employees to be more forward-thinking in their reactions to a new way of doing things requires an understanding of the change process, which occurs in three stages, according to psychologist Kurt Lewin.[6] First of all, we must unfreeze the current frozen philosophies and ways of thinking/behaving. This is probably the hardest of the three stages and the most important. If we are not successful in explaining the rationale behind the change, the next two steps cannot be fully accomplished. Unfreezing calls forth fear of the unknown and often its attendant banes: declining productivity, rumor, conflict, and accusations.

However, this pre-change state of flux also provides an ideal opportunity to examine the systems that are not working, to provide assurances, to point out the advantages of the new way of doing things. Philip Crosby states unequivocally that changing mindsets is the hardest of all management tasks, and the leader who can heighten awareness of the positive aspects of the forthcoming change will find that the second step, that of actually introducing the change, is facilitated immensely. Determining the most propitious time requires a judgment call on the leader's part, of course, but he must make certain that old attitudes are completely defrosted, thoroughly thawed before the new processes are put into place.

FIGURE 5

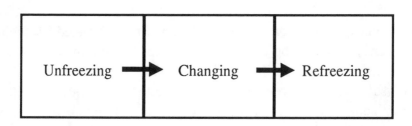

Once the new routines become established, managers must next seek to solidify the new ways of doing things. Sharing the successes of the new way, finding causes for celebration, publicizing and publicly recognizing efforts, continually providing feedback and assistance—all of these acts will help the new process to become ingrained in the collective mindset.

Misner cites a specific example of the need for leaders to do some comfort re-zoning:

> *One of my supervisors was excellent at doing things by the book and so when the TQM changes were introduced, she experienced some discomfort. In time, she realized she could do an even better job using Quality tools and she wound up being committed to TQM hook, line, and sinker.*

> *We have not had any failures yet, as far as implementing these principles is concerned. I would not say that we have had 100 percent success—some people are still sitting on the fence, trying to make up their minds—but the education process is going on. I understand their worry. It's easy for people at the top to say, "We will do such and such a thing." After all, we at the top are used to dealing with changes.*

> *But people at other levels need to see that 100 percent of their co-workers are accepting the change or they need to be convinced that the new way is really a better way before they will buy into it.*

Bringing Quality into an organization or a department is never an easy process. And managers need to expend their best efforts to instill commonality and constancy of purpose as far as Quality is concerned. However, best efforts are not enough. As Dr. Deming cautions

> One could announce an important theorem: we are being ruined by best efforts directed the wrong way. We need best efforts directed by a theory of management.[7]

He calls for managers to acquire a system of "profound knowledge"—made up of appreciation for a system, statistical theory, theory of knowledge, and psychology.[8] He also regards hard work and best efforts as necessary but not sufficient conditions for successful management of Quality.

> Hard work and best efforts, put forth without guidance of profound knowledge, leads to ruin in the world that we are in today. There is no substitute for knowledge.[9]

The difficulty of acquiring a profundity of knowledge is compounded by the *amount* of knowledge in the world today. Every day in America, 3,000 publications are issued and the amount of knowledge in the world doubles every 20 months. Knowledge, like life, is in a constant state of flux. Certainly, there are some cerebral constants, but the wise leader will embellish the essential core of his knowledge with refinements from time to time. Dr. Deming himself has done this, for example, with the inclusion of psychology into the body of his works.

Dinosaur Mentalities

Given the flux in our worlds, the more readily we can accommodate ourselves to those forces over which we have little or no control, the less stress we are likely to have. Resisting the inevitable is not only foolhardy, it can even be hazardous to your professional life. Some organizations are still laboring with a dinosaur mentality, still trying to accommodate Quality in a cumbersome dinosaur bureaucracy. It's impossible to do. The two concepts are antithetical.

Misner noted that middle managers have had many opportunities to acclimate themselves to change—beginning with their first promotion into supervisory ranks—and so are probably more willing to travel new organizational paths than are individuals who take a defensive stance. The defensiveness must be viewed as a self-protective measure, and the knowledgeable supervisor will make repeated efforts to vitiate defenses. Managers have the burden on their collective shoulders of providing ongoing encouragement and support. Misner observes, "We can simply not do it once and then quit. Our efforts have to be continuous."

With the Quality movement taking us into the twenty-first century, he notes:

Companies that assume their product or services are good enough and that intend to keep it that way, without making any changes, will probably go out of business, because someone will come along and find a way to do it better.

Another cogent statement of the absolute necessity to change is provided by Peter Drucker, who equates the beginning of obsolescence with the beginning of a new product's profits.

Thus, your being the one who makes your product, process or service obsolete is the only way to prevent your competitor from doing so.[10]

While the initial import of his words is a radical one at first glance, the truth is, we must simply assess the processes continually and make changes and improvement as often as we can. Misner recommends this:

Lower expenses so we can lower prices and remain competitive. Find new ways to do things quickly. Accept the fact that we will never get to the point of perfection, but we will keep on trying to reach it.

Suggestion Systems

The reach for perfection means involving employees at all levels. And one of the least expensive yet paradoxically most financially rewarding means of involving employees is the suggestion system. It is worth noting some of the basic differences between the way American and Japanese firms elicit recommendations from employees.

In America, the most successful systems often have monetary rewards associated with them. In fact, when the tangible rewards are minimal (such as pens that are given out by the mayor in one large American city to employees who suggest workable ideas for improving the processes of government), employees often feel diminished and are not inclined to submit further suggestions. Another flaw in the improvement system is the amount of paperwork associated with many suggestion procedures.

According to Misner,

There is a right way and a wrong way to go about the suggestion process, which can be bureaucratic. When it is, though, we lose the purpose behind the process. Asking employees to fill out forms in triplicate discourages suggestions. We should be asking people to come up with good ideas informally. Some of these can be implemented without ever having been written down.

(The ideal system is probably one that lies between the extremes of excessive paperwork and no paperwork.)

The emphasis on the Japanese suggestion procedure is less extrinsically and more intrinsically focused. The intrinsic motivation is the satisfaction derived from working toward the common goal or improving the morale of co-workers. There are some Japanese firms, such as the Matsushita Company, that have more than six million suggestions a year by employees motivated to share in the corporate wellness.

Eiji Toyoda, chairman of Toyota Motor Company, has been quoted as saying,

One of the features of the Japanese workers is that they use their brains as well as their hands. Our workers provide 1.5 million suggestions a year, and 95 percent of them are put to practical use. There is an almost tangible concern for improvement in the air at Toyota.[11]

But American business also has a long and proud history of brain use. Henry Ford, as historians have recounted, was once called an ignoramus in an article written by a *Chicago Tribune* reporter. Ford actually sued the newspaper and issued a public challenge for the paper to prove that he was, in fact, ignorant. The suit, believe it or not, made it to court. During the course of the trial, defense attorneys asked Ford dozens of questions that most people with formal schooling would have been able to answer. He was asked about the years in which famous historical events occurred; he was asked the names of Presidents, etc.

Ford was at a disadvantage since he had had very little schooling. He finally admitted, "I don't know the answers to those questions, but I could find a man in five minutes who does. I use my brain to *think*, not to store up a lot of useless facts." When suggestion systems operate as they should, a great deal of thinking—based on fact-storage—occurs.

The suggestion system works only when there truly is a system, a system to which top management responds. A well-defined procedure should be in place and incentives should be provided to both individuals and groups who suggest improvements or savings. The quality of the suggestions submitted is more important than the quantity, naturally. And management can take an active role in heightening awareness of the suggestion process, in enhancing the quality of the ideas.

If training is needed so that employees will have sharper analytical skills for assessing the current, and helping transform it into the future, condition, then management must provide that training. The suggestions need not center merely on increased profitability. Rather, ways to make the job less tedious or safer or more efficient or enjoyable could also be encouraged.

A review process must be included in the system. Depending on a number of variables, the review could be a team of peers, or first-line supervision, or any of the various levels of management. Enhanced dialogue between submitter and reviewer is only one of the benefits to be derived from a formal suggestion program.

The high percentage of employee suggestions that are actually implemented in Japan suggests feedback and follow-through are part of the suggestion system. In some plants, supervisors are evaluated on the number of suggestions submitted by subordinates. While such policies might be viewed by Americans as unfair, the fact remains that we can do more to encourage feasible suggestions from our employees. Less threatening than having supervisors appraised according to the number of suggestions submitted by employees, is the Japanese practice of having families participate in the suggestion-making process.

Misner warms to the practice of having rewards more intrinsic than extrinsic, especially in view of the budgetary restraints the government is now experiencing. With internally motivated ideas being presented, the suggestion process can succeed, even if cash awards are not given as frequently as they were in the past. He says:

Intrinsic rewards are better. Recognition by peers and superiors is quite meaningful in people's lives. We actually can ask the work force, "How would you like to be recognized by each other?" This aspect of TQM allows us ways to give employees more pride in the work they do.

Training

Subordinates and supervisors alike receive training at DLA. Everyone, of course, has received or will receive training on the basic tenets of TQM. In addition, there is leadership training for supervisors and motivation and communication training for both supervisors and employees. Problem-solving, effective speaking, and effective writing are additional skill areas that are stressed.

On the topic of the skills needed by the incoming work force, particularly for entry level positions, Misner expressed some dismay:

We invited local high schools to submit essays in celebration of the birthday of Martin Luther King, Jr. We selected three and awarded a savings bond to those students. Overall, we were disappointed in the quality of writing we saw.

Recent statistics from the National Center for Education Statistics would make that concern warranted. They describe the eighth-graders in their study as being in dismal academic condition.

- American eighth-graders spend four times as many hours a week watching television as doing homework.
- Those same eighth-graders read only two hours a week outside school.
- One out of five eighth-graders is able to solve simple arithmetic problems requiring use of the basic functions of addition, subtraction, multiplication, and division.
- 14 percent of those eighth-graders are unable to read at even a basic level.

Further evidence from the National Assessment of Educational Progress (sometimes referred to as the Nation's Report Card) was derived from a nationwide study, which found that

- Only 36 percent of fourth-graders knew why Columbus sailed to America.
- Fewer than half of eighth-graders knew that Martin Luther King, Jr., advocated non-violence.
- Only 38 percent of eighth-graders knew that Congress makes laws.
- More than half were unable to define the phrase "separation of powers."
- Only 50 percent recognized that the United States is a representative democracy.

TQM will not solve all the problems of the working classes in America or of the managerial strata that supervise them. However, with its emphasis on a solidly trained work force, TQM may help to overcome the deficits that young people are bringing with them when they walk through the door for their first job.

Summary

Executive Order #12637 has made the practice of Total Quality Management mandatory in all federal agencies. Michael Pepe, Brigadier General for TQM, affirms universal involvement in TQM, and emphasizes other key words: measurement, analysis, profound knowledge, and continuous improvement of processes.

Colonel Dale Misner explains that one of the ways he translates the abstract concepts into concrete behaviors is to encourage his staff to look for better ways of doing things. The regulations required for the procurement process do mean a great deal of paperwork, but TQM is helping to reduce that paperwork. Other wastefulness is being reduced, in part, by TQM's encouragement of visible management and by training in problem-solving techniques. These techniques define the difference between what is and what should be and transform that difference into the achieved desired state.

The Ishikawa or fishbone diagram is an excellent, easy-to-use analytical tool. It not only helps groups solve problems but also helps "create" problems. That is, the cause-and-effect analysis can examine a process that "ain't broke" and actually suggest ways to prevent it from becoming broken, or to have contingency plans ready when it does break, or simply to make the process better than it currently is.

Although group efforts and common language are fostered with TQM, groupthink is not. Differences of opinion are encouraged and diversity is valued, but once a plan of action has been agreed upon, all are expected to incorporate it into their daily work activities.

Changing mindsets is a formidable managerial task, but by examining critical aspects of the work environment—Machinery, Methods, Measurement, Materials, Mission, Milieu, Money and People—we often find ways to make work easier and the work environment safer or more pleasant. And such enhancements usually engender a willingness to work with the changed system. The change process is usually easier for middle managers, who have had to change on numerous occasions, than it is for front-line employees, who have not had many changes foisted upon them. The leader must facilitate the change by taking advantage of opportunities to eliminate the worst and keep the best of the old way of doing things.

Best efforts, though, are not enough. Dr. Deming maintains that a theory of knowledge must accompany the manager's efforts to introduce Quality into the environment. And the more cumbersome the hierarchy, the more unwieldy the bureaucracy, the less likely will be the opportunity for Quality thinking to permeate dinosaur mentalities. Streamlined structures are vital if American businesses are to change, to become instruments of their obsolescence, as Peter Drucker suggests they do.

The Quality quest is a never-ending one. Perfection will never be attained, but Quality employees never stop seeking it. One way to lower expenses and thereby lower prices and thereby acquire or retain a competitive status is to utilize a suggestion system. Ideally, such a system will elicit ideas from intrinsically motivated employees. Training in Quality concepts is one way employees can refine their skills and thus be in a better position to refine the processes in which they are engaged.

For Further Consideration

1. What key words do you associate with TQM?

2. Has TQM in your organization given you "permission to deviate from formalities"? Explain.

3. What aspects of your job could you describe as being over-regulated?

4. How visible is the management of your organization?

5. To what problem-solving methods have you been introduced as a result of TQM training?

6. Compare "what is" in your company to what "should be."

7. Relate Quality to the phrase, "Pay me now or pay me later."

8. What can a supervisor do to ensure the assignments he gives are clearly understood?

9. How does groupthink differ from cohesive teamwork?

10. Discuss Tom Peters' contention that learning to love change is the only survival course.

11. What are the critical elements in your organization or in the way the organization does business?

12. How do you deal with the inertia that usually accompanies change?

13. Can you cite an example of best efforts not yielding best results?

14. What are you doing to refine your body of knowledge?

15. How can dinosaur mentalities be lobotomized?

16. What are you doing to make "your product, process or service obsolete"?

17. How can your suggestion system be improved?

18. How would you like to be recognized for your work?

19. How do you translate abstract TQM concepts into concrete behaviors?

20. What step(s) follows your identification of waste?

References

[1] GOAL/QPC, *Memory Jogger™ (GOAL/QPC [13 Branch Street, Methuen, Maine 01844], 1989), p. 1.*

[2] *Ibid.*, p. 3.

[3] Mann, Nancy R. *The Keys to Excellence: The Story of the Deming Philosophy* (Tokyo: Diamond Publishing Company, 1989), p. 155.

[4] *Ibid.*, p. 113.

[5] Scherkenbach, William W. *The Deming Route to Quality and Productivity: Road Maps and Roadblocks* (Washington: CEEPress Books, 1990), pp. 105–106.

[6] Lewin, Kurt. "Group Decision and Social Change," In G.E. Swanson *et al.* (eds.), *Readings in Social Psychology* (New York: Holt, Rinehart, 1952), pp. 459–473.

[7] Deming, W. Edwards. "Foundation for Management of Quality in the Western World," Paper delivered at a meeting of the Institute of Management Sciences in Osaka, Japan, July 24, 1989, p. 7.

[8] *Ibid.*, p. 11.

[9] *Ibid.*, p. 10.

[10] Drucker, Peter F. "The 10 Rules of Effective Research," *The Wall Street Journal* (May 30, 1989), p. A16. Reprinted with permission of *The Wall Street Journal*, © 1989, Dow Jones & Company, Inc. All rights reserved.

[11] Imai, Masaaki. *Kaizen: The Key to Japan's Competitive Success* (New York: Random House, 1986), p. 15.

Dr. A. Blanton Godfrey, Chairman, CEO
Juran Institute

"We just cannot live on borrowed
money and imported goods. We
have got to become a strong nation
again and this includes not only the
quality of our products and services,
but also the quality of our schools,
the quality of our political processes,
and the quality of the way we treat
each other."

Background

Dr. Blanton Godfrey earned his Bachelor's Degree in physics from Virginia Technical Institute "back in the Dark Ages," as he puts it, "when you could still understand physics." The year was 1963. He went into the Army immediately afterwards and wound up as a captain in Viet Nam. Following his military service, he returned to graduate school and earned his doctorate in statistics from Florida State.

From there he went to his "first real job" with AT&T's Bell Laboratories in Homedale, New Jersey. He started out in the Theoretical Studies Group, working mainly in Quality Assurance. Over the years, he was promoted to various jobs and finally to head of the Quality Theory and Technology Department, which is the descendent of the Quality Theory Department started back in 1924 by Dr. Walter Shewhart. Says Godfrey,

This department had an illustrious history with the work of Shewhart, Dodge and others. We like to think that in the 80's we continued in that tradition. The department was very strong in both theoretical methods and applied methods and the teaching of Quality throughout AT&T. We taught employees in the service areas, the manufacturing areas, and the business process areas about reliability and experimental designs. We were the ones that started working with Dr. Taguchi in 1980 when he first came to the United States.

We not only brought things to AT&T but we arranged the Quality Production and Research Conference that the American Statistical Association now sponsors. We also had very strong groups within the department who developed software for Quality control, reliability, prediction, and for reliability estimation throughout AT&T.

We supplied product tools for people and training and consulting and direction support. So, all these things that I have been talking about that managers need (the support, the resources, the skills

*and tools), were a function of my department. We also organized
and provided the three-day training course for all top managers
in the company from the president on down. (They are still using
that course we put together.) By understanding competitive positions and Quality productivity, you understand Quality improvement.*

It was at one of the thirteen three-day training programs that Godfrey
first made the acquaintance of Dr. Joseph M. Juran, who had been invited
as a speaker. (Dr. Juran, along with Peter Drucker and W. Edwards
Deming, has had considerable impact on American productivity. The
octogenarian triumvirate has been responsible for awakening Americans
to the need for higher quality workmanship and service. Dr. Juran was
awarded The Order of the Sacred Treasure by Emperor Hirohito "for the
development of quality control in Japan and the facilitation of U.S. and
Japanese friendship." This award is the highest honor that can be given
to non-native citizens.)

Dr. Juran spoke to the AT&T team about Quality improvement to more
than 500 top managers in those seminars. Often, he would meet with
Godfrey to plan the presentations. Recalls Godfrey,

*We got to know each other pretty well and he asked me to come
here to the Juran Institute [located in Wilton, Connecticut]. When
he stepped up to the position of Chairman Emeritus, he asked me
to become Chairman and Chief Executive Officer.*

The Juran Influence

The Juran Institute's management seminars have their genesis in the
work Dr. Juran did with Japanese managers in the late 1940's and early
1950's. And, in confirmation of the Institute's recognition of Quality as
a "global issue," about one-third of their consulting work is for foreign
clients. Juran moved from Quality Manager at the Hawthorne Works of
the Bell System to administrative wartime positions, to a career of
management training and consultant. He founded the Institute in 1979.
Continuing the vision of its founder, the Juran Institute states its mission

as one of providing its clients "with the concepts, methods, and guidance for attaining leadership in quality."

In an article for *Boardroom Reports*,[1] Juran tells top management the obligation for elevating the corporate levels of quality is theirs and theirs alone. The responsibility cannot be shifted to the shoulders of subordinates. Like Dr. Deming, he disdains exhortations and the ephemeral efforts of indiscriminately hired consultants. He also has harsh words for the "do-it-right-the-first-time" philosophy, claiming that such a philosophy suggests that "it" hasn't been done right in the past or that "it" was done several times before it was done right. And yet, he asserts, many people have been promoted and rewarded for these past behaviors that apparently were the wrong way to do what is now being done right the first time.

He draws a distinction between "leading" and "cheerleading," and warns that senior managers must do even more than they are now doing if they wish to have their companies meet world-class quality standards. Those world-class standards have been defined by the International Standardization Organization (ISO).* Among the general guidelines of the organization are these requirements for successful companies:

In order to be successful, a company must offer products or services that

- meet a well-defined need, use or purpose;
- satisfy customers' expectations;
- comply with applicable standards and specifications;
- comply with statutory (and other) requirements of society;
- are made available—at competitive prices;
- are provided at a cost that will yield a profit.[2]

---

*I am indebted to John Heberling, Senior Quality Engineering Specialist at AiResearch, Los Angeles Division of Allied-Signal Corporation, for sharing this information about ISO9004. ANSI/ASQC Q94-1987 is reprinted with the permission of ASQC.

Juran has four basic recommendations for those managers who aspire to world-class quality:

- Undergo training in how to think about quality, how to plan for quality, and how to measure improvement.

- Take a leading and permanent role in creating the quality-improvement program.

- Make the organizational changes necessary to meet these policies and goals. [He adds that the traditional sequence of product development must be replaced by cross-functional efforts.] "Department turf wars," he declares, "must be eliminated."

- Personally review and reward performance.[3]

Training Managers for Leadership

When I asked Godfrey how tomorrow's managers should be trained, he gave a thoughtful and comprehensive response:

There are several things we need to worry about with our managers. First of all, I am speaking very much from my own expertise and I will talk not about everything they need but what they need with respect to Quality. The managers of tomorrow really need to understand their role in leadership for Quality. Management now has a rather wide role. They need to understand how to set goals, how to deploy these goals throughout the organization, how to break these down into specific tasks, so that the members of the organization have both the responsibility and the authority, as well as the training and capability to do what needs to be done.

In reference to goals, Dr. Juran says the Quality goal must be "a specific target which focuses the energies of all employees on achieving that target, and on doing so within a specified period of time." He adds that senior management must remain visibly committed as the goals are shared with supporting layers of the corporate pyramid. The need for clear communications is critical, with specific tasks identified for meeting the goals. This goal-meeting process will be expensive, he warns, especially the training part of it, but these goal-meeting expenditures should be approved (and policy and structural changes made) before the process begins.[4]

Godfrey echoes this viewpoint:

And that is another thing they need to understand: when they get these assignments, they have to make sure the resources are in place: resources meaning the people but also meaning the skills of the people, the training of the people so that employees are never asked to do things they are unequipped to do or that run into organizational barriers.

Another aspect of leadership for managers is understanding their own organizational structure and understanding where the organization has built barriers...barriers between departments where we get a lot of suboptimization rather than optimization. And so the leaders must work very hard to break down these barriers. They must work very hard to make sure that the people have the training they need to do their jobs and so they know what these jobs are.

So that when people at all levels of the company meet their goals, they are meeting the needs and expectations of the customer. Then, we are all working toward the customer and avoiding some of this internal suboptimization we have when we are all doing pieces of something but the pieces just don't add up to anything. Of course, this also means getting many people involved with the customers; it means getting many people involved working together; it means empowering people to do things they have not done before—not only giving them the responsibility, not only giving them the authority, but also giving them the resources, the training, the skills to do these things.

That is a major change from what many of the managers have defined as their jobs in the past. It is much more than commitment and much more than involvement. It really is leadership because leadership implies that the people know what is to be done; they know how it is to be done and they actually provide the leadership for others to be able to do this.

Graphically, the understandings management needs for Quality leadership, are these:

FIGURE 1

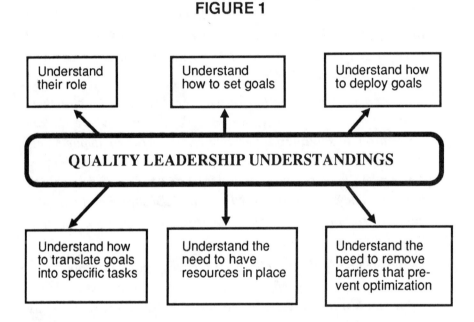

Parallel Views

An interview with Sharon Sarris, Community Relations/General Affairs Manager for the New United Motor Manufacturing, Inc. (NUMMI) plant in Fremont, California, yielded a concurrent viewpoint. (Sarris is one of sixteen GM people assigned to the NUMMI plant to learn firsthand about the Toyota production line. Following their assignment at NUMMI, they will return to GM and apply what they have learned. "It's a tremendous job," she declares emphatically.)

Management has to be clear on basic goals and objectives. "Our goal is to produce the highest-quality product." I have heard this so often from our president. When NUMMI was started, the clear message was that quality is the most important thing. A very simple message, really. By words and practice, we in management demonstrated that quality was a key focus and that we support it, at all management levels.

And the turnaround in thought and behavior at NUMMI is directly attributable to training, according to Bertha Davis in *Crisis in Industry*:

Without changes in the way workers are trained, organized, and supervised, without changes in worker attitudes, today's sophisticated technology cannot work its potential wonders. Trouble at the GM Hamtramck, Michigan, plant—a luxury-car plant considered a showcase for high technology—was repeatedly contrasted with the situation in Fremont, California. Located there is the plant of New United Motor Manufacturing, Inc. (NUMMI), a joint venture of Toyota and GM, operated under Japanese management. With far less money spent on new technology at NUMMI, the cars it produces are deemed of higher quality than those produced at any other GM plant.

The critical difference, it is agreed, is that the workers went through weeks of intensive training before production began. Japanese-style labor-management relations prevail. For example, Toyota management pledged that in a business downturn, management salaries would be cut first before asking for wage concessions from union workers. In return, the union permitted reorganization of job categories from twenty-six to four broad groups, permitting a flexibility in the management of labor that increased productivity. There are no reserved parking spots for management in the company parking lot; there is no executive dining room, just a cafeteria for everybody.[5]

Quantitative-Skills Training

In a promotional piece that describes the purpose of the Juran Institute, Godfrey predicts manager changes in quality management for the next century. He envisions the concern for customers as being paramount, even passionate in some cases. He also foresees a great deal more benchmarking and the development of better methods for identifying poor quality. Advancing the belief that training will provide the "competitive edge," he writes:

> Companies will use training as a strategic weapon. They will train all of their people in the basic concepts of quality management, tied closely to job function and individual need. Organizations will invest heavily in educating their most valuable resource. This will become their competitive edge.[6]

Godfrey continues in his enumeration of what leaders will have to do to manage quality well:

> *Another thing they need to be able to do is manage more quantitatively. We have had too much "seat-of-the-pants" flying in this country, with people making snap judgments based on opinion or on—as David Garvin calls it—"gut fact," which is a gut feeling that has been held for five years and now is treated as a fact.*
>
> *You really need to have the data available, a good analysis made of the data, information that people understand, cutting through the variation, cutting through the noise and the smoke and the incomplete reports; really understand the aspects of the business, really understand how a company could be compared to the customer needs, compared to the competition, compared to what is going on in the world. Then make clear and clean decisions based on those facts.*
>
> *Most of our managers have not been trained adequately in quantitative skills. Some people will object and say that even engineers, who have an incredible amount of training in quantitative skills, may have still missed much of the more statistical type of train-*

ing—the probability training, the data-analysis training that they need to operate.

A quick review of the indexes of management texts from the last decade will underscore the truth of Godfrey's observation. Very few of them bring statistical process control into the management science discipline. But quantification is a concept that has come and gone and come back again. American managers are finally beginning to accord measurement the status it deserves. In the words of Dr. Juran:

> Finally, top management must develop and adhere to accurate measures for evaluating performance. *Key:* Data on productivity, defect rates, etc., must be summarized into ratios and indexes that can easily be used by senior managers to track and control performance on the way to the new company quality goals.[7]

Creating Partnerships

Business Week's cover story for the week of March 12, 1990, is entitled "King Customer." In it, James M. Hulbert, a marketing professor at Columbia Business School, is quoted as saying, "More top managers are recognizing they have to be customer-focused, but they don't always recognize the way the organization has to change."[8] The article describes a 1980 focus group of car buyers that Ford Motor company assembled in California. They were shocked when college-age buyers admitted never having been in a Ford and not knowing anyone who even owned a Ford.

The feedback led Ford to listen more to customers, even to invite them to evaluate prototypes. In the sharp words of Ford's chairman, Donald E. Petersen: "If we aren't customer-driven, our cars won't be either."[9]

In his work with managers, Godfrey, too, stresses the importance of customer relations,

> *I work with these people all of the time and I am just stressing some of the things that we have observed, in their companies and in other companies, that have made positive changes in the lives and businesses of the people involved.*

Beyond statistical training, Godfrey cites other important aspects of managerial functions:

The other things are much more obvious: the idea of working more closely with people, of working more closely with customers, of creating partnerships between the suppliers in the company and the customers in the company, creating self-directing work teams where we reduce the amount of management needed, the amount of management given, the amount of overhead in organizations.

The ideal is a group of people who have a very easy time working together, they have the data they need, they have the tools they need, the support they need to make clean decisions and implement them themselves. There is not a huge amount of bureaucracy or a huge amount of going through the multiple layers in the company.

Not surprisingly, there is congruence to be found in Dr. Juran's responses to *New York Times* interview questions:

Q. What is the outlook for quality improvement at American companies?

A. The major phenomenon of the 1980's is that top managers began to take charge of quality the way they have always taken care of finance. They realize that the influence of quality on sales was profound and that it could not be left to underlings. In the decade to come, they will include quality in their basic business plans. That was never true before.

Q. What approaches should American managers focus on? Are statistical process controls and quality circles the answer?

A. Those are tools, and a good way to lose time in improving quality is to focus on tools and try to apply them. Statistics are the fundamental science in quality, just as mathematics is the fundamental science of physics, but that is not all that is involved. The real issue is to decide when to apply the tools and who is to use them. There is no such thing as a single magic tool that you can train 100 percent of the people to use and solve all your problems.

Q. Anything else?

A. Yes, relations with the work force are changing. The old system of close control is giving way to this concept of self-managing teams. It has two aspects. Self-control, in which people have more control over their own jobs. And there are self-directing teams, where groups of people literally design their own jobs. It is restoring the planning to where it once was, but at a much higher level of sophistication. Best-in-class competitive benchmarking will also be big in the 1990's. Unfortunately, some people will probably latch onto it as a magic bullet.[10]

With this greater emphasis on self-management, companies can afford to do away with some of the layers that separate the bottom from the top. However, the "doing-away" must be done carefully. As Godfrey sees it,

Managers are finding out that flat organizations do work, but they require information-technology beyond what most companies have. They require training the people to make decisions and use this information far beyond what they have been doing.

Companies that just cut out without thinking through what the organization needs to have in the way of resources to operate with fewer levels of managers—these companies just run into all sorts of trouble. What we have to do is understand what it takes to work with a flat organization, to work with an organization that is very flexible, very responsive to the customers, where decisions are made at very low levels, where everyone in the organization is thinking, rather than having planners who plan and workers who do what they are told.

The Japanese say, "Let's hire them for their hands and feet, because we get their heads for free." The same thought is shared by many American managers, but it is really not put to very much use. Most of our managers believe in this but they just do not know how to implement it.

Scientific Management

Around the turn of the last century, conditions were ripe in America for the advent of "scientific management," a system espoused by Frederick Taylor, and designed to separate the planner/managers from the workers. Free enterprise, coupled with the Protestant work ethic, gave Americans the perfect soil in which the factory system could flourish. Technology was growing rapidly and our natural resources were abundant. The management system that evolved capitalized on the willingness of workers to work. It was a system that literally managed the masses of willing employees. It emphasized and increased their productivity and—given the lack of precedent on which to build—could be considered successful in helping the free enterprise system to take root in this country.

However, it was not a perfect system. The negative consequences of it are depicted in Figure 2.

FIGURE 2

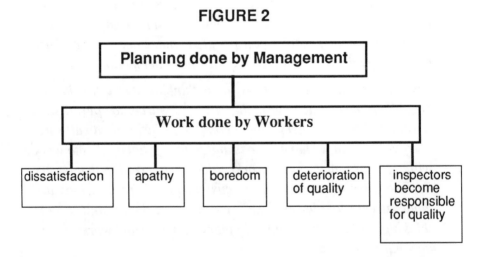

A publication of the Community Relations Department at NUMMI is equally severe in its description of Taylor's "division of labor" approach:

Along with the Taylor approach went an underlying attitude that production-line workers were lazy and not very smart. Many managers shared the attitude of Henry Ford, who said at the time he announced the $5/day wage—"The assembly line is a haven for those who haven't got the brains to do anything else"—and treated production-line workers accordingly. Not surprisingly, workers have long fought against the monotony and mindless nature of traditional assembly line work in which they were treated as so many cogs in a wheel. The inevitable result was a labor relations structure based on antagonism, confrontation, and mistrust, as typified by GM's Fremont plant [before its joint venture with Toyota Motor Corporation].[11]

Today, of course, the American worker is respected for the contribution he is able to make, putting to full use his hands and feet, as well as his brain. More and more organizations are encouraging team-based management and the creation of working partnerships.

Kaizen

The sense of partnership permeates the NUMMI plant, to the extent that it has been built into the union contract in the form of "kaizen," a Japanese word meaning "improvement." As Sharon Sarris puts it,

Kaizen is a very important part of the company. It is one of the fundamentals here. It means that we are always looking for improvement, continuous improvement, involvement of all our team members in looking for ways to enhance processes, either to assure quality or to make the job safer, make it more efficient.

The word "kaizen" is used in our contract in lieu of the work "improvement." We regard it as a basic commitment here and are constantly seeking improvement in quality, efficiency and work environment through kaizen, Quality Control circles, and suggestion programs. Both negotiating parties are bound to kaizen.

The suggestion program supports the whole kaizen philosophy. Basically, the program rewards and encourages people to make improvements by writing them up on short, simple suggestion forms. Their ideas are for improving cost, safety efficiency, quality. The program has the full support of management. The suggestion goes to the group leader, who works with the team member to refine it before it is passed along so that the idea has a better chance for acceptance and implementation. Points are given based on the merit of the idea. Each point is worth one dollar. We give out gift certificates for purchases at a local store.

Masaaki Imai lauds NUMMI's efforts in his book *Kaizen: The Key to Japan's Competitive Success.*[12] He speaks of work standardization as a critical element in the Toyota manufacturing process and uses the Toyota definition of standardization: "the optimum combination of workers, machines, and material." He also mentions the multiple job assignments NUMMI workers have. Labor and management have opted to define fewer job categories and to encourage employees, as Sarris confirms, to engage in many different job functions.

The three ingredients of work standardization are shown in Figure 3.

FIGURE 3

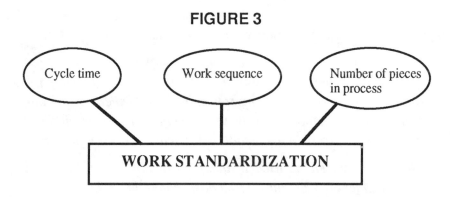

Imai speaks of the need for supervisors to help those employees who may be having difficulty doing the standardized work. Once the employee can meet the standard, the standard is raised—usually with employees' input. Kaizen is a simple concept, one that involves constant improvement. Citing the NUMMI experience, Imai discusses the synthesis that has evolved from two forces previously viewed antithetically: labor and management. The NUMMI union has agreed to the fact that management will have some role in raising standards, and management has agreed to the fact that workers will participate in the kaizen process.

"This is the first instance in Western labor relations," Imai relates, "where there has been accord on the joint commitment to KAIZEN in the work place." A constant concern in auto workers' negotiations is job security. The fear that kaizen may lead to a reduced work force has been offset by management's commitment to maintaining jobs. Many of NUMMI's employees had previously worked at the GM plant, which was shut down when GM sales sagged. These employees have no trouble accepting the fact that kaizen will lead to better-quality cars, which will lead to continued employment. It is little wonder, Imai points out, that employees willingly participate in kaizen practices.

Rewards

Although Dr. Juran states that reward systems are needed to "drive people to meet quality goals,"[13] Godfrey prefers the word "recognition."

I would use the word "recognition" more strongly than I would use the word "reward." Recognition is constant. When people do something that is good, and you want to recognize it quickly, you want to have recognition among their peers, you want to have recognition from the corporation at all levels. You want to have recognition, of course, in the company newsletter, the company magazine, the local press. You want to make sure that those things that are contributing to the success of the company are recognized clearly, and that credit is given freely.

The rewards I have recommended have been more on a profit-sharing basis, more on a team basis when people are rewarded as a group. If you can, get away from some of these individual rewards and especially get away from some of the rewards that are tied closely to perceived savings in the first year. Things like that just create nightmares of bureaucracy.

I think quick, small rewards that are more in the way of recogni-tion than they are in the way of rewards are to be preferred. Din-

ner for two, $100 presented in a small meeting after a special event. Those are fine, but when you get into huge bonuses that are attached to one person's particular contribution, you run into all sorts of problems because very few contributions are made by one person. Almost all contributions are made with the contributions of many people in varying degrees, varying time. Most good ideas have many, many mothers and fathers.

We really should recognize the multiple contributions. To single out one person for something and to ignore the rest is to create problems. We really are working together in most companies and I think we should encourage that.

Developing Trust

As Godfrey points out, the intrinsic rewards are usually more meaningful than the extrinsic ones. At Edson International, a New Bedford, Massachusetts, firm that makes steering systems for yachts, employees who have been with the company at least five years are given keys to the machine shop. The policy lets employees who can't afford their own workshop use the shop on weekends as long as another person is with them in case of injury. President Will Keene comments on his employees: "They've made it known they plan to stay with our company for the long haul. They aren't out to rip us off."[14]

That same sense of trust is addressed by Sarris. She believes that

Changing how management thinks and operates is the key. From that change flows a system that supports the change. If a manager really believes in something, he or she must also believe in the steps to get from seeing how this works, to asking how the plant must be changed. Do we implement a just-in-time delivery system? Do we build relationships with the union? How do we get trust and respect so they believe me when I say we are going to allow them to stop the line?

Increased employee participation at NUMMI is a function of several forces, not the least of which is the rejection of the Taylor system and its dependence on precisely defined jobs. The precision leaves little room for worker independence of thought or action. Mr. Konosuke Matsushita, Executive Advisor of the Matsushita Electric Company, in his address to a group of Western industrialists more than a decade ago, predicted failure for the industrial West if attitudes were not altered. "Your firms are built on the Taylor model," he noted, "where your bosses do the thinking while your workers wield the screwdrivers. You're convinced, deep down, that this is the right way to run a business."

At NUMMI, the sharp distinctions between labor and management are blurred, creating a sense of unity rather than division. The 100 job classifications have been reduced into a single job description for multi-skilled workers who work in teams to improve processes. Their improvements are more the result of their own observations, judgments and subsequent actions than the result of management-imposed alterations. The trust that is placed in them results in greater pride, a prerequisite for quality.

Sarris defines the "traditional" limits to workers' involvement:

In the old days, stopping the line was equivalent to, was translated to, work stoppage. We had to shift, to tell workers that, in order to build in quality, "It is your responsibility, team leader. If you see a problem that has reached your work station, or if you cannot get the bolt screwed in the right way, you do not say, 'Oh, well, too bad. Somebody else will catch it later down the line.' Instead, you pull the cord, you signal the need for help. When the supervisor responds, the problem will be fixed.

"If you cannot fix it in time, you stop the line or flag it so it will be corrected before it leaves the plant." And we have had absolutely no problem with that. We still have 85 percent of the work force that in the old days would have viewed work stoppage as a way to give management a hard time.

We have a production system that supports kaizen by assuring everybody's job is defined and there is a standardized work practice for every job level, so that you do not have inequity as far as job difficulty is concerned. We have what amounts to job classifications so that people can help each other. They can do other jobs and not just narrowly defined jobs.

If a line does stop—for example because of a problem in the paint department—then people can be cleaning the work area or doing minor maintenance rather than waiting for the guy whose job it is to clean the area or to do the minor maintenance to come over. We release people in a given department, keep skills where needed for higher-level jobs and allow others to do lower-level jobs.

I asked Godfrey to discuss these paradigm shifts that upset traditional views of employer/employee relationships, as far as the Juran Institute is concerned. He replies that they believe in everything they preach and they try to practice it carefully.

We have had incredible teamwork and a feeling of esprit de corps among the people like I have never seen in any other company I have worked with or worked in. The teamwork is evident even in simple projects. For example, we wanted to improve the graphics that we use. We had a team actually headed by my secretary—a quality-improvement team of people from different levels including senior consultants and some of our people from sales and service.

They went to trade shows and looked at hardware and software. They got the names of people using various products and actually interviewed those people at companies like IBM and Xerox—companies much bigger than we are but nonetheless, it is still people doing the same type of thing. They then made their decisions about the hardware and the software we would buy. We asked for volunteers to take over this new job involving the creation of graphics. One of our people volunteered and we sent her off for training. We created a small office with this equipment in it and now, we generate graphics of a much higher quality than we ever have before—at about half the cost.

Quality Implementation

Lawrence Holpp has identified ten saboteurs that can hamper Quality implementation efforts.[15] In isolation, he says, the factors are "irritants." Combined, they are "deadly."

1. UNCORRECTED VISION
Vision statements must be closely coupled with behavior.

2. POOR OBJECTIVES
Policy deployment is a specific management method that can help link customer needs to daily activities within even the most layered organizations.

3. LOOSE CANNONS
The first are people who use quality as an excuse to establish fiefdoms. The second are people who remain in powerful positions but don't get with the program.

4. WANDERING TEAMS AND LOST SUPERVISORS
Organizations must either develop a new role for supervisors and team leaders in managing the quality-improvement activities of various groups of people, or they must abandon the traditional role of supervisor entirely and move toward semiautonomous teams.

5. NONSTATISTICAL THINKING
To learn to use statistics comfortably, participants need practice with realistic solutions.

6. NEW-PROGRAM SYNDROME
The goal now is to quit calling it a program and instill quality thinking, techniques, vocabulary and systems into everybody's day-to-day work.

7. WHAT, MORE TRAINING?
Unfortunately, past practices of ignoring performance objectives when designing courses have not helped training departments attain the prestige they must have to drive Total Quality Improvement.

8. DOUBLE-CROSSED FUNCTIONAL MANAGEMENT

The real problem hindering cross-functional management is not the ability or willingness of team members to cooperate. It is the long history of not being rewarded for cooperation, or being punished for sharing information or involving others.

9. ELECTRONIC MANAGEMENT

Total Quality Improvement is not something for caretaker managers. It is a full-time job and, for many, becomes a personal crusade.

10. 1, 2, 3...CHANGE

We don't resist (for long) changes that benefit us.

This same careful attention to the pitfalls awaiting Quality implementers is evident in the approach taken by Godfrey and his associates at the Juran Institute.

We work with people throughout the organization. We do a seminar with the top people at which we talk about the basic concepts that they need to know. We talk about what they need to do. We create an action plan; we decide on some of the things they may want to do to get started. How are they going to manage this? What does the Quality Council do? Who is going to be on the Council?

At the end of those three days, they have an action plan that they can then implement. Then we come back and work with the middle managers so that they understand what is going on, to make sure the top managers who took part in that course know why they were doing this, what they are doing, how they should schedule, etc. And as they pick specific projects, specific things to do, we provide their training, usually for the trainers. Then we decide on the people who will train the teams, the facilitators and the in-house consultants.

Next, we provide the training for those people. We teach statistical tools as well as the problem-solving methodology, everything from simple statistical graphics to statistical quality control to quality planning, asking: What are the teams focusing on? What direction is the company taking? We provide support all the way down through the workers.

The people we have trained subsequently train the actual team members, working with them to the completion of a successful project. Then they select new people, train them, etc. We provide ongoing support, returning to do some reviews, training the next set of middle managers, the next set of trainers.

Our philosophy and our goal is to transfer this technology to the company as fast as possible, to make the company as self-sufficient as possible. We never go away. We are there for help, for their reviews. We are there to do assessments to see what level they are at. We are working for them and with them. They are doing the hard work; they are the ones achieving the results. We are just helping them do it over the several years that it takes for the thinking process to be turned around.

Like Holpp, Godfrey stresses that successful Quality implementation is more than just training. The participants must become involved; they have to see the successes and understand how they were achieved. Then they must make similar success happen throughout the company. Godfrey is adamant in stressing the need to take Quality out of manufacturing and get it into the business process, the financial organization, into purchasing, into personnel. Quality implementers must bring the philosophy and the practices into business plans and into strategic planning. He asserts,

It's not enough just to hear about it. You have got to do it. Most of us learn by doing and we have got to give personnel the confidence that they can do it. It takes awhile for this realization to sink in.

The Juran Institute training focuses on simple statistical graphics like flowcharts, cause-and-effect diagrams, histograms, run charts, analyses of needs, simple control charts and experiments, box plots—the tools employees could use to solve problems. Their intent is to help people change at the level of their performance. But team skills, according to Godfrey, are as important as the statistical skills and so they work with employees on team building, critiquing skills, positive feedback, and constructive feedback so that people will be comfortable sharing expression and working as a group.

Quality and the High School Curriculum

Sharon Sarris points out that team building can be emphasized in the high school curriculum.

Better communication skills can be taught. We train kids to be individualistic by way of IQ tests, honor roll, etc. Instead, we can be emphasizing the team approach to acquiring knowledge. Young people move into the workplace and there, they are supposed to share their knowledge, using problem-solving processes to make improvements, using a more systematic approach to a given situation through the process of how to approach problems. We need to learn how to accept people's differences, how to listen to other people's ideas.

And Godfrey, too, sees possibilities for pushing Quality down to pre-employment levels. Asked what aspects of the Quality movement could be introduced to the high school curriculum, he replies,

As a matter of fact, all of them. All of the basic tools really have to be introduced. Dick Schaeffer at the University of Florida, chairman for several years of the Quantitative Literacy Project, a project funded by the National Science Foundation, joined with the American Statistical Association and the National Council of Teachers of Mathematics. They are trying to introduce more quantitative methods into the high school curriculum. He and I have spoken recently about incorporating Quality methods into educational programs. I volunteered to send him our materials for their use. As many as they would like.

They are training several of the top teachers from each state, each summer. Then these teachers go back and introduce what they have learned into their schools and provide resource people to train other teachers.

It's been a beautiful program. So far, it's received very good press. It has been launched very well. The first programs brought teachers into Princeton during the summers. It has become a great honor to be part of this program. They are a very strong force. Of course, it is only a drop in the bucket compared to the total number of school teachers, but they are off to a good start and there are some other organizations at the state level that are picking up.

Governor Bill Clinton of Arkansas has been a real leader in all of this. There is some very good work that Arkansas Eastman (a division of the Eastman Kodak Company) has done. They have worked in several cities and schools in Arkansas. Both Governor Clinton and Eastman Kodak have been strong supporters of these efforts.

Quality and the Future

Says Godfrey, "The biggest challenge facing American industry is getting our act together, defining what is important, getting our people prepared for this challenge and getting companies organized in such a way that we can meet the challenges."

We have got to get back to the basics. We have got to get back to products that people want and are willing to pay a good price for. We have to get back to providing the services that customers really do want, customers who are all of us.

We have got to get back to a long-term focus on the health—not only of industry but also of America. We just cannot live on borrowed money and imported goods. We have got to become a strong nation again and this includes not only the quality of our products and services, but also the quality of our schools. The quality of our political processes, and the quality of the way we treat each other.

When we treat the earth badly, we are treating everybody in future generations badly, not just the people who live here now. I think that people are beginning to realize this. It sounds almost trivial to say "back to basics" but we need to get back to making things that really meet our needs and do not destroy our environment.

We can all have a good life. This country is so rich and so filled with talented people that some of the problems we allow ourselves to have are ridiculous.

Summary

Ever since their association at AT&T's Bell Labs, Dr. A. Blanton Godfrey has worked closely with Dr. Joseph M. Juran, ultimately succeeding him as Chairman and CEO of the Juran Institute. In their work with firms undergoing Quality transformations, Godfrey and his associates place responsibility for Quality squarely on the shoulders of top managers. They talk constantly of meeting world-class standards and teach companies how to reach those higher standards.

Tomorrow's managers, Godfrey emphasizes, must understand their roles and must establish goals so all employees can help move the company toward world-class levels of competition. He predicts tomorrow's managers will demonstrate a greater concern for customers, that they will benchmark more extensively, that they will find better ways to identify poor quality.

Such efforts will be expensive, Dr. Juran cautions, especially in terms of training. But companies that are serious about moving ahead must commit policies, budgets and staffs—*before* the Quality effort is begun. It is the leader's job to break down any barriers that stand in the way of goal-accomplishment.

Sharon Sarris, Manager, Community Relations/General Affairs for NUMMI, speaks of the extent to which the Quality message is repeated at her joint-venture facility. And Bertha Davis echoes the impact training has had on bringing about change at NUMMI. When training is appropriate and thorough, particularly for quantitative skills, it will eliminate the "seat-of-the-pants" flying and the "gut-facts" that Godfrey scorns.

If we are serious about quality, Dr. Juran insists, we will accord it as much importance as we have accorded finance in the past. We will recognize the value of statistical tools, as well as the need to unify relations with the work force, engage in competitive benchmarking, and promote self-management. We will move away from Taylor's "scientific management" and will instead form partnerships both inside and outside the company.

Masaaki Imai applauds Toyota's work standardization, an "optimum combination of workers, machines and materials," which is currently in use at the NUMMI plant. There, labor and management have agreed to the use of *kaizen,* or constant improvement, as the best way to save jobs and perhaps save the plant itself. The suggestion system is an effective kaizen medium.

When employees do make valuable suggestions or otherwise demonstrate exceptional performance, Godfrey feels it is more important to recognize than to reward them; and trust and empowerment are two intrinsic means of reward. Godfrey cites an empowerment example from the Juran Institute to illustrate how they practice the concepts they teach, one of which is self-sufficiency.

Lawrence Holpp warns of saboteurs that could diminish Quality improvement endeavors: uncorrected vision, poor objectives, loose cannons, wandering teams and lost supervisors, nonstatistical thinking, the new-program syndrome, poor training, double-crossed functional management, electronic management, and too-rapid change.

Many Quality principles could be introduced to the high school curriculum, especially the cooperative aspects of learning and working toward a goal. Making educational systems healthier—as well as industrial, political and ecological systems—is the primary challenge before us, as far as Godfrey is concerned.

For Further Consideration

1. If you were asked to help design a three-day training course on quality improvement, what elements would be included? In what sequence?

2. What are some other "global issues" that we face?

3. Carefully delineate the differences between leading and cheerleading, from a managerial point of view. If you can, cite examples.

4. Compare the product or service your company provides to the ISO success standards listed on page 123.

5. How are you—individually and as a company—measuring improvement?

6. How are you—individually and as a company—planning for Quality?

7. What organizational changes can you point to that have been made in order to achieve Quality policies and goals?

8. Is performance rewarded or recognized in your firm? Explain.

9. Specifically, how should management demonstrate visible commitment?

10. What has your department been asked to do to achieve Quality improvement? Are the department members equipped to do what they have been asked? Elaborate.

11. What barriers stand in the way of your making the best possible Quality contribution?

12. What things have you not done before that you think you could now handle—given the responsibility, authority, resources, training and skills?

13. What are your personal Quality goals?

14. If you had to issue a Quality message, what would it be?

15. Japanese-style management seems to be working well at NUMMI. From your knowledge of such management, what practices do you think would work and which would not?

16. What are *your* predictions about Quality and the future?

17. To what extent have quantification skills been part of your management or business training?

18. How do you feel your company should change to better meet customer needs?

19. How does one bring about self-directing work teams?

20. List the "business partnerships" you have formed with individuals inside and outside the company.

21. What kinds of benchmarking does your company do? Could it do more?

22. What would be "the optimum combination of workers, machines, and material," as far as you are concerned?

23. If your job could be broadened to include several additional job functions, what would the revised job include?

24. If you were in charge of the reward/recognition system at your firm, how would you fashion it?

25. In what specific ways could trust be increased in your company?

26. How could the traditional distinctions between workers and managers be made less sharp?

27. What saboteurs could you identify that may be lessening the impact of Quality improvement efforts in your firm?

28. As far as supervisory positions are concerned, Holpp thinks they should either be redefined or else eliminated. What do you think?

29. What are the advantages of Quality improvement programs? The disadvantages?

30. If your company does not have a Quality Council, how would you go about forming one?

31. What does (or should) a Quality action plan contain?

References

[1] "How to Manage for World Class Quality," *Boardroom Reports,* Vol. 10, No. 9 (May 1, 1990), pp. 1, 6.

[2] "Quality Management and Quality System Elements—Guidelines," a publication of International Standards Organization (ISO), ISO #9004: 1987 (E), first edition 1987-03-15, p. 4. Reprinted with the permission of ASQC.

[3] *Boardroom Reports, op. cit.,* p. 6.

[4] *Ibid.*

[5] Davis, Bertha. *Crisis in Industry: Can America Compete?* (New York: Franklin Watts, Inc., 1989), p. 66.

[6] Godfrey, A. Blanton. "Managing Quality in the 1990's," *Juran Institute* (Wilton, Connecticut: Juran Institute, Inc., 1990), p. 5.

[7] *Boardroom Reports, op. cit.,* p. 6.

[8] Phillips, Stephen *et al.,* "King Customer," *Business Week,* No. 3149 (March 12, 1990), p. 89.

[9] *Ibid.,* p. 90.

[10] "Talking Business—With Juran of the Juran Institute," *New York Times* (February 6, 1990), p. C2.

[11] Community Relations Department, "New United Motor Manufacturing, Inc.," a publication of New United Motor Manufacturing, Inc. (January 1989), p. 18.

[12] Imai, Masaaki. *Kaizen: The Key to Japan's Competitive Success* (New York: Random House, 1986), p. 169.

[13] *New York Times, op. cit.*

[14] "Building Trust," *Inc.,* Vol. 12, No. 8, p. 108. Reprinted with permission, *Inc.* magazine (August 1990). Copyright © 1990 by Goldhirsh Group, Inc., 38 Commercial Wharf, Boston, MA 02110.

[15] Holpp, Lawrence. "10 Reasons Why Total Quality Is Less Than Total," *Total Quality Handbook* (Minneapolis: Lakewood Books, 1990), pp. 109–118. Reprinted with permission from Lakewood Publications, 50 South Ninth St., Minneapolis, MN 55402. All rights reserved.

Shirley L. Powell, Quality Assurance— Total Quality Management (TQM) Coordinator
AiResearch — Los Angeles Division of Allied-Signal

"Many of the concepts implemented by the Japanese during the past 40 years were basically American....concepts that we Americans had rejected, convinced we were and would always be, the world's best."

Background

"I'm a paradigm-shifter." Shirley Powell, AiResearch Quality Assurance—TQM Coordinator for the Los Angeles Division of Allied-Signal (ALAD), describes herself this way. "Ever since we put a man on the moon and my grandfather assured me it was just a Hollywood hoax, I determined it would behoove me to stay open to change. Not to accept all change but to question and accept it when necessary. This thinking has helped me in shifting paradigms," she reveals.

She has been involved with shifting paradigms devoid of TQM to paradigms that embrace it since 1969, when she worked to start up a new company in Irvine, California. They operated then according to A.V. Feigenbaum's Total Quality Control principles.

We put a quality program together at that company and then moved on with the same group of professionals to two other companies using the successful methods and systems we had developed. So I have actually had an opportunity to help set up ground-floor quality programs in three companies, each with different environments. I then worked as a consultant for eight years. I began at AiResearch as a field representative of General Dynamics in 1984 and was then hired full-time by AiResearch in 1988.

AiResearch embraced the concepts of TQM in 1986 and has expended considerable effort to provide an environment that promotes continuous improvement. Early success with Taguchi Experiments and various SPC techniques convinced ALAD to "go ahead with the TQM process."

With encouragement from Quality Assurance (QA) management, a full-blown, customer-focused pilot package was developed and implemented within the Research and Development Quality Engineering group with a staff of 30. The group was given two hours of formal training in various subjects each week. Teaming was encouraged, which meant, in part, we regarded each person in the group as an equal member. A major part of the pilot package included individual development planning. Each individual was encouraged, but not forced, to participate in the process of developing his/her own position description, including job expectations and targeted completion dates. It was difficult because it was a big change from previous supervisory techniques.

The Research and Development (R & D) Quality Engineering Group of Quality Assurance at ALAD provide various QA support functions, including Inspection Planning, Gauge and Tooling Planning, Development Program support, and Proposal and Contract Review activities.

The parent company, Allied-Signal, has gone from producing commodity chemicals, oil and gas to producing advanced technological products. With worldwide markets (over 100 countries), Allied-Signal is one of America's thirty largest industries. Its product lines are centered on aerospace, automotive and engineered materials. Headquartered in Morris Township, New Jersey, Allied-Signal is an $11 billion company with 113,000 employees working in 45 nations and territories outside the United States.

ALAD is a division of Allied-Signal Aerospace Company, headquartered at the Torrance, California, facility along with ALAD. Powell works here with Quality Engineers who are assigned to the Product and Procurement Quality Assurance department.

Job Satisfaction

Powell has been active in bringing Quality precepts to educational settings beyond her workplace. She did seminars with junior-year high school students in the 1960's and 1970's, encouraging them to acquire work experience so that when they left high school and entered the work force, they would be able to use basic tools, especially with electronic and mechanical assemblies.

She speaks of once asking an auditorium of 600 youngsters how many of them believed their parents really enjoyed their jobs. Every hand went up. Powell knew the research showed that as many as 80 percent of working adults are dissatisfied with their jobs and may be considering a career or job change. It was clear to Powell then that parents often keep from their children the extent of their dislike for their jobs. Perhaps, she offers, they keep it from themselves as well.

Career changes can rend the emotional materials of individuals as well as whole families. Reluctance to engage in the upheaval that normally ensues from such changes may be keeping people in unsatisfying jobs. They either don't have the courage or the ability to switch jobs. Powell comments, "Once you have been in a job for ten years, making any change can be traumatic."

There are a lot of stressed and unhappy people here because of that constant conflict. Instead of being comfortable or enjoying what they are doing, they remain in jobs that don't give the needed satisfaction.

I enjoy what I do more than most people. I do encounter difficulty trying to make long-term employees see that there are options. It took me eight years working in consulting to work through those insecurities myself, to understand that there would always be another job and I did not have to work where I would stagnate.

Fear

Dr. Deming speaks of this fear in *Out of the Crisis*. He considers the etymology of the word *secure* (from the Latin "se" meaning "without" and "cura" meaning "care") and asserts that without work-related security, employees cannot give peak performance. He elaborates,

Secure means without fear, not afraid to express ideas, not afraid to ask questions. Fear takes on many faces. A common denominator of fear in any form, anywhere, is loss from impaired performance and padded figures.

There is widespread resistance of knowledge. Advances of the kind needed in Western industry require knowledge, yet people are afraid of knowledge. New knowledge brought into the company might disclose some of our failings. A better outlook is, of course, to embrace new knowledge because it might help us to do a better job.

Some people may wonder whether at this stage of life they can learn something new. If there were a change, where would I be?

New knowledge would cost money. Would we get our money back?[1]

One of the goals Powell and her team have set for themselves is the elimination of stress and fear, a task she regards as formidable and at which she admits they have not been fully successful. When fear is present, it serves to block the implementation of TQM. Employees cannot give wholehearted support to change when their jobs are on the line. And the number of jobs that appear on that line is growing steadily in defense-related firms due to current Congressional budget discussions.

Instead of trying to control the forces over which she has no control, Powell brings her intensity to bear on the successes that can be and have been wrought among her staff, the support staff in particular. She encourages inverting the organization chart as a way of disarming fears. "Supervision is almost invisible," she chortles. "Our staff remains in control. We are the fixers. We concentrate on system-related problems and remove obstacles that our staff identify during brainstorming sessions."

Developing Potential

"Shining stars" is the phrase she uses to describe the support staff. She believes, and encourages them to believe as well, that they have made significant strides in developing their potential and sharing their developed potential with the team as a whole. Many have come to realize they are capable of much more than clerical functions and are often counted on to collect and analyze data.

Also, the experience is bi-directional. The Quality Engineers are learning to appreciate the support staff as more than clerical support. She places emphasis on the individual first and job second. "What counts," she tells staff members, "is that you do your best work." Being in an environment that is free of fear allows for this positive interaction.

It is encouragement of this nature that enables employees to know their work is important and their ideas have merit. When individuals feel they are valued for what they are able to do with their mental as well as their manual abilities, they release the ideas and creative suggestions that may have been stultified until such an appreciation is shown. Bertrand Russell referred to fear as "the main source of superstition, and one of the main sources of cruelty. To conquer fear," he declared, "is the beginning of wisdom." Synonymous with that wisdom are creativity and innovation.

Figure 1 shows the ways in which fear can impact employees and the organization as a whole.

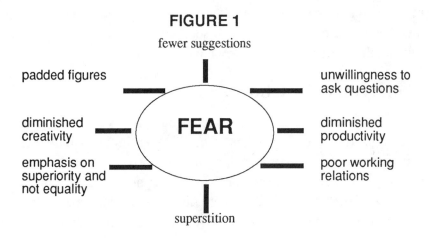

FIGURE 1

When the culture encourages the idea that the boss is being paid to think and subordinates are being paid to do what they are told by the omniscient superior, workers will stop suggesting good ideas and will turn off emotionally to the organization's mission.

In the egalitarian environment Powell has attempted to create, position titles are less important than contributions individuals can make. Acknowledging that her efforts might run contrary to the efforts of personnel and human resource departments, she shares the essence of her message to employees:

"Look, your labor grade and title are not indicators of your future. We would like you to tell us your perception of how your job should be done. If you participate in the development of your own goals and objectives, you will be evaluated against those, not against what Mary Jane does over here or what John does over there. We are not going to line you all up and evaluate you against each other. You will be evaluated against your own standards. If something prevents you from meeting your objectives, like a special project pulling you away so you cannot meet a target date, let us know and we will adjust."

Acknowledging that individuals need to set their own goals, she concedes that sometimes the goals are unrealistic. Sometimes, she claims, they are too hard on themselves or set themselves up for more than they can handle in the time frame they have established.

Management by Objectives

Powell is adamant about the deleterious effects of management by objectives (MBO). She echoes Dr. Deming in describing MBO as management by fear. His eighth point is to "drive out fear. Create trust. Create a climate for innovation." Powell is doing exactly that as she decries the MBO focus on the bottom line, a focus that creates a negative environment, in her opinion. She does not equivocate about the effects of fear:

Hierarchies developed under MBO organizations have become counterproductive. There must be a person in a position of superiority over every position. That is how we were taught in the existing culture. It just doesn't work anymore.

It's terrible in a TQM environment because every position is important. We all make valuable contributions. Everyone, no matter what the job, is important. Europe is a step ahead of us in this regard. After World Wars I and II, they were down to basic levels. They know firsthand that certain things are petty; they just don't deal with them. We're not there yet, and I sincerely hope it won't take that level of desecration for America.

It's the same thing with the Japanese. They were devastated after World War II. Subsequently, though, they requested and were given wonderful tools and techniques to rebuild their industries. As Chief of the Occupational Forces, General MacArthur did a great service by helping Japan. He provided them with the best... ideas that we Americans wouldn't accept.

In an equally forceful diatribe against MBO, Dr. Deming asserts:

The job of management is not supervision, but leadership. Management must work on sources of improvement, the intent of quality of product and of service, and on the translation of the intent into design and actual product. The required transformation of Western style of management requires that managers be leaders. Focus on outcome (management by numbers, MBO, work standards, specifications met, zero defects, appraisal of performance) must be abolished, leadership put in place.[2]

Self-Knowledge

You are better able to do your best work, Powell contends, if you know about yourself and how others perceive you. If you have difficulty relating to others, or if you hesitate to share your opinion at meetings, or if you believe you have an extroverted personality yet others perceive you as introverted, you cannot make the greatest possible contribution to your team. And if you cannot share, Powell insists, you'll have problems teaming well. She tries to make all persons aware of who they are; she also tries to make each individual realize how his or her efforts contribute to the whole.

Sometimes, such awareness will lead to behavioral or cognitive shifts. Other times, individuals find the information creates such dissonance in their perception of themselves that they reject it and go on thinking and behaving as they have always done. Powell comments,

Sometimes they like what they hear and sometimes they do not, but self-awareness tools are as important as any technical tools that can be provided. Unfortunately, no part of our education or training has provided us with this knowledge. We end up finding out who we are through practical experience and the proverbial school of hard knocks. This method of learning establishes a mindset of survival techniques that can be detrimental to teaming environments.

One way to acquire self-knowledge is through surveys and Powell has taken advantage of what she is learning in her classes at the University of Redlands. She has transferred her new knowledge of evaluation, appraisals, training theory and techniques to her work at ALAD, passing along current methodologies to the group often before the "ink dries." Powell interacts with Quality engineers and describes them as one of the best groups to work with when tasked with making changes in an organization. Admitting that the engineers themselves may not share her conviction, she observes that her work with them is not really experimental because she is "making an impact upon them even though they may not be aware of it."

Additionally, she shares surveys related to leadership styles, learning skills, listening habits. The emphasis with these instruments is not on grading or comparisons but rather on aiding people to know more about themselves. As shown in Figure 2, Powell depends on a number of factors that will give employees knowledge about themselves and the way they perform their jobs.

The initial survey for the pilot program was an attitude survey, given to both the controlled engineering group and a non-controlled engineering group. The former rated themselves low in their knowledge of TQM; the latter, Powell reveals, thought they knew everything. As the training program continued, the experimental group realized the accuracy of their own assessment: once they began to acquire a "profound knowledge" (as Dr. Deming describes it), they realized how little they truly did know.

FIGURE 2

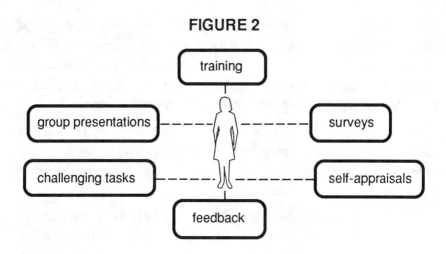

Removing Barriers

To nurture both employees and a democratic structure, Powell works to encourage employee participation in training, which is conducted in one-hour sessions twice a week. The programs include her entire group and occasionally outside staff from other Quality Assurance departments. In an effort to promote teamwork and understanding of internal customer needs, she will often invite employees to do an hour presentation that focuses on what they do in their jobs.

The usual response from a designated employee will be, "I don't do enough to fill up a whole hour talking about it!" Powell works synaptically with such an employee—linking neurons of ideas in a mind mapping process until there is a realization by the employee that he does have a comprehensive grasp of what the job entails. The end product is inevitably a sophisticated one.

A good example is the company Soldering Instructor, who has been with ALAD 14 years. When initially asked to make a one-hour presentation, she was reluctant, but finally did put together a demonstration/ lecture. On the morning the presentation was to be made, she called Powell to advise she could not go through with it. However, after being subjected to Powellian affirmations, she agreed. At the session, she explained processes with such clarity that everyone understood. It was among the best and most informative sessions in the series. Subsequently, the ALAD Training and Development Department asked to use her "Mind Maps" as an example of new technique utilization.

Powell, in her ancillary role, works on developing employees' self-worth. She expresses concern for individuals who go to work every day not really understanding what their purpose or role is or how their efforts (or lack of efforts) affect the organization's success.

We have been trying to turn around the negativism by saying, "Look, you do a lot. You have a lot of useful information." Most of these people have more information about this company and about the evolution of the company and how it got where it is going than I will ever know. They remember Cliff Garrett [the company founder] walking the halls and knowing everyone by name.

While such seniority brings many advantages—continuity, a pride in having been associated with start-up, a memory bank for reminiscing and making comparisons to the good old days—there are some disadvantages as well. The average person in Powell's department has nearly 20 years' seniority. She speaks of celebrating 31-year anniversaries with the company. Such constancy, of course, reduces personnel problems and makes turnover virtually non-existent. But this very constancy implies a paradigmatic rigidity, a dedication to continuing behaviors that have meant survival over the years.

It also implies difficulty in planning career paths. On more than one occasion, Powell has had subordinates tell her they are exactly where they want to be and are not concerned with upward mobility, to which Powell simply replies, "Good. Enjoy it."

Dr. Deming, in his twelfth point, urges the removal of barriers that rob people of pride of workmanship. He speaks of procedures or practices or policies that strip hourly workers of the natural desire to take pride in their work, a desire that is squelched if there are not criteria for acceptable performance. Another complaint common among hourly workers is the lack of certainty regarding continued employment, a feeling that can create the feeling of being a "commodity."[3]

Powell addresses some of the barriers she has encountered:

> *You are not only dealing with an insecure work force but also with paralyzed paradigms and age groups in which it is hard to accept change. Even when we show them how good it is, buying in causes them severe discomfort. So, we have been taking it a step at a time.*

> *It has become an emotionally heavy burden to bear. When we can't deliver, it becomes our responsibility [to do something, even if it is not what was originally hoped for]. We encourage the teams, motivate them to a certain point, and then sometimes can't deliver for various reasons. Often, the reason is fixed human resources policy, limited resources or individuals with fixed paradigms on what can and cannot be accomplished.*

Another barrier encountered by the company as a whole is the control of profit margins by the Department of Defense. Powell explains the negligible difference between the two types of markets her company serves.

> *When we say "commercial," we actually mean both military and commercial. To define us as commercial is not to perceive us correctly. We run a single-standard quality system. It doesn't matter whether you buy a part for a civilian aircraft or a military aircraft. You are going to get the same level of part with slightly different levels of documentation.*

> *When you are in a Department of Defense [DOD] environment, such as we have, you struggle to justify every person that you have on board and every dollar that you spend. Stress and fear enter in, too. How in the world do you provide a stable environment in such a variable atmosphere? That's the challenge.*

> *Even if you did away with MBO today, the challenge is to provide a stable environment when we are so susceptible to political decisions made by governments—not just our government, but*

world governments (Europe, the Middle East, Soviet Union, Japan, and so on) as well.

Beyond these barriers, depicted in Figure 3, perception presents another barrier as well. When Quality efforts are perceived as falling only under the auspices of the Quality department as opposed to falling into every employee's domain, the Quality environment will not thrive.

FIGURE 3

BARRIERS TO QUALITY

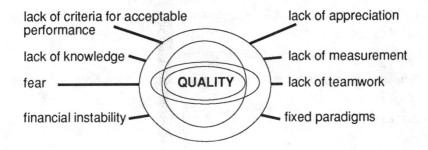

Powell cites Quality Engineers who have been working in detection and who consequently have earned the reputation of being "just part of an inspection department." That perception has become ingrained so that when these engineers are promoted from the ranks of inspection, they bring their mindsets toward Quality with them.

Proclaims Powell, "Training is the only way to alter those perceptions." In so doing, she believes, employees will not be engaging in Quality engineering per se, but rather in reject- and defect-identification. Quality Engineering, she contends, means prevention, and producing a product that has a consistent, acceptable quality level. Acknowledging how difficult it is to alter perceptions in an established company, she cites the genesis of the widely held perception about Quality engineering:

*Cliff Garrett and Howard Hughes and Jack Northrop—they all
had technical secrets and became entrepreneurs on a big scale in
the late 30's and 40's. They had very strong engineering groups
and engineering in this environment did not include TQM. When
you say Quality Control or Quality Assurance to these groups,
they often think "inspection."*

Integration

The company is working toward the integration of leadership, customer satisfaction, and continuous improvement objectives. So, too, is
Powell. She explains that they are trying to deal with individuals within
the various organizations on a one-on-one basis. They regard the Engineering Department, for example, as a customer. Contracts, Quota-
tions, Sales—all are customers. Powell goes to them and asks what those
customers need. She asks for honest dialogue so she can determine what
Quality Engineering has and has not been doing to satisfy their needs.

Not surprisingly, Powell has found others hold some inaccurate notions
about how her department functions. The narrower the communications
channels, she has found, the greater the likelihood that misperceptions or
misunderstandings will occur. She is now assembling a program to be
given to those internal customer groups in order to correct erroneous
impressions. The program will define what Quality Assurance means
today.

"We are not just a group of 350 inspectors," Powell avers, "trying to
inspect Quality into our product." She has found it most effective to deal
directly with the individuals at the top of each of these customer groups
as she tries to widen communication lines. Correct information will more
easily cascade through a given department if there is a single recipient of
it—namely, the person in charge. Through trial and error, Powell has
learned to place the responsibility for proper dissemination of information on the shoulders of the person in charge of those other functional
areas until the total organization has the posture of continuous improvement.

Controlling Quality

For most companies, an analysis of data on the quality of products is used to determine trends or to recommend changes in technology. Such data are hard to acquire in a timely fashion, Powell notes, when a firm is doing leading-edge work, as hers is. Limited production figures in a research and development environment can present a barrier, but not necessarily a barrier that is impossible to deal with.

> *When you only make two or three of something—a conceptual model, a development model, and production unit—it's very hard to have people think in terms of statistical process control [SPC]. Often people think quantities when assessing quality. So we concentrate on the common processes. This assures overall control of our products.*

The function of the R & D Quality Engineering Group—preparing the documentation for the product prior to its introduction to the manufacturing line—sometimes takes two years. She cites the work they have been doing for the space station as an example. The result of this extensive time and effort by numerous people may be a single product, such as one system for a space station environment. Of course, they also monitor the product after release and installation.

In distinguishing between **Quality Control** and **Quality Assurance,** Schermerhorn defines the former as the process of "*checking* products or services to ensure that they meet certain standards" and the latter as the process of "*preventing* the production of defective products or services."[4]

He speaks of the need to apply Quality Control to all stages of production so that waste can be reduced at the beginning, and rejects can be reduced at the end of the process, thereby increasing productivity throughout. One of the driving forces behind the acceptance of Quality Assurance has been the inevitable comparisons made between Japanese products and American ones. Several such comparisons are cited by Schermerhorn:

1. A new American car is almost twice as likely to have a problem as a Japanese car.

2. An American color television needs repairs twice as often as a Japanese set.

3. American-made computer memory chips were found in one test to be three times as likely to fail as Japanese-made chips.

4. During the first year of average use, there were seventeen service calls on American-made air conditioners for every one on a Japanese-made unit.[5]

Meeting the Challenge

Powell alludes to the possibility that an awareness of such comparisons may be enough to unite Americans. She speaks of the need for unity in our country, a unity resulting from response to a commonly perceived danger. The threat of foreign competition may be a sufficient stimulus to bring about the needed commonality of purpose. Americans seem to need a common cause, she contends, if we are to coalesce the current fragments littering the national scene.

Any time you mix something new with something old, Americans have this ability to come out with something really precious. But, it takes us awhile. It's like war. We don't want it. We will be isolationist until the end. But when the time comes, we are the toughest fighters on the earth.

Right now I think many feel TQM and statistical process control are Japanese concepts that are being forced on us. That, of course, is not true. Many of the concepts implemented by the Japanese during the past 40 years were basically American. Concepts that we Americans had rejected...convinced we were and would always be the world's best, only to realize in the early 80's that we were falling seriously behind, and not just behind Japan!

Convinced that American business will do what has to be done, Powell expresses her absolute certainty that we can recapture our position of prominence in the world. She cautions that we may have to redefine what our position is, though, since we are becoming more service-oriented.

The loss of an inexpensive labor base, she proposes, is one reason for the change in orientation.

By comparison, the Japanese do not have an inexpensive labor base either, she notes, despite what Americans believe.

We are not looking for slave labor. We are looking for all of us to do what we are doing right, the first time, the first pass. Then we can be as competitive with better quality, no matter the cost of labor. We can still pay a high salary to do the job if we would do it right the first time and if we do not have a hidden factor to deal with. And when the product is shipped, our customers will be satisfied—no returns, no complaints. It will not matter if it is a product or a service!

Cultural Changes

With wry amusement, Powell speaks of the meaning some people associate with cultural change. There are some, she notes, who think, "I am still going to the same church, and still going to the same job, and still working 9 to 5 each day. What in the world do you mean by a cultural change?" She speaks of ALAD having made changes subtly, having begun to transform the division culture with bits and pieces rather than an overnight replacement of the old with the new.

When the change is made too abruptly, she contends, disaster can follow. Powell compares the gradual way ALAD introduced its employees to the TQM methodologies, to the approach taken by another firm in the aerospace industry. "Phenomenal" is the word she employs to describe the resistance of those other employees to the change foisted upon them. Unless drastic measures are taken, she predicts, the resistance is going to bankrupt that other company. She chronicles the worst possible change scenario, the one that caused such employee resistance:

They closed down on Friday and opened up on Monday and they said, "TQM is here." They changed entire manufacturing lines and all the organizational structures. But because they didn't get their suppliers and employees to buy in, they cannot meet their commit-

ments. The suppliers are not delivering, their employees are unhappy, and the airplanes just sit there.

In her typically penetrating style, Powell observes that the company may have dedicated itself to TQM, but they did not get a real commitment from all their suppliers. It is the little parts and pieces, she claims, that are preventing them from turning out hardware. By contrast, she lauds ALAD's efforts to enhance the bottom line by doing things in a smarter fashion, not cheaper or quicker necessarily, but smarter.

Believing that knowledge is power, she attempts to share with her staff information about the various product lines in the company, attempts to develop pride by taking them on tours so they will more fully understand the complexity and far-ranging interests of the company. Because the product lines are so varied, though, it is difficult to engage in full-scale benchmarking (the process of acquiring information about the competitive practices used by the best in a given field).

Instead, Powell tries to provide internal data. She views the diversity of product lines as an advantage, for it enables them to deal with the entire process of manufacturing in a self-sufficient manner. ALAD, in a sense, is a more often than not a holistic manufacturer: it begins with raw materials, machining, and processing, and ends with a finished product.

Even though the division's culture is not yet fully engaged in Quality methodologies, Powell feels her efforts have brought considerable satisfaction to her and some degree of enrichment to participating employees. She denigrates the American mystique encased in the phrase, "Do it all or don't do it at all." In her words, "Anything that you do to modify any one person's behavior or attitude for the better, even slightly, makes the effort worth it!"

As a result of taking classes at a local university, Powell has encountered many people from the company described earlier, the company that attempted a radical crossover to a TQM environment. When they tell her they want to go back to the way things were, she logically asks them how they are going to do that. She counsels them to accept the change by asking, "Don't you think it would be easier to buy into what the company is trying to do than trying to go backwards?"

In time, Powell believes employees in that other company will realize there is nothing to go back to, that the old structure has been destroyed. When companies bring Quality into the way things are done, their decision is never based on whimsy, she points out. It is usually based on extensive study, extensive deliberation.

Supplier Relationships

Dr. Deming asserts that long-term relationships between company and supplier are needed for the best possible economic reasons. Such relationships clearly have advantages for both parties. The supplier can anticipate some stability in his cash flow, at least for that account, and therefore is probably more willing to help a large account realize some special savings. As far as purchases are concerned, the variation between lots is diminished and accounting procedures are streamlined.

ALAD, too, is working to address relationships with suppliers. The supplier base has been consolidated and streamlined, says Powell, so the division can participate with its suppliers in the TQM process. She elaborates:

Our suppliers are our life's blood. In recognizing this fact, our suppliers are encouraged to participate in the TQM process. We now purchase with long-term commitment from them so that they may know we are seriously committed to them.

We have reduced our sub-tier base enormously and are dedicating more business to those remaining by using long-term purchase orders so they truly know they are partners in what we do.

We are going more and more toward "just-in-time" inventory. We must. We can't keep gigantic inventories. It's neither prudent nor cost-effective in today's economy.

Layne Taylor, a procurement specialist at AiResearch, has been in charge of setting up supplier conferences for the past several years. Over 100 suppliers participate in the conferences, primarily those who do the highest volume of work with ALAD. Often suppliers that are being developed to do work with the company are invited to participate in the conferences as well. They are companies that management has identified as worth pursuing, as having the potential to become part of the ALAD network.

The primary motivation behind the conferences came from managers in the Procurement and Quality Assurance departments. It is they, she explains, who have the most direct dealings with suppliers. The decision to have such conferences was based on an awareness that several of ALAD's buyers and procurement people were having the same problems with suppliers. Taylor expands upon the genesis of the supplier conferences:

> *We realized perhaps there were some common misunderstandings that might apply to our entire supplier base. As in any relationship, communication is probably the most important thing. We realized that somehow communication had broken down in a lot of areas.*
>
> *In many ways, the relationship between the corporation and its suppliers is comparable to the relationship between a parent and a child. You cannot continually discipline a child. And, it seemed that the only time we communicated with our suppliers was when there was a problem. Such an approach was neither productive nor progressive.*

Taylor advocates letting suppliers know what is expected of them. They cannot be "disciplined" for not meeting standards if they are not aware of what the standards are. Expressing a belief that a company is only as strong as the people who support it, Taylor observes that the suppliers are the supporting basis of the work that AiResearch does. With justifiable pride, she discusses the supplier rating system AiResearch has established for tracking the progress of its suppliers. Half the criteria in the system pertain to Quality (number of rejections versus the number of acceptances) and the other half pertain to the delivery time, which is the other most important aspect of the products coming in.

The company sent out letters telling suppliers that they were either on the approved list or on the "need-to-improve" list. Naturally, the letters generated considerable interest in the vendor community. At that point, ALAD decided they needed to get all the vendors together so they could tell them exactly what the letters meant and how they could move from the need-to-improve category to the approved one. One of the ways recommended for improvement was the use of statistical process control (SPC).

For the suppliers who were designated as approved suppliers, being on the list was a stroke. We would put their names upon a plaque in our lobby each month, showing they were our preferred vendors. We would also send them out a letter. Some suppliers would have their letters framed.

The first year that we did this, we awarded plaques to twenty of our top suppliers who were selected by the management and by their ratings and by the dollar amount that they were doing. The president of the company went out to some of the presentations, but primarily the Procurement and Quality Assurance managers went to the supplier's site and awarded the plaques to the company.

Some of our supplier companies made the award ceremony quite a celebration. They would bring all of their employees in and serve cake and really treat it as a special event.

As depicted in Figure 4, the one-day conference proved to be a successful alternative to dialogue based on criticism of sellers by buyers.

FIGURE 4

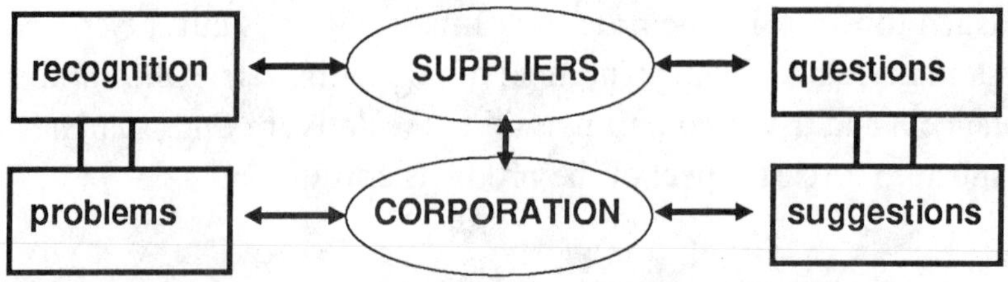

It was divided into four workshops covering topics such as "What does it take to become a preferred supplier?" and "What are ALAD's expectations for the future?" and "Where is the company headed?"

At the conference, the company president would address the assembled vendors, stressing the importance of their inclusion in ALAD's picture. Suppliers were shown an exhibit that depicted where the part they produced finally wound up on the aircraft. Taylor discusses the rationale behind such exhibits:

The workers who are sitting there in the shop, making a bolt or a nut, do not really understand the big picture. So we showed them exhibits of the final aircraft that their part went into. We had their names up there and their parts. What we were saying was, "You made this for us and it goes into what we build and the end result goes into this aircraft."

The public relations people from the firm put together a big display that essentially said, according to Taylor, "This is what you do and this is why it is important to us." With this expression of faith, ALAD was in a better position to emphasize its need to have work done correctly by supplier firms. In some cases, the company even provided assistance and tools to its vendors. Taylor amplifies on the cooperative relations theme:

After the supplier conference, we continued the rapport. We took some of our experts and they went to some of the shops and did seminars on SPC to try to continue the momentum initiated with the conference.

Psychologists speak of the emotional disequilibrium that ensues from learning something that is at odds with the comfortable knowledge we possess. After considerable discussion and some apprehension, Ai-Research willingly opened itself up to potentially disquieting knowledge. They invited "cognitive dissonance" at the conference by putting managers (from Quality Assurance, Procurement, Accounting, Engineering and Manufacturing Engineering departments) on a panel. At some risk to the panelists, suppliers were invited to address specific problems they were having with a given department, to the manager of that department. The risk paid off. As Taylor tells it,

That was the single most successful aspect of the conference. Suppliers came up to us afterwards and said, "No one has ever really listened before to our side of it. No one has ever really clearly answered our questions. We never really had a forum for our concerns.

Reverting back to the parent-child analogy, Taylor mentions the importance of rewards as a means of recognizing work that is well done, as a means of showing appreciation. It is all a question of letting people know what is expected of them, she contends.

Positive energy has been one of the most valuable derivatives from the conferences, in Taylor's opinion. Good will resulted between company and suppliers when the latter finally felt they were being listened to.

It goes back to communication. I do not think there is anything more important that you can do for someone than to make them feel as if they are being listened to.

Taylor also comments on the mutuality of the buyer-supplier relationships and regrets they are so often viewed as one-sided relationships. When the dialogue is an exchange as opposed to a mere sending and receiving, the rewards are multiplicative. Admittedly, quantitative gains from such occasions as the supplier conferences are difficult to asses. However, Taylor feels the qualitative gains—the deepening of cooperation, the sense of appreciation on both sides, the enhanced communications—are very much in evidence.

Of late, because ALAD has split into two divisions, smaller seminars are being held instead of one large one as in the past. Groups of suppliers that do similar work or groups that have similar concerns (e.g., small businesses) are being targeted for "mini-conferences." Despite the uncertainty engendered by restructuring, the value of the interactions is so important to ALAD that they are determined to continue the rapport-building with suppliers.

The ALAD organization as a whole has been developing a Quality management system. The phrase they have coined is "commitment to continuous improvement" or CCI. That has become the catchword and it has come all the way down from Allied-Signal corporation. The thrust is coming from our customer, the federal government, which has tried to instill CCI in us as suppliers. We are doing the flowdown to our suppliers.

Taylor cites the progress that can be made when buyers and sellers are aware of common goals. She says again, "Communication is probably the most important part of any relationship, but especially a business one."

Summary

Paradigm-shifting, according to Shirley Powell, is easier when employees are satisfied and secure with their jobs. Our real challenge today, particularly in defense-related industries, is to foster job security despite the impact of decisions over which employees have no control. As Dr. Deming points out, new knowledge is especially resisted in a fearful environment.

Powell encourages knowing what forces are controllable and working with those instead of worrying about the ones that are uncontrollable. Controllable, from her perspective, would be efforts to encourage employees' self-worth and self-knowledge. She makes these efforts by inverting the organizational chart and by helping staff members to develop their potential.

Fear stultifies creativity; it crushes innovation. And one fear-imbedded practice, Powell asserts, is the Management by Objective (MBO) approach. It requires managers to constantly supervise, when—according to Dr. Deming—they should be leading. Leader-managers should be breaking down barriers. Among those barriers are not knowing the organizational aim, not feeling appreciated, not being able to express one's ideas.

Another potential barrier, Powell notes, is departmental longevity. While long-term employees can bring many advantages to a department, they are also prone to employ the techniques that have helped them survive over the years. To change those techniques, to attempt to introduce Quality practices, is often a difficult task. Longevity can create paradigm paralysis. Opening the lines of communication is one way to minimize the distortion, to support the introduction of new ideas. Leadership is required, as are a focus on customers and a continual analysis of the processes being used.

Limited production figures can represent another barrier but are workable if anticipated and accommodated. With diverse product lines and a manufacturing self-sufficiency, it is difficult to acquire benchmarking data. But there are other ways to encourage improvements—by rallying around a common purpose, by introducing change slowly, by deepening pride. We must appreciate small successes, especially because they are not easily won in environments that have employees clinging to the old ways, even though they admit some of the old ways never really worked.

Powell feels what she coins "Integrated TQM" (a combination of the best of participative and leadership styles) will help the nation regain its competitive position, but cautions that it is not enough for a company to dedicate itself to a TQM process. The company must ensure that its employees and suppliers are equally committed. To help develop supplier relationships, ALAD holds supplier conferences, the most critical aspect of which, says organizer Layne Taylor, is communication.

To give momentum to communication efforts, ALAD invites suppliers to address their concerns to departmental managers at the conference. The company also has the Public Relations department make displays showing where the suppliers' parts wind up in the final product, the aircraft itself. Following the conference, ALAD will often send its engineering experts out to a supplier's facility to teach SPC practices, hoping to assure quality, as John Schermerhorn says, by "preventing the production of defective products or services."

For Further Consideration

1. In what ways have your paradigms regarding Quality shifted?

2. Explore the feasibility—within your own company—of having people do their own job descriptions, set their own goals, appraise their own performance.

3. Have you known people who stay in jobs that do not satisfy them? Why do you think they stay?

4. Dr. Deming states that people resist knowledge. What causes this resistance?

5. What could you and your team or department do to eliminate work-related stress and fear?

6. In what specific ways have you worked to help your team members or subordinates develop their potential?

7. How would you go about creating a "climate for innovation"?

8. Why has the MBO approach become so ingrained in our business psyches?

9. How profound is your knowledge of TQM?

10. What are the strengths of your department/team? The weaknesses?

11. What, if anything, is robbing you and/or your co-workers of the "pride of workmanship"?

12. If you were in charge of the Quality implementation program in your firm, what would you do to extricate Quality from the domain of the Quality Control and Quality Assurance departments and make it the responsibility of every employee?

13. What inaccurate notions do you think other departments may have of you and your team or department? What can you do about dispelling those notions?

14. How is the Quality transformation being handled in your company?

15. What can you do to instill pride in your teams?

16. What are the barriers to Quality that you have encountered?

17. Could your company make (or has it made) the transition to sole-source suppliers? Explain.

18. What have you done to improve supplier relationships?

References

[1] Deming, W. Edwards. *Out of the Crisis* (Cambridge: Massachusetts Institute of Technology, Center for Advanced Engineering Study, 1986), pp. 59–60. Reprinted from *Out of the Crisis* by W. Edwards Deming by permission of MIT and W. Edwards Deming. Published by MIT, Center for Advanced Engineering Study, Cambridge, MA 02139. Copyright © 1986 by W. Edwards Deming,

[2] *Ibid.*, p. 54.

[3] *Ibid.*, p. 77.

[4] Schermerhorn, John R. Jr., *Managing for Productivity, 2nd edition* (New York: John Wiley & Sons, Inc., 1986), pp. 482–483.

[5] *Ibid.*, p. 483.

Mark E. Crumly, Chairman
American Society for Quality Control

"The most valuable contribution Training Departments can make is providing general overall awareness training. This would include communicating the vision of the company and outlining general programs that impact all departments within the company."

Background

Mark E. Crumly is the manager of Equipment Services/Quality Assurance for GTE California Incorporated. He is also chairman of the American Society for Quality Control (ASQC), which is an organization with over 63,000 individual members and over 600 corporate members. ASQC has a worldwide membership dedicated to the advancement of quality, a dedication articulated in 1946 when the organization was founded. Seeking to lead people in turning quality commitments into action, the organization espouses improving quality by helping people help themselves.

Statistical Quality Control (SQC) was not widely employed in America prior to World War II, except in the Bell Telephone Laboratories. But when the War thrust upon our nation the need to reduce scrap, it also thrust upon us the need to reduce the number of people assigned to inspection. Sampling practices were instituted then and they served well in place of the previously time-consuming process of examining every single piece of every single product coming off the manufacturing lines.

The Office of Production Research and Development, under the auspices of the War Production Board, worked with the United States Office of Education to deliver instruction to personnel from businesses vital to the war efforts. Even when the war was over, the companies with defense contracts continued to employ the statistical tools they had been given. And, as the benefits of Statistical Process Control (SPC) were publicized, it was not long before numerous American industries were learning and applying the statistical techniques.

It is not surprising that ASQC was formed in the postwar years; nor is it surprising that its membership ranks have continued to swell. ASQC offers its membership reading material, certification programs, conferences, surveys conducted by the Gallup organization (usually published in October to celebrate National Quality Month), and sponsorship (along with *Fortune* magazine) of the annual National Quality Forum.

ASQC also provides corporate members unique opportunities for training. For example, the Electronics Division of the Coors Ceramic Company (a subsidiary of Adolph Coors Co.) has decided to enroll every employee in training leading to a professional certification offered by ASQC.[1] In an effort to make all employees Quality-conscious, Coors Ceramics will pay $300 to employees who pass the ASQC examination and thereby earn a Certified Quality Engineer certificate. Intense study of quality assurance engineering and statistical methodologies is required in order to qualify for the certification.

The company encourages employees to take classes offered both on-site and through a home-study program. It also helps employees/students to form study groups and pays the membership and examination fees that are part of the ASQC certification. Bruce Goral, Coors' Quality Control Manager, cites the numerous benefits to the employees who take part in the program:

- a clearly defined goal
- enhanced performance of cross-functional teams
- pride in workmanship and in personal accomplishment
- a significant reward system
- measurable improvements in product and process quality
- the adoption of a common language

Corporate Cultures

When asked what training departments within a corporation could do to advance the kind of self-improvement advocated by ASQC, Crumly replies,

The most valuable contribution Training can make is providing general overall awareness training. This would include communicating the vision of the company and outlining general programs that impact all departments within the company. This ensures rapid and consistent deployment of the company's vision, policies and goals throughout the company. This is the first step to changing corporate culture.

The culture that is to embrace a new definition of itself must take steps to ensure that definition is a clear one. In *Waging Business Warfare,* David J. Rogers speaks of the need to have a corporate mindset, a uniform animus shared by all members of the organization:

> Studies of business enterprises are loudly proclaiming the need to define "corporate cultures" clearly. Twenty-three hundred years ago a Spartan general wrote that the safest course for a great army was to be animated by one spirit; and while many corporations are beginning to learn that small, semiautonomous groups can increase productivity, the Romans had well documented the fact a few thousand years ago. That the military masters came upon insights into competitive superiority before the art of management did shouldn't be surprising. The study of business management as we know it really only began in the twentieth century, while masters of war started to give serious thought to organizing and managing about the time Pharaoh Thutmore III devised a special formation to beat the Syrians in 1439 B.C.[2]

Overcoming Resistance

Given the history of culture-establishment, it is not surprising that those who are trying to provide awareness training are met with "I've-heard-it-all-before" attitudes among employees. Doxologies to the Quality god will have no effect if only one or two voices are raised in praise. There must be concurrence with the corporation mission from all levels.

Management consultant Donald J. Ford feels that cynicism is usually bred from past failures or from the conviction that top management does not really support a given program. Overcoming such attitudes, he maintains,

> *is largely a matter of top management taking specific actions to visibly demonstrate its support, such as speaking out on the issue at management and employee meetings, modeling TQM behavior in their own work, devoting resources to the effort, actively participating in training and group meetings, etc.*

If cynicism is bred from a past failure, it is important to carefully analyze what went wrong previously and to deliberately plan to correct those errors.

Training

Assuming the corporate culture is a receptive one and that employees are eager to learn more about Quality, what are some fundamental concepts, I asked Crumly, of which they should be aware? What are cognitive bulwarks that must be established to defend against ignorance or misunderstanding? What is the vocabulary of the common language we have to speak? His response includes eight specific points, as depicted in the following diagram.

FIGURE 1

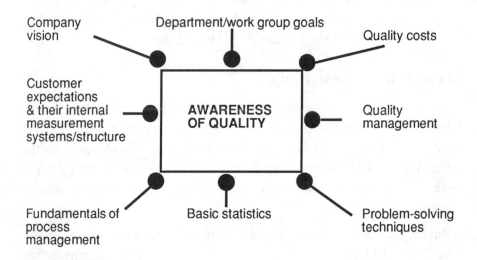

Control Charts

Crumly includes the "basic statistics" aspect of Quality Awareness "with great reluctance." He explains:

Most courses today are based on theory and not practical application. For example, with little or no arithmetic, I can train a shop operator to obtain and record data. These data elements, either discrete or attribute, can be graphically recorded, and the operator can determine when the process is out of control.

Control charts have been used in American business for nearly seventy years now. The first one appeared in an unpublished memorandum in 1924 and was written by Dr. Walter A. Shewhart of the Bell Laboratories.

Harrison Wadsworth *et al.* point out that everything that is reproduced has variation.[3] Just as there are no two identical snowflakes in the natural world, there are no two products of manufacturing processes that are identical. Control charts review how variation—the differences in the basic traits or products—impacts quality. A given process, they declare, can be considered stable or in control if the samplings continually fall within the upper control limits and the lower control limits. When the sampling reveal an unstable process, steps must be taken to bring the process back into control.

A.V. Feigenbaum, one of the most respected names in the quality-control field and a former president of ASQC, defines the control chart this way:

A chronological (hour-by-hour, day-by-day) graphical comparison of actual product-quality characteristics with limits reflecting the ability to produce as shown by past experience on the product characteristics.[4]

Since single observations of variance yield no predictable data, it is necessary to conduct numerous chronological observations in order to discern patterns or the absence of patterns. Variation can be shown by plotting the statistics obtained from observed values. The control chart has statistically calculated limits (upper and lower) around the fluctuating pattern of measurement, as shown in Figure 2.

The control chart helps us understand variation that is due to common causes and variation that may be due to special causes. The common causes of variation fall within the managerial control and so we turn to

FIGURE 2

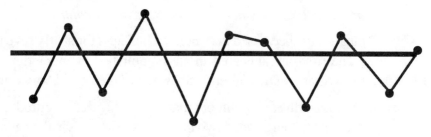

Upper Control Limits (UCL) -----------------

Lower Control Limits (LCL) -----------------

management for correction. Special causes also need correction. However, since the special causes are not typical of all operations, the correction of the cause may or may not fall within the managerial domain. More often than not, the special cause can be fixed by the individual most closely associated with the process. But the special cause must be dealt with before the control chart can be used again to determine if the process is consistent in the results it yields.

Dr. Deming cautions against misinterpreting the causes for variation:

We may now formulate two sources of loss from confusion of special causes with common causes of variation.

1. Ascribe a variation or a mistake to a special cause when in fact the cause belongs to the system (common causes).

2. Ascribe a variation or a mistake to the system (common causes) when in fact the cause was special.

Overadjustment is a common example of mistake No. 1. Never doing anything to try to find a special cause is a common example of mistake No. 2.[5]

William Scherkenbach discusses the familiar belief that 85 percent of the responsibility for making improvements falls to managers, who control systems and so bear the burden of altering systems.[6] It follows, according to popular perception, that responsibility for investigating special causes falls to workers 15 percent of the time. He addresses the pitfall of assuming that the process is in control 85 percent of the time and of assuming that special causes (workers' responsibility) are evident 15 percent of the time.

The percentages are guidelines and not hard-and-fast attributions of accountability. The 85/15 percent divisions are only immutable if there is no communication between management and workers. Scherkenbach uses as an example a change of material that will be shown as a special cause on control charts. And yet, he says, the machinist is not responsible for the special cause, since upper management makes the decisions about purchasing.

When there is no communication, workers are left feeling impotent. Fifteen percent represents, after all, a limited control. While management may be ultimately responsible for resolving problems associated with the common causes of variation, workers can and should have impact upon management's information and actions regarding the causes.

Since this book is essentially a series of interviews with Quality figures and not a textbook on Statistical Process Control (SPC), I recommend the interested reader pursue other texts for further information. (In addition to the Wadsworth, Deming, Scherkenbach, and Feigenbaum texts, there are any number of excellent resources, including *Statistical Process Control,* 3rd ed., by Eugene L. Grant [published by McGraw-Hill Book Company, New York 1964]; *The Deming Management Method* by Mary Walton [published by Dodd, Mead & Company, 1986], and *Quality Control and Application* by Bertran L. Hanse and Prabhakar M. Ghare [published by Prentice-Hall, Inc., Englewood Cliffs, New Jersey, 1987]).

These books, for those who wish to learn more, will provide the extensive examination that Statistical Process Control deserves. It is not the intent of this book to discourse upon quantitative methods, a decision that seems especially appropriate considering what a General Motors president shared in a speech before an audience of GM vendors.[7]

He related the story of three auto executives who were sentenced to be shot by a firing squad. One of the executives was French, and when asked if he had a last request, he pleaded for one final bottle of Lafite Rothschild wine, 1938. The second executive was Japanese and his last request was a little different. He just wanted to deliver one last lecture on the importance of Statistical Process Control.

Finally, they asked the American if *he* had a last request. He replied without hesitation, "Please. Shoot me first. I just can't handle another lecture on SPC!"

If you choose to pursue your knowledge of the statistical control of processes, however, by enrolling in courses instead of reading on your own, bear in mind Dr. Deming's lamentation:

> Awakening to the need for quality, and with no idea what quality means now or how to achieve it, American management have resorted to mass assemblies for crash courses in statistical methods, employing hacks for teachers, being unable to discriminate between competence and ignorance. The result is that hundreds of people are learning what is wrong.
>
> No one should teach the theory and use of control charts without knowledge of statistical theory through at least the masters' level, supplemented by experience under a master. I make this statement on the basis of experience, seeing every day the devastating effects of incompetent teaching and faulty application.[8]

Crumly, too, discusses the dangers of instruction conducted by unqualified instructors. (In this scenario, however, more damage was done to the instructor than to the instructees.)

> *I was present at a training session where the trainer was attempting to teach overall quality principles including vendor management techniques and basic statistics. The audience had many jeers and snickers for some of the proposed techniques. During the second day, the class finally felt sorry for the instructor and indicated that they were all Certified Quality Engineers responsible for vendor quality management!*

This points to a fatal flaw in typical company training. The trainers are not professional educators, and the company does little to enhance the abilities of the trainer. In addition, the typical trainer has little experience across many of the company's service or product delivery processes. This poor soul didn't even bother to identify her audience, let alone determine what they do for the company.

Tripartite Training

Crumly asserts that training departments should be engaged in providing training to all levels within the company. Sometimes, however, the best way to deliver that training, especially for small and medium-sized companies, is to have the training department identify, qualify, and then negotiate with consulting organizations. He proposes that in most cases, an outside consultant can provide the training faster, at a reduced cost, and at a higher quality than can internal consultants.

By contrast, large companies with large training responsibilities and large budgets can hire full-time educators and have them develop courses in order to avoid some of the pitfalls described above.

No matter the source of the training, American businesses are footing a large bill each year to make employees proficient at their jobs. David Kearns, CEO of the Xerox Corporation and author of *Winning the Brain Race,* estimates it costs companies $25 billion a year (some estimates are as high as $30 billion) to do the remedial training needed to compensate for educational deficiencies. More and more, we see businesses making overtures to improve public education.

Apart from obvious benefits to business of having better prepared employees, there are humanitarian issues that transcend corporate profitability.

- Children today account for the poorest segment in our nation. And, a preschool child who is poor today is six times more likely to be poor in the future than a person over 65.

- In 1965, half the adults in America had children in school. Today, that figure is only 24 percent.

It is clear that support for education will have to come from sources other than those with a vested interest (their own children) in education. We need coalitions that will bring power through knowledge in order to reify James Madison's prediction: "Knowledge will forever govern ignorance, and a people who mean to be their own governors must arm themselves with the power which knowledge gives."

Power-giving coalitions must be formed to bring educators, business people and Quality professionals together—not only to save our schools but also (many would say, not hyperbolically) to save our country. One such coalition involves ASQC, which worked with Corning Inc. to sponsor a "Koalaty Kid" (symbolized by a bespectacled koala bear reading a book) conference in the spring of 1990. ASQC's aim is to "extend the Society's influence in the area of education." The Koalaty Kid program, ASQC feels, has "significant potential to improve education through quality improvement techniques, and to increase public awareness of the quality imperative through its exposure in classroom and students' homes."[9]

Among the participants were school district educators and administrators, business people and Quality professionals. The Koalaty Kid program is not new: it began in 1975 at Carder Elementary School in Corning, New York, with the aim of having students aware of and abiding by Quality concepts. Teachers and administrators also subscribe to the Quality philosophy.

Among the Quality concepts encouraged in the classroom are these:
- taking pride in workmanship
- recognizing individual and group efforts
- developing a work ethic
- doing the right thing at the right time in the right way
- accepting responsibility

- being aware of a mission
- seeing that Quality is an ongoing process

In 1988, ASQC initiated a two-year pilot project to determine if the Carder School experience could be replicated in twenty-six other schools across the country.

The results of that pilot project were shared at the Koalaty Kid conference. Seventy-five participants met to

1. share the lessons and insights of individuals participating in the pilot program;

2. describe in real terms what value the program brings to students, to schools, and to society in general; and to

3. consider the future course of this effort.[10]

Based on the feedback from participants, ASQC has decided to continue hosting conferences and to continue supporting the Koalaty Kid project. In fact, there are now more than 600 schools, business partners and ASQC chapters interested in the program.

Michael MacDonald, manager of Quality for the Telecommunications Products Division of Corning Glass Works specifies the elements that constitute Quality:

- Total Quality is meeting the requirements of your customer.

- Total Quality also is having an attitude of error-free work.

- Managing by prevention is the method used to ensure that errors do not occur.

- Measuring by the cost of quality is used to determine how well we are preventing error.

- Commitment to relentless daily improvement, teamwork, communication, corrective action, recognition, and education/training are the cornerstones of quality improvement.[11]

These Quality concepts can be fostered in the workplace environment as easily as in the classroom environment—elementary, secondary, or college level. This fostering needs to occur if we are to reduce the gap between what is, and what should be, possessed by workers. In response to a question about the introduction of Total Quality Management (TQM) principles into the high school curriculum, Crumly has this to say:

The high school level should have a basic definition of quality, i.e., customer satisfaction. I believe this is intuitive, and it may even be fun talking about specific examples that relate to student activities or experiences. This topic may not be appropriate until junior or senior status. The student at this time may be able to grasp not only the philosophical aspects but may also appreciate the practical statistical nature and application within differing industries.

The difficulty comes from where to place the course. Quality extends across all activities in our daily lives. If we decide to place the course work in a specific elective, all students not taking that elective will not have the opportunity to learn the techniques.

(One possible solution would be to have some of the Quality principles made part of the curriculum for a course that *is* mandated for all four years of secondary education. That course in most states is English.)

Ford, when posed the same question, replies that the public education system itself needs revitalization desperately and that revitalization, he asserts, could be brought about by TQM. Considering not the entire system, though, but merely the curriculum, Ford comments:

Let me focus on some of the "basics" that businesses complain are lacking in many employees. If the schools could provide these prerequisite skills, TQM would be a lot easier to implement.

Among the basic skills that are needed, statistics and mathematics stand out. In my work with major corporations, we found that many hourly production employees lacked sufficient basic math skills to enable them to implement SPC or other statistical tools of TQM. I've even heard of college graduates who had to be sent to basic math classes before attempting SPC.

A close second to math skills would be communication and inter-personal skills. The ability to listen, speak, and write clearly, is no longer a given. Without these basic communication skills, TQM implementation runs into a wall or even a Tower of Babel in the multicultural milieu of California. Interpersonal skills like being a team player, participating in group processes and problem-solving, brainstorming, etc. are often lacking in the workplace. These basic social skills should be taught in the schools, starting from the earliest grades. The closest that today's high schools come to teaching these things are extracurricular activities like athletics and social clubs. These skills should be part of the regular curriculum for every student.

There are other ways to prepare the incoming work force to be Quality-conscious. Crumly cites three of them:

1. Support the American Society for Quality Control. This professional society is working with the education community to develop curricula at all levels. I would refer you to their International Headquarters for a complete description of their "Koalaty Kid" program. This is aimed at supporting schools across the country.

2. Support local schools to ensure they have the proper curricula and wherewithal to provide a sound educational foundation.

3. Provide an incoming orientation that clearly defines the company vision and employee support mechanisms that ensure implementation of the vision. This step of orienting and training, up front, will ensure that employees perform at a distinct level of service.

Performance at both a distinct and distinctive level of service requires employees to work with both their hands and their heads. If an under-standing of Quality has not been acquired prior to their assuming a place in the work force, employees can acquire such an understanding through self-initiative and company-sponsored opportunities. Quality-driven employees do not shirk the responsibility for further education. They ask for training when management fails to arrange it; they discuss quality with co-workers; they read as much as they can; they share what they know with friends and family members; they benchmark with associates in comparable firms to learn how processes are improved elsewhere.

Kaizen-driven Responsibilities

As Masaaki Imai notes in *Kaizen: The Key to Japan's Competitive Success,*[12] employees have a responsibility to their employer: to comply with the standards and practices instituted by management. Occasionally, an employee may have difficulty abiding by established criteria. In such cases, management must assume the responsibility for either training the employee or for transferring the employees to a job for which he is better suited, or for altering the standard. If an employee should actually refuse to abide by standards, then the employee must be disciplined.

In America, we tend to ascribe a negative connotation to the word "discipline" until we think of the word "disciple," which comes from the Latin *discipulus,* meaning "student." A disciple is one who follows the principles of, and learns from, a leader or instructor. To say that an athlete or musician is well-disciplined is to pay him a compliment. In academic settings, a "discipline" is a course of study.

So, disciplining an employee should not mean punitive measures—at least not in the beginning. Disciplining should mean instructing and showing and explaining so the employee can become disciplined, as far as workplace/management expectations are concerned. Ultimately, of course, if an employee continues to defy management requests, that employee may have to be let go.

In the following charts,[13] Imai depicts the differences between the Japanese perception of employees' responsibility and the Western perception of that responsibility. In Figure 3, we see that management has two essential responsibilities: improvement and maintenance, with the former more dominant than the latter. Workers are more concerned with amerliorating standards. Imai bisects the work "improvement": it can either mean *kaizen,* small enhancements in the status quo; or, it can mean

FIGURE 3*

JAPANESE PERCEPTIONS OF JOB FUNCTIONS

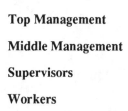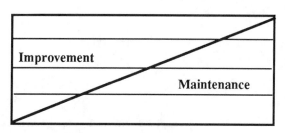

Top Management

Middle Management

Supervisors

Workers

innovation, dramatic improvements in the status quo, resulting from technological advancements.

The more unskilled a worker is, the less opportunity he has to contribute to innovation. Rather, until he learns the rudiments of the job and develops proficiency in performing it, his contribution is not in the improvement or "kaizen" category but in the category of directions-following and standards-maintaining.

When we break down the word "improvement," the new depiction looks like this:

FIGURE 4*

JAPANESE PERCEPTIONS OF JOB FUNCTIONS

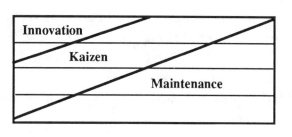

Top Management

Middle Management

Supervisors

Workers

*Reprinted with permission, Random House

According to Imai, the typical Western perception of job responsibilities has the preponderance of responsibilities of middle managers and their subordinates devoted to maintenance functions, as depicted in Figure 5, and the responsibility for innovation being relegated to uppermost managerial echelons.

FIGURE 5*

WESTERN PERCEPTIONS OF JOB FUNCTIONS

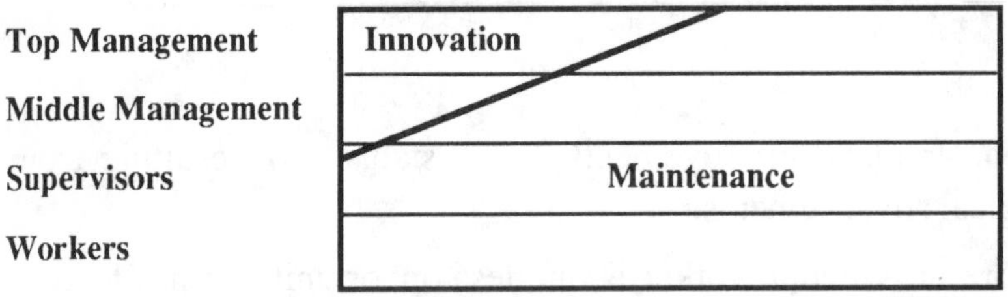

Crumly alludes to the kaizen type of improvement, which clearly cuts across the hierarchical levels of corporate structures, as he discusses his own contribution at GTE California:

My most successful effort has been in vendor management. The ability to motivate GTE vendors from overall 15 percent defective to 0 percent defective across a three-year span was very rewarding. The dollars saved through this quality improvement effort amounted to over $180,000 per quarter for only six vendors!

Other success stories revolve around introduction of process management and the ability to establish functional teams to improve performance. These teams have enjoyed varying degrees of success. Most notable was a cross-functional service provisioning team that reduced time of delivery from 30 days to 13.

*Reprinted with permission, Random House

The efforts that were not so successful have revolved around globalization of the problem. Quality management begins at the grass roots of an organization. The typical TQC approach is to develop macro customer satisfaction measures and tie individual rewards to the macro measures. This creates frustration within the individuals because they do not control the entire quality delivery process.

Grass Roots Reactions

In *The Reckoning,* David Halberstam discusses at length the grass-roots versus the top-of-the-tree input. He denounces the arrogance that is so often associated with being on top. Halberstam parallels the macrocosmic American smugness with the microcosmic managerial smugness of those managers who come not from the shop floor but from the nation's leading business schools.

Bloated with a sense of its own superiority, Halberstam claims, America had no need to listen to the theories of W. Edwards Deming, thus forcing him to take his ideas about Quality to Eastern minds. Forty years later, the arrogance is being supplanted by an overwhelming eagerness to learn from Dr. Deming lessons that were available but ignored scores of years ago.

Often, Quality is imposed, rather than implanted, in the grassroots soil. When that happens, frustration will indeed result. Halberstam writes:

True quality demanded a totality of commitment that began at the very top: if top management was committed to the idea of quality and if executive promotions were tied to quality, then the priority would seep down into the middle and lower levels of management, and thus inevitably to the workers. It could not, as so many American companies seemed to expect, be imposed at the bottom. American companies could not appoint some medium-level executive, usually one whom no division of the company particularly wanted, and, for lack of something better to do with him, put him in charge of something called quality. The first thing that an executive like that would do, Deming said, and quite possibly the only thing, was to come up with slogans and display them on banners. If the company treated quality as a gimmick or an after-thought, then true quality would never result. Above all, he was saying, quality had to be central to the purpose of a company.[14]

Summary

World War II made American industries more efficient by reducing scrap and reducing mass inspections. In place of total inspection, sampling techniques were introduced. Their effectiveness outlasted the war effort and they were soon incorporated into post-war manufacturing. It was in this SPC-endorsed era that the American Society for Quality Control was born, an organization designed to help people help themselves in their quality-improvement efforts.

Within the corporate culture, training is the favored way to make employees aware of Quality. But training is often met with cynicism. When it is, Donald Ford advises, management must be exemplars of Quality behavior; they must actively speak and participate and behave in ways that demonstrate their commitment to Quality.

Mark Crumly concurs, saying that such awareness will be the result of eight factors: a company vision; department and work group goals; Quality costs; customer expectations and their internal measurement systems and structure; Quality management; fundamentals of process management; basic statistics; and problem-solving techniques.

Control charts are integral to the stabilization of processes. First employed by Walter Shewhart seventy years ago, such charts establish upper control limits and lower control limits. When values consistently fall within these ranges, a process can be declared stable. When an isolated occurrence falls outside the limits, investigation must follow to determine if that variance is a special cause or a common cause. If it is a special cause, that cause must be dealt with, usually by the person closest to the process. If the special cause is found to be a rare one and is not repeated over a period of time, the system can be considered stable once the special cause has been attended to or eliminated.

If the variation is the result of a common cause and is happening repeatedly, the source of the variation must be investigated so the system can be brought back under control. Decisions about what should be done are ordinarily made by management, ideally with input from workers. Special care must be taken, Dr. Deming cautions, in labeling the source of the variation.

More and more efforts are underway to bring Quality concepts, SPC among them, into the nation's classrooms. Often, these efforts are undertaken by consortia composed of educators, businesses, and Quality advocates. One such program is the Koalaty Kid program, operating under the joint aegis of Corning Glass and ASQC.

Quality concepts are encouraged at home, at school, and at work when concerned societal elements merge to make our work force better prepared for meeting its responsibilities. Crumly encourages those who are concerned with Quality, education, and America's competitive position to support ASQC, to support local schools, and to ensure thorough orientation programs are offered to new employees.

Masaaki Imai speaks of the responsibilities toward maintaining standards and improving standards on the parts of both employees and management. In Japan, he points out, *kaizen* or improvement responsibilities are expected of both workers and managers, whereas in Western organizations, the responsibility for innovation lies exclusively with management. He espouses cross-functional efforts to improve processes.

Crumly speaks of improvement endeavors and successes in dealing with GTE vendors and notes the importance of working cooperatively with individuals at grass-roots levels of companies. Management must recognize that employees have contributions to make with both their heads and their hands.

Without such recognition, there is usually arrogance on the management level, an arrogance which has proven to be toxic in the corporate ecosystem following the second World War. It was then that Dr. W. Edwards Deming, long ignored by his own countrymen, took his Quality theories to Japan and aided that nation in its revitalization of a war-devastated economy. America is belatedly learning Quality lessons from the man who, his followers maintain, has done more than any other person to help the world.

For Further Consideration

1. Is the common language of Quality being spoken in your company? Discuss.

2. What do you think is the best way to overcome jaded or cynical attitudes toward TQM?

3. To what extent are control charts used in your organization? Do you know of cases in which the cause was mislabeled (special for common or vice versa)?

4. What steps do you think trainers must undertake before attempting to provide training on Quality principles?

5. What would you list as the cornerstones of Quality improvement?

6. What percentage of your job is improvement, as opposed to maintenance?

7. In reference to the work of your team or department, what kaizen successes (small enhancements) were made in the last six months?

8. What dramatic improvements were made in the last two years?

9. What cross-functional efforts are you (or have you been) engaged in?

10. Dr. Deming advises us to eliminate exhortations (Point #1). What is the status of exhortations in your company?

References

[1] "Certifying Quality," *Total Quality Newsletter,* Vol. 1, No. 3 (June 1990), p. 8. Reprinted with permission from Lakewood Publications, 50 South Ninth St., Minneapolis, MN 55402. All rights reserved.

[2] Rogers, David J. *Waging Business Warfare: Lessons from the Military Masters in Achieving Corporate Superiority* (New York: Charles Scribner's Sons, 1987), p. 22.

[3] Harrison, Wadsworth, *et al., Modern Methods for Quality Control and Improvement* (New York: John Wiley & Sons, 1986), pp. 115–124.

[4] Feigenbaum, A.V. *Total Quality Control* (New York: McGraw-Hill Book Company, 1961), p. 250.

[5] Deming, W. Edwards. *Out of the Crisis* (Cambridge: Massachusetts Institute of Technology, Center for Advanced Engineering Study, 1986), p. 318. Reprinted from *Out of the Crisis* by W. Edwards Deming by permission of MIT and W. Edwards Deming. Published by MIT, Center for Advanced Engineering Study, Cambridge, MA 02139. Copyright © 1986 by W. Edwards Deming.

[6] Scherkenbach, William W. *The Deming Route to Quality and Productivity: Roadmaps and Roadblocks* (Washington: CEEPress Books, 1990), p. 101.

[7] Keller, MaryAnn. *Rude Awakening* (New York: William Morrow and Company, 1989), p. 26.

[8] Deming, *op. cit.,* p. 131.

[9] American Society for Quality Control, "ASQC and Koalaty Kid" Bulletin (Milwaukee: ASQC), p. 1.

[10] American Society for Quality Control, *Koalaty Kid Pilot Program* (Milwaukee: ASQC, 1988), p. 1.

[11] McDonald, Michael. "A Definition of Quality and a Quality Professional's Point of View," *Ibid.,* p. III.

[12] Imai, Masaaki. *Kaizen: The Key to Japan's Competitive Success* (New York: Random House, Inc., 1986), p. 6.

[13] *Ibid.,* pp. 5, 7.

[14] Halberstam, David. *The Reckoning* (New York: William Morrow and Company, Inc., 1986), p. 313.

William B. Bullock
Vice President, Operations
Lockheed Aeronautical Systems Company

"There isn't any pat list of tools that deal with all situations, and so to train all employees in all tools can become very inefficient and add waste rather than eliminate it."

Background

One hears a sincere concern for the worker and for the fears of the worker in William B. Bullock's comments. In an interview with the company newsletter, the *Star*, Bullock is quoted as saying: "On a larger scale, we have to make sure that we provide our people with the best training, job instructions, tools, plans and leadership to perform the way they want to perform."[1] He speaks too of the challenge of breaking down turf-protection barriers. With admirable insight into the rationale behind turf-protection—the fear of change as an eroder of that which is known and understood—Bullock observes that such singular preoccupation prevents true teamwork from happening.

Change is not a new element in the tableau of Bullock's career. His appointment in 1987 to the position of vice president of operations was an appointment that highlighted a career begun thirty years earlier when he joined the firm as an aeronautical engineer. Seven years after he started, Bullock was stationed in Washington, D.C., where he worked closely as the official liaison between Lockheed and the Department of Defense. Bullock's career has also taken him to Paris, where he coordinated JetStar sales for Europe and Africa.

In 1971, he was appointed to the position of manager of the JetStar Commercial Sales Department; three years later, he was promoted to the director of the JetStar project and subcontracts department. He also served as director of the L-400 project for a brief period in 1980 before being selected as deputy program manager of the Hercules programs. He served in that later capacity until his appointment as director of the Hercules programs in 1980.

His Bachelor of Science degree in mechanical engineering was earned in 1957 at North Carolina State University. Other accolades in Bullock's illustrious career include his selection by the Massachusetts Institute of Technology as a Sloan Fellow in 1969. Bullock's Master's Degree is in the management field, a field that he has explored further through attendance at the Lockheed Executive Institute and Senior Management Institute.

In terms of company-wide revenues for public companies head-quartered in Los Angeles County, Lockheed Corporation is fourth largest, preceded only by Occidental Petroleum, Atlantic Richfield and Rockwell International.[2] The company underwent major restructuring in 1989 and emerged, according to the company's annual report, as "a leaner, more competitive company with good earnings potential in the new defense environment."

According to that report, the company anticipates 50 percent of its total future revenues will come from missile and space systems. It also expects expansion in civil space, commercial, and foreign revenues to constitute one-third of its sales before the decade is over. The company prides itself on its diversity in defense—high priority national programs, an extensive customer base, a range of vital defense technologies—and points to this diversity as the primary reason for its strong position in the defense industry.

In the shared view of Daniel M. Tellep, Chairman of the Board, and Robert A. Fuhrman, Vice Chairman of the Board and Chief Operating Officer, that position is based on distinct growth initiatives that form the diverse infrastructure:

> First, we have combined five separate companies to form our new Technology Services Group. Its revenues grew 26 percent in 1989. The group has made great progress in new areas such as aircraft modification and maintenance, environmental services, and airport development and operation.

> Antisubmarine warfare is another new long-term initiative. We have captured eight key technology contracts which position us well for the future.

> A third initiative centers on our efforts to attract commercial aircraft subcontracting work for our facilities in Georgia. We are continuing discussions with potential customers and expect to build this base significantly.

Our fourth initiative adapts our computer systems integration skills to enter nondefense government markets as well as selected commercial sectors. Although this initiative has just started, our experience shows that we are capable of generating high competitive proposals.[3]

Need for Optimism

In an era when critics of American industry are repeatedly taking shots, Quality improvement can provide the bulletproof vest that means survival. In a poll of senior executives in 298 companies, the Gallup survey organization, working with the American Society for Quality Control (ASQC),[4] found that the majority of companies—72 percent—no longer believe Japan is the single greatest competitive threat. In fact, only 9 percent list Japan as the biggest challenge to the success of the American enterprise system.

Few would argue that America weakened its own competitive power by a failure to attend to quality. And choosing to attend to quality is a question of attitudes. In *The Technology Edge,* Gerard K. O'Neill discusses the production of "semiconductor-on-sapphire" [SOS], which both Japan and America rushed to produce since the material conducts heat well but insulates against the flow of electric current, thereby increasing the power output derived from an integrated circuit.[5]

Patience is required in the production of SOS because it is exposed to high temperatures and then cooled very slowly. In the American factories, the quality was substandard. When the cause of the defective chips was discovered, it proved to be a question of attitude rather than capability: most of the defects were made near the end of the working day. In order to get out of work on time, employees were cooling the furnaces too fast. By comparison, the Japanese workers would complete the process as they were supposed to, regardless of the hour.

Because Japanese workers identify so closely with their companies, they worry about the company's reputation. And because emotions and attitudes are so closely entwined with physical work, the final product is one in which they take considerable pride. One Nissan executive explained why Japanese products are held in such high regard when he noted that their quality came from the heart of the worker.

When we seek to improve quality, we must seek to improve attitudes as well. In sharing the Gallup findings, John E. Condon, president of ASQC, spoke of the awareness most companies have today of the importance of quality as a competitive issue.[6] He cited the belief 73 percent of the respondents have in the protection afforded by Quality in a recession era. Only 19 percent of those interviewed felt that America was falling behind foreign competitors as far as Quality is concerned. ASQC also asked about the relative merits of the ways Quality could be enhanced within a given company.

As Figure 1 shows, "more inspection" received the lowest number of endorsements among those surveyed, while employee motivation, involved corporate leadership, and employee education were listed as the top three ways to improve quality.

Corporate leadership is the most important item in Figure 1, for it impacts all other means of improving quality. In their study of corporate leadership,[7] Harry Levinson and Stuart Rosenthal learned that leaders have the ability to take charge. Their self-images are strong and they have a powerful sense of self, a powerful ego ideal. Their interactions with others are supportive and they provide subordinates with the authority and encouragement to take risks. Finally, they found that leaders are thinkers as well as doers.

Reflecting that optimism in Quality as a means—perhaps the only means—of survival, Tellep, Fuhrman, and Vincent N. Marafino (Vice Chairman of the Board and Chief Financial and Administrative Officer) issued a "CORPMEMO" calling for support of the company's mission.[8]

That mission is "...to meet the needs of our United States and foreign customers with high-quality products and services...." The new management policy statement encourages all employees to focus on the customer and ensures that the policy will be management-led and will be a long-term commitment. The company has begun to assess its internal operations in terms of the standards defined in the Malcolm Baldrige

FIGURE 1

THE BEST WAYS TO IMPROVE QUALITY

Please rate the following in terms of their importance as ways to improve Quality throughout American business.

* EMPLOYEE MOTIVATION
* INVOLVED CORPORATE LEADERSHIP
* EMPLOYEE EDUCATION
* PROCESS CONTROL
* QUALITY IMPROVEMENT TEAMS
* CAPITAL EQUIPMENT EXPENDITURES
* MORE CONTROL OVER SUPPLIERS
* IMPROVED ADMINISTRATIVE SUPPORT
* MORE INSPECTION

0 10 20 30 40 50 60 70 80 90 100

National Quality Award. Lockheed, at least as far as its executive echelon is concerned, is determined to reduce costs, to make the Quality effort a company-wide effort and to concentrate on teamwork, strategic planning, and appropriate measurement of work processes.

Training Department Support

Bullock was asked what training departments can do to bring about company-wide receptivity to change and to continuous evaluation of the

FIGURE 2

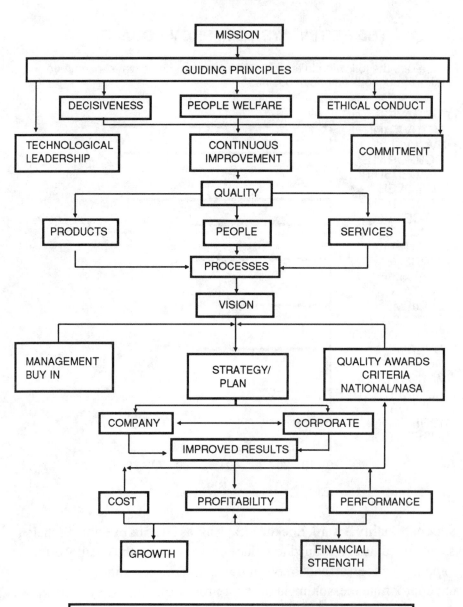

Continuous improvement is linked to Lockheed's mission and guiding principles.

status quo. Adamantly, he asserted his belief in the need for training departments to serve in ancillary roles. He spoke of their function as assisting management wherever possible:

> *My view is that one of the reasons for a lack of success in implementing changes and quality improvement is that training gets assigned to people other than the doers. All too often, such training is assigned to someone in the training organization and it turns out the person tries to do it rather than to facilitate it.*

He feels the primary responsibility of training departments is responsiveness to line management. Since training department staff members cannot truly know what the needs of line management are, they must support what line management deems important rather than attempt to tell line managers what the training department believes is important. There must be cooperation and communication before training on Quality issues can be conducted.

Clearly, Bullock has a finger on the manpower pulse:

> *In a large organization, the employees tend to listen to the people that they work for. They pay attention to, and are responsive to, the people they report to. Things that come to them from other areas are sometimes listened to but become somewhat academic. To me, that is typically true of large manufacturing organizations.*

His views on what statistical tools should be "taught" to employees are equally realistic. Bullock does not believe it is appropriate to teach all tools to all employees. Instead, he asserts that employees should be made aware of the existence of tools and their possible application to the work being done.

Ever cognizant of the need to eliminate waste, Bullock points out,

> *There isn't any pat list of tools that deal with all situations and so to train all employees in all tools can become very inefficient and add waste rather than eliminate it. I cannot say any one tool is useful for all people. Statistical Process Control (SPC) is not useful for everything. Pareto analysis is not appropriate for everything. The tools should be tailored to the application.*

Line Management Training

If line workers can learn best from line management, who trains line management? A number of sources can be used to provide the fundamentals of Quality concepts. One such source is the training department, fulfilling a facilitative role. But learning can also come from books (Bullock has purchased copies of Dr. Deming's *Out of the Crisis* for each of his managers) and from exposure to outside experts. Bullock has had William Conway of Conway Quality, Inc. conduct seminars for Lockheed employees in both Marietta, Georgia, and Burbank, California.

In an address to 2,000 Lockheed personnel, Conway asserted the need to satisfy the bill-paying customer, who is the ultimate arbiter of Quality. In Lockheed's case, the U.S. government is the external, bill-paying customer. Conway posed a simple question, to be used to ascertain what the external customer would view as added value: "Would the external customer pay for it if he knew what we were doing?"

Getting employees to ask themselves questions such as these is a matter of changing mindsets, and Philip Crosby has noted that changing mindsets is the hardest of all management jobs. When I asked Bullock what training departments could do to bring about mindsets receptive to Total Quality Management (TQM) principles, he responded with several ideas. Training departments, he observed, have to stay abreast of techniques, of technological developments. He expects them to bring knowledge of tools to the line management. Regardless of who is bringing what, though, commitment is the key that unlocks all the improvement doors.

> *If the line management starting at the very top is not committed, then it is hard for an outside organization to cause them to change.*

Upon reflection, Bullock qualifies his point by citing leaders like Conway or Dr. Deming who can have a powerful impact, as outside agents, on alchemizing resistance into commitment. Bullock speaks of his own conversion to Deming-style religion.

> *Dr. Deming's seminar really made a lot of difference to me. However, before I went, I had already been baptized. I had already made the commitment that we were going to improve quality and*

so, going to the seminar did not really accomplish that [turn-around in thinking]. In fact, I suspect there are people who go to a Deming or a Conway and nothing changes. They go back home and they go back to work. Hopefully, there are not many, but I know there are some.

Transferring Quality concepts into everyday operations falls into the line manager's domain Bullock feels.

Line management has to make it happen, has to be a part of planning and structuring so the right training is given to the right people at the right time. Because training that is given to the wrong people at the wrong time is more waste, rather than value added. Sometimes we do not plan or structure the training that is appropriate as well as we should. Consequently, we train people and they go back to work and nothing happens. The application of training is what is important.

Communication

Learning and awareness can also be encouraged by ongoing communications about the Quality thrusts in an organization. The Lockheed newsletter, *The Star,* has articles about Quality in every issue. In addition, *Star Quality* is published quarterly; it reports exclusively on the Quality efforts underway at Lockheed.

It is this kind of top-down communication cascade that ultimately will anoint every employee. Such publications serve not only to promulgate the corporate Quality drives, but also to make employees aware of what is being done elsewhere. For example, in a recent issue of *Star Quality* is an article entitled "National Top Companies Get the Quality Message."[9] The article reports on the fifth annual National Quality Forum, which assembles business leaders of major American corporations to discuss quality improvements. David T. Kearns, former CEO of the Xerox Corporation, is quoted as saying that "American business must understand that quality improvement is a continuous process. We are in a race in which there is no finish line."

Quality and the Future

Resistance to change is often reduced when individuals realize the change is here to stay and that it is making its residence permanent in numerous other organizations. Conveying the message that Quality is not a fad, that it is not an isolated corporate theme, that it *is* an ongoing race, will help persuade those who may feel they need not listen to corporate messages. When I asked Bullock about the future of the Quality movement, he enunciated his conviction quite clearly:

> *I do not think there is any question about the fact that Quality is here to stay. The reason I say that is that the whole world has seen vivid and absolute examples in the place where it matters the most to most people—in business success and financial success.*

> *American industry has lost out on all too many areas to the Japanese. Though it has taken a long time, I think people have become aware of why we lost out. I think once that awareness comes, then the recognition is there that in order to both improve and survive, and succeed financially, Quality is absolutely essential. Quality improvement is absolutely essential and not just a one-time thing. Because our competitors across the Pacific did not just do it once—it absolutely continues.*

> *I know examples where the Japanese continue to astound American management by decreasing the prices on items they supply—enough to offset inflation year after year. Whereas in this country, that is almost unheard of.*

> *Quality is here to stay, without a doubt.*

Helping to spread the Quality word at Lockheed are reprints of employees' views. The last page of *Star Quality* often asks a "Quality Question." Here are response to the question, "What do you think of when you hear the word 'quality'?"[10]

- It is building a product with pride and integrity. An excellent example is the C-130 that we've been building for 34 years.

  —*A.L. Eubanks, inspector*

- We've got to have pride in the job we do. Quality is not engineered in—it's built in. —*J.R. McClure, supervisor*

- Quality to me is doing a job I can be proud of. It's doing the kind of job you would hope somebody would do for you.

  —*Weldon Crenshaw II, shear operator*

- Doing it right. I'm an engineer, and if I put out a drawing that doesn't require changes, that's quality. It doesn't always happen, but you keep on trying.

  —*Loretta Duzan, electrical engineer*

Building Blocks for a Quality Structure

Since management direction of the Quality initiatives is vital to eliciting the kind of universal participation displayed in the above responses, I asked Bullock what building blocks management has to establish in order to have a Quality structure.

I think the four key phrases are "management commitment, continuous process improvement, perpetual curiosity, and no hypocrisy." As far as that last one is concerned, I think the problem is that when senior management says, "We are going to improve Quality," people down the line fall in step and say, "Yes sir."

Then they begin to generate reports and things that on the surface tend to imply that things are changing, but, in fact, nothing is changing. Posting artificial records and data on improvement and changes is hypocritical. Employees do know the difference. They know when things are improving and changing. If they see management at any level bragging to or reporting to its higher level of management about what they are accomplishing—and in fact it is not being accomplished—that becomes absolutely counterproductive. All it does is harden and deaden the workforce toward any serious commitment. (See Figure 3.)

FIGURE 3

BUILDING BLOCKS NEEDED FOR CORPORATE QUALITY STRUCTURE

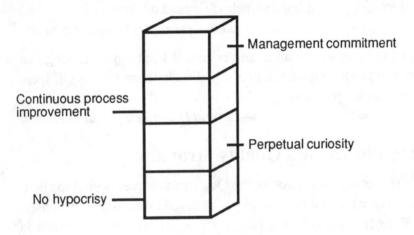

The Fear Factor

The falsified figures are not always promoted by ego gratification. As Dr. Deming says, "Where there is fear, there will be wrong figures." Bullock admits it is a challenge to overcome fear but feels the way to deal with it is to have a "flowdown" at every level.

The v. p. has to convince the directors. The directors have to convince the division heads and then the managers and then the first-line supervisors and they all have to become believers. Then they have to convince the workers that fear is not necessary. And that is tough, because in large organizations, it is hard to know just how committed people are.

One of Dr. Deming's Fourteen Points is the command to drive out fear. He believes that most people experience confusion about what their employers expect of them, and the fear factor prevents them from asking questions to clarify their doubts. There is concomitant fear of creating conflict or of being blamed, fear of being embarrassed or punished, fear of jobs being lost or promotions being denied. And the cost of such fears is exorbitant.

While economic uncertainty, especially in the aerospace industry of which Bullock is a part, may be overshadowing any light TQM may be shedding upon ways to improve work practices, that uncertainty is a cyclical fact of life in American business. To be sure, the Japanese system of lifetime employment may be what has enabled them to embrace Quality practices since their introduction to them and to Dr. Deming back in 1950.

Lifetime employment eliminates the fear of unemployment but not all other fears. Peter Drucker speaks of a unique fear experienced by Japanese employees.

> ...the fear of losing one's job for the ordinary economic reasons, because of technological changes, or because of arbitrary management action, is largely absent in Japan. There is haunting fear in the Japanese system, the fear of losing one's membership in the employing institution. In the Japanese tradition there is no place for *ronin,* the masterless man. Nor, if only because of the seniority system of wages, is it possible, as a rule, for a man to find a job except on the entrance level, so that anyone who is unemployed past age thirty is practically unemployable. This creates tremendous fear of the consequences of personal misbehavior, i.e., tremendous pressure for conformity. It also creates genuine fear lest the enterprise itself may go under—which, in turn, then makes the Japanese willing to go to very great lengths to maintain the competitive position of their employer, whether the competitive position of a business in the market, or the competitive position of a government agency in the continuous infighting of Japanese politics.[11]

While lifetime employment may sound enticing, its corollary is life-times tied to one particular employer, one particular industry. With the American penchant for mobility, such a system, in its purest form, could never work. And Americans would probably not want it to work, for it would mean denial of certain freedoms to which we have become inextricably accustomed. Modified forms of job security can work, however, and many labor union contracts and management policies are now experimenting with ways to ensure longevity of job life.

In an effort to safeguard jobs, some companies are deliberately understaffing, at least as far as their full-time employees are concerned. By hiring more part-time workers or temporary workers, companies are not forced to lay off their full-time employees when the economic pendulum is swinging more slowly. Other companies are trying shorter work weeks or worksharing situations. When an industry experiences hard times, some firms will take employees from their usual jobs and assign them to other tasks, often those that will bring in increased business. Other companies are taking special care in the hiring process to ensure the best possible fit between the expectations of both applicant and organization.

Performance Measurements

Bullock views change and continuous improvement as prerequisites for survival in today's market, which he characterizes as having customers who "demand and deserve higher quality and lower costs." He is hopeful that American business, which ignored for too long the dangers of foreign competition, will be able to compete on equal terms with foreign firms. Once that stage has been achieved, then America must aggressively seek ways to stay ahead.

Performance enhancement, Bullock claims, is one way Lockheed can better compete against other American firms vying for the lessened defense dollars.

The other part of fear is that it is difficult to convince all managers at all levels that, in fact, the old performance measurements are not any longer the important performance measurements, that schedule and cost are what matters. It is difficult because we teach quality, we preach quality, we meet on it, we discuss it, we have projects, but on Fridays, when the work week is coming to an end, the culture says, "We have got to sell off more work."

Bullock notes the difficulty of changing the mindset that measures worth by measuring numbers. He explains,

Many people believe that is the way they should measure performance. It takes constant education and training and demonstration of commitment to make people believe we really are changing.

In *Out of the Crisis*, Dr. Deming discusses "deadly diseases" that blockade the necessary transformation of the Western way of managing.[12] He maintains that the only way to cure those who are suffering from these diseases is to completely overhaul the current way we are doing business. These diseases, he contends, differ from mere obstacles in that the diseases are more difficult to get rid of and more injurious.

There are seven of them, one of which is the performance appraisal system. He describes the effects of such a system in vitriolic terms.

It nourishes short-term performance, annihilates long-term planning, builds fear, demolishes teamwork, nourishes rivalry and politics.

It leaves people bitter, crushed, bruised, battered, desolate, despondent, dejected, feeling inferior, some even depressed, unfit for work for weeks after receipt of rating, unable to comprehend why they are inferior. It is unfair, as it ascribes to the people in a group differences that may be caused totally by the system that they work in.[13]

Dr. Deming condemns such ratings for not encouraging leaders to help people. Instead, managers are expected, in a sense, to discover and deal with defects, namely the perceived inadequacies of employees. He has equally harsh words for merit ratings, as they encourage individuals to improve themselves or their positions, rather than try to improve the system.

An attendant side effect of the ratings system is diminished pride. Deming asserts that when we use performance appraisals, we are encouraging short-term thinking and even "short-time performance." Our national obsession with numbers allows bosses to require quantitative proof that we have done something. Such counting, says Dr. Deming, actually diminishes the pride of performance. The doctor who can examine six patients in just one hour is not the kind of doctor most of us would like to claim as our own.

Bullock says,

I agree with him. I do not think that institutionalized reviews are very useful. They have become sort of artificial; they are forced. I think the only effective performance reviews or performance counseling come through genuine discussions with employees at a time that is appropriate. It does not necessarily mean twice a year or once a year on June 15.

Fortunately, people get so preoccupied with getting the job done that sometimes I guess you need to force some structure. Idealistically, I believe that forcing it makes it less effective.

Preparing the Work Force

On the subject of bringing about widespread acceptance of ideas such as these—ideas that will, as Dr. Deming claims, take us out of the crisis—Bullock feels that high school is the ideal place to introduce an awareness of the tools and some survey-level exposure to applications of the tools, such as Pareto analysis. Certain SPC techniques and fishboning are very appropriate, he contends, for introduction at entry level points.

He comments that because of the lack of such exposure at the high school level, many companies are publishing their own dictionaries of tools and terms. The Boeing Company has one, Lockheed has one—a number of organizations are putting out their own textbooks because there is no common language being spoken, using the discrete TQM vocabulary.

Working with Suppliers

Including suppliers in the argot and syntax used by the corporation itself is another way to achieve unanimity of effort. Bullock speaks of having "a long way to go in that arena," but admits Lockheed is beginning to make inroads with their supplier network.

Just this week, our people were out making awards to a couple of suppliers who have perennially been low-quality performers, but who began turning around a couple of years ago.

K. Theodor Krantz, in an article playfully titled "How Velcro Got Hooked on Quality," tells of a similar interest taken by a buyer in a seller. General Motors (GM) informed Velcro in August 1985, that they had to set up a total quality control program within 90 days or else lose GM's business. GM purchases Velcro tape for binding different parts of the car seat and also for binding fabric to car roofs. GM was not upset about delivery schedules or the quality of the Velcro product; rather, the giant automaker was concerned because of the quality process at Velcro. GM charged that Velcro was *inspecting* quality instead of *manufacturing* quality. Krantz reveals:

> They were dissatisfied with the fact that we were throwing away 5% or 6% or 8% of the tape, depending on the product. They wanted quality maintained up and down the line to prevent such waste. And they said that to have the head QC person report to the head of manufacturing was unacceptable.[14]

Velcro was duly alarmed to find that GM had given Velcro the next-to-lowest quality rating for its suppliers. Radical action was called for, including the training of 500 employees at Velcro's only facility in the United States, the one in Manchester, New Hampshire. Velcro has managed to clean up its act. Their waste reduction efforts now show outstanding success. They have gone from 23 quality control people to 12. And, in a reluctant but necessary move, they have terminated veteran supervisors who could not seem to get the Quality message.

As we have seen, the Quality message is one that is being delivered both internally and externally. At Lockheed, corporate officers are expected to recognize that they are both customers and suppliers, that they are forces in both internal and external environments. If the Quality mission is to succeed, improvements must be made in all the processes that relate to this recognition.

Summary

Whatever barriers are preventing Quality endeavors from succeeding must be identified and reduced or altogether eliminated. For companies to remain competitive, for teamwork to optimize employees' potential, for bold restructuring plans to succeed, the barriers to efficiency and profitability must be spotted and then broken down. Particularly in these defense-reduction times, companies such as Lockheed Aeronautical Systems must continue with what has worked, improve or eliminate what has not, and venture into new arenas if they are to win their share of the global marketplace profits.

Diversity in product line accompanies the restructuring of organizational charts and the redesign of facilities. Through all of these changes, a company needs to convey its frailty in the capability of the work force to make the future a bright one. Quality concepts, introduced and sustained with management commitment, will help corporations move into the future that strategic planning has envisioned. That future will no doubt have higher standards than does the present, but as an American statesman noted 200 years ago, there is no gain without some pain.

Corporations may have to, as Dr. Deming asserts, reconsider the performance appraisal system, for it invariably creates the kind of fear that stifles productivity. They may also have to look at their supplier relationships and find new ways to work cooperatively so standards can be met, waste can be eliminated, and processes can be facilitated.

Communication and training, as William Bullock tells us, are the means for winning converts to this new Quality religion. The training should be done by line managers, with the support and cooperation of training departments. Workers respond better to direction from those to whom they report, Bullock feels.

But all the training and all the proselytizing will be to no avail if employees sense hypocrisy or a lack of commitment from upper-level managers. Managers must be sincere about their Quality sermons; if they are not or if they choose not to accept the new religion, they may have to be let go, as they were in the Velcro organization. For those who are committed and who choose to endorse the Quality plans, perpetual curiosity, according to Bullock, is the trait that will enable individuals to continuously improve the processes of their work.

For Further Consideration

1. What are the sources of fear?

2. Other than turf-protection, what other behaviors obstruct true teamwork?

3. Is diversity of product line a wise option for your company? If so, in what ways could you or do you diversify?

4. Does your company need a new management policy? If so, what should it include?

5. Specifically, how can we establish ongoing dialogue to find out what the needs of line management are?

6. Bullock asserts that—in terms of acquiring new knowledge/skills—employees "pay attention to and are responsive to, the people they report to." Do you agree? What are some advantages and disadvantages of having outside experts address employees?

7. Has the training department ever presented classes that you felt were a waste? If so, what were the circumstances surrounding this wasteful expenditure of individual and corporate time/money/efforts? What can you do to eliminate such waste in the future?

8. If you were (are) in a position to do so, what book would you give to each of your company's managers?

9. Specifically, what have you done (are you doing, will you do) to create mindsets that are receptive to TQM?

10. How committed are you to the Quality movement? How committed is your company? Your department?

11. Bullock alludes to the waste incurred in sending to outside seminars employees who subsequently do nothing differently. Why do you think intellectual and/or behavioral inertia sets in?

12. How could a company ensure that training is being put to use?

13. How can you translate Quality concepts into everyday operations?

14. What do you think of when you think of the word "customer"? Give details.

15. How do we increase the pride of workmanship and the pride of being associated with the company employing us?

16. What do you think a Quality structure rests on?

17. What examples of corporate hypocrisy do you know about?

18. Can you think of situations in which fear caused problems? Does management by fear ever work?

19. How do we encourage "perpetual curiosity"?

20. Can you think of any other forces that "harden and deaden the work force toward any serious commitment"?

21. How long do you think it will be before workers really believe that "fear is not necessary"?

22. Compare the Japanese and likely American reaction to the idea of a "masterless man."

23. To what lengths would you be willing to go to "maintain the competitive position" of your employer?

24. What are some of the pressures upon employees to conform?

25. What are the consequences—both immediate and far-ranging—of personal misbehavior?

26. Unions often regard job security as an important bargaining point. What are your views about such security?

27. What prerequisites for survival can you cite?

28. Will your company ever reach the point at which performance counseling replaces performance review?

References

1 "Operations Takes Hands-On Approach to Improvement," *Lockheed Star,* Vol. 2, No. 21 (October 19, 1989), pp. 1–2.

2 "The 1990 Book of Lists," *Los Angeles Business Journal,* Vol. 4, p. 126.

3 Tellep, Daniel M. and Robert A. Fuhrman. "To Our Shareholders," *Lockheed Corporation 1989 Annual Report,* pp. 3–4.

4 "Biggest Challenge to Corporate America Is Within, Survey Says," *Star Quality,* October 19, 1989, p. A.

5 O'Neill, Gerard K. *The Technology Edge* (New York: Simon and Schuster, 1983), pp. 20–21.

6 *Star Quality, op. cit.*

7 Levinson, Harry and Stuart Rosenthal. *CEO: Corporate Leadership in Action* (New York: Basic Books, Inc., 1984).

8 Daniel Tellep *et al.* "Continuous Quality Improvement," *Lockheed CORPMEMO,* No. 709 (November 15, 1989), p. 1.

9 *Star Quality, op. cit.,* p. C.

10 *Ibid.,* p. D.

11 Drucker, Peter. *Management: Tasks, Responsibilities, Practices* (New York: Harper & Row, 1974), p. 249.

12 Deming, W. Edwards. *Out of the Crisis* (Cambridge: Massachusetts Institute of Technology, Center for Advanced Engineering Study, 1986), pp. 97–148. Reprinted from *Out of the Crisis* by W. Edwards Deming by permission of MIT and W. Edwards Deming. Published by MIT, Center for Advanced Engineering Study, Cambridge, MA 02139. Copyright © 1986 by W. Edwards Deming.

13 *Ibid.,* p. 102.

14 Krantz, K. Theodor. "How Velcro Got Hooked on Quality," *Total Quality Handbook* (Minneapolis: Lakewood Books, 1990), p. 162. Reprinted with permission from Lakewood Publications, 50 South Ninth Street, Minneapolis, MN 55402. All rights reserved.

Carl G. Thor, President
American Productivity and Quality Center

"The first and obvious thing is that satisfaction of the customer is critical in all aspects of Quality. All the gurus and all the approaches end up with customer orientation as the absolute driving force."

Background

Carl G. Thor is a director of the Malcolm Baldrige National Quality Award Consortium. He is also president of the American Productivity and Quality Center, a position he has held since 1987. Thor's name is a familiar one in Quality circles, for he has published extensively and has led several industry studies and statistical research projects. Additionally, he has worked with a wide variety of organizations to create and improve productivity and Quality management, and measurement and reward systems.

Having earned his MBA in statistics from the University of Chicago, Thor began working at Humble Oil and Refining Company, where he was involved in product trading, regional logistics, and investment studies. From there, he went to Anderson Clayton and Company. In 1977, Thor joined the American Productivity and Quality Center, located in Houston, Texas.

The Center defines as its mission the intent to improve productivity, quality, and quality of work life by "providing educational, advisory, and information services of exceptional value; and researching new methods of improvement on both domestic and international fronts and broadly disseminating its findings." Structured as a nonprofit, nonpartisan organization, the Center has made contributions to business, government, academic institutions, and labor unions.

With a professional staff numbering sixty employees, the Center provides various services for both national and international clients. Those services include

- publications
- information service
- education and training
- consulting
- involvement with national affairs
- research
- networking

The Center's chairman, C. Jackson Grayson, Jr., founded the organization in 1977 in response to a growing concern that the rate of productivity in America was declining. Grayson believes that the standard of living is measured in terms of productivity—not in terms of currency values or trade surpluses. He also believes that the impetus for increasing productivity must come from both the employer and the employee level.

More than one hundred organizations participated in the founding of the American Productivity Center, as it was first called. The inclusion of the word "Quality" eleven years later was a reflection of the crucial interrelationship of quality and productivity.

One of the most important milestones in the Center's history was its participation in the 1983 White House Conference on Productivity. The Center worked to bring together nearly 200 business, government, academic, and union leaders to share recommendations for improving national productivity levels.

In 1987, the Department of Commerce, in establishing the Malcolm Baldrige National Quality Award, hired the Center and its partner, the American Society for Quality Control, to form the consortium that administers the National Quality Award. Two years later, the Center sponsored the first national conference to share information about the companies selected to receive the Baldrige Award.

Training

A recent article in *Total Quality Newsletter*[1] discusses the difficulty of providing Quality training, particularly when the word "quality" does not have a universally shared denotation. It is agreed, however, that for Quality initiatives to succeed, there must be willing participation from every level of the organization, starting at the uppermost rung of the ladder. There must also be sufficient time and training accorded employees if the corporate culture is to undergo serious change.

The *Newsletter* interviewed David Luther, senior vice president and corporate director of Quality at Corning Inc., where a comprehensive quality improvement effort was instituted several years ago. That effort, claims Luther, is at least partially responsible for the company's 100 percent increase in profits over the last seven years. Luther says their quality efforts are predicated on a strong commitment to training.

Corning's goal for its Quality training is to have all of its 26,000 employees worldwide move from the current figure of 4 percent of working hours spent in training to 5 percent. The training program at Corning begins with mandatory Quality awareness orientation. In 1986, there was disagreement about the extent to which the Quality improvement program was dependent on training. Today, according to Luther, there is no such disagreement.

Among the points they are trying to establish in their Quality-conscious credo are these:

- The customer is Number 1.
- Error-free work is not only possible but expected.
- Error prevention is essential.

Thor, too, concurs with the need for training to reflect corporate directions and corporate emphases. "Training should be in sync with what the company is saying Quality management is," he confirms. The very fact that management is emphasizing certain concepts tells us that the company regards certain issues as critical ones.

The first and obvious thing is that satisfaction of the customer is critical in all aspects of Quality. All the gurus and all the approaches end up with customer orientation as the absolute driving force.

Now there are some Quality programs that just talk "customer" as if they are talking about the person who buys their toothpaste or comes to their ballpark or whatever, as if the external customer is the only person everybody has to satisfy.

Thor regards the product-purchaser as one of many vital links in the Quality chain.

Recognize that when you start talking about the average company, you have a business that has both production and support. The

*support people very often aren't dealing with the outside customer
or the external customer. The finance department provides reports
for the operating people. The HR people hire people for other
areas. The concept of internal customers is something relatively
new to an organization; most corporations are very cognizant of
the importance of servicing the external customer only.*

The results of a recent study by the Zenger-Miller consulting firm lend survey figures that support Thor's assertion.[2] Respondents in the survey spend an average of only $2.58 on service training for front-line employees. And the majority of that money is spent on teaching employees how to cross-sell and how to handle complainers, but not on how to really work with customers to ensure their satisfaction on a daily basis. Other factors that run through the training programs of the surveyed companies show limited management involvement, training limited to customer service personnel, and limited follow-up.

Training Goals

Thor, like other Quality leaders I interviewed, has demanding standards for those who would train others on Quality precepts. He is adamant in his view that they should first train themselves.

*It's going to sound obvious but it doesn't always happen. Understand Quality yourself before you go off and start listing curricula
you think would be great. Get some Quality training yourself—not
only going to courses, but even going down into the plant to see
what Quality people do.*

*Spend a few hours with inspectors, go along on a call to the
supplier and see what the supplier relationship looks like, go with
a couple of hourlies to a community college training course and
see what the level of training is like there. Listen on the floor to
some of the so-called on-the-job training episodes and see what
those are like. In other words, understand it yourself first before
you train it. I have seen some corporate training people who never
leave the office claim to understand what is needed when they
clearly do not.*

We are very much believers in needs analysis thinking. After you have come to know Quality yourself, identify your internal customers from all over the organization. Sit down with them and find out what they think and want. They often don't know. They can talk in terms of "This is what we would like people to do better," without really knowing the name of what they want. It is this kind of need you might never realize unless such dialogue is going on.

Thor is committed to training that cuts across employee classification. If it is important to know who the customer is, then it is important for *all* employees to know that. If it is valuable to know how the system operates, then it is valuable for affected employees in several different functions to have such information.

The companies often mess up the interface between white-collar workers and blue-collar workers. Trainers sometimes segregate the courses. "Oh, you are an hourly—you go to these. You are a support person, you go to those." Such a policy works against the integration you are trying to achieve. If customer identification and system identification are the prime things, you will defeat your purpose by separating employees.

I think Quality training could be done very usefully and most appropriately in a mixed manner. Everybody can be involved in data generation, for example, whether they are clerks or executives.

Thor illustrates with a situation from his own office: those who do keyboard work get keyboard training, but those who ask the keyboarders to do things don't get training, not even general, introductory information. Pointing the finger at himself, he admits, "I have no idea what the capability of my secretary's computer is, but I ask her to do things with it that I don't understand well myself."

Customer Orientation

Thor views employees' unfamiliarity with the needs of internal customers as a subset of the problem of system-identification. He laments the fact that many people simply do not have an understanding of the overarching system of which they are part. If every employee in an organization comprehended the nature of systems—what system they were part of, where that system started, where it progressed to, where it ended—there would then be a better knowledge of both the internal and external customer and of the employee's place in that relationship.

Control Points

Related to an orientation toward the customer is Thor's "favorite phrase": "Every work station is a control point." He believes that if somebody could do a good job of teaching everyone in the organization that work stations are control points that are directly related to several other systems that impinge upon a work location, the Quality performance and increased productivity would not be problems in the workplace. And by work stations, Thor means the jobs of the floor sweeper and the mail clerk as well as the jobs of middle managers and executives.

That is getting back to the same point that the main thing to teach is that everybody is part of a system. If you have knowledge of the systems that run through your office, that will be emotionally satisfying to you but also practically satisfying to you because it means a positive part of the continuous correction process.

Such an understanding guarantees that you understand the system, that you understand your control point. Such knowledge means immediately that you are going to demand measures of performance, measures of control, measures of resources used.

A corollary to this idea is the belief that everyone needs feedback data from the system he is part of. Thor contends that managers have responsibility to know what their subordinates are doing, in order to determine if serious efforts to improve are being made. If they are, then such efforts become a justification for further training—not just statistical training but other kinds of training as well. Not everyone needs sophisticated statistical training, declares Thor, but people do need to understand charts and some of the numbers associated with the systems of which they are a part.

Empowerment

Simple knowledge of customers and of systems is not enough, he maintains, if workers do not feel empowered. Employees need to feel integrated with the system, need to feel good about themselves and the work they do. "You need to inculcate in people's minds the idea that they *are* the system; they *are* the active agent," he insists. It is management's responsibility, according to Thor, to make workers feel empowered, with respect to the system of which they are part.

These four components—control points, systems, empowerment, customer orientation—as depicted in Figure 1, represent the basis of Thor's Quality philosophy.

FIGURE 1

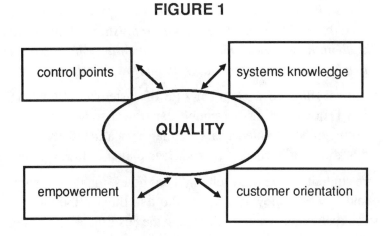

Quality and the High School Curriculum

Thor is of the opinion that some rudiments of the Quality movement can be introduced to the high school curriculum without difficulty. Just as many school districts are experimenting with empowerment in the form of school-based management team (as opposed to central-office administration of schools), so, too, can students be encouraged to assume greater responsibility for their own learning.

He uses the example of the right guard on a football team who needs to be empowered in the same sense that adults are empowered when a task and corresponding authority are delegated to them. Part of the delegatee's responsibility is not only to do the job well but to do it better than it has been done in the past. That betterment is a consequence of continuously examining the process and seeking to ameliorate it. Thor observes,

> *It is hard to say into what curriculum Quality concepts would fit but it is possible to encourage system thinking, to encourage the realization that you are part of a network. Whether that is part of mathematics or science or social studies, I'm not sure, but it is probably part of all three.*
>
> *The scientific method involves cause and effect linkages, which you try to teach in science. Fairly unsophisticated mathematics talks about networks. Computer programming, which is increasingly a high school subject, talks about flowcharts.*

The closest thing to a practical side of system thinking, in Thor's estimation, is flowcharting. If a student can flowchart how to get to school each morning or how to plan a party or plan a vacation, then he possesses the kind of thinking needed to be an active player in the systems game.

Before students leave high school, Thor notes, many of them work at McDonald's, where they are exposed to two other principles in which Thor strongly believes: being oriented to the customer and making every work station a control point.

> *They've certainly been exposed to customer service. At McDonald's, they are encouraged to try their best to serve the customer. They are made aware, too, of the system: they are taught there are eight steps to preparing a Big Mac. In fact, it's possible that students have seen more of these two Quality concepts than have their teachers.*

Thor recalls when he was teaching Program Evaluation and Review Technique (PERT) and critical path analysis courses to graduate students, he would often go home after his classes and work with his own high school-aged children. "The more I think about it," he deliberates, "the more I realize I could just as well teach the same concepts to my own children using pretty much the same words. As a matter of fact, the high school kids might even be a little less inhibited in considering how to organize that kind of thinking."

The majority of activities that constitute basic TQM involvement, agrees management consultant Donald J. Ford, could be taught to high school students:

> *Some of the ones that are part of nearly everybody's TQM tool kit are brainstorming, flowcharting work processes, cause-and-effect diagrams (fishbone and Pareto), benchmarking, Statistical Process Control, and quality function deployment. To me, the essence of TQM can be summarized by the following activities:*
>
> - *Brainstorm a list of "problems."*
> - *Prioritize them.*
> - *Analyze and flowchart the current process.*
> - *Look for inefficiencies or opportunities to improve.*
> - *Brainstorm possible solutions.*
> - *Compile an action plan.*
> - *Try it out.*
> - *Evaluate the results.*

When we look for inefficiencies or opportunities to improve, as Ford recommends we do, four key words should be kept in mind: synthesize, minimize, optimize, and alter. Considering ways to do each of these will lead to simplification of work processes and identification of waste of energy, time, money, and/or personnel.

Synthesize:

Can one of the processes be combined with another?
Can approaches or uses be combined?
Can steps be combined?

Minimize:

Can the process be made less complex?
Can some steps be eliminated?
Can some requirements be condensed?
If the process, or some aspect of it, did not exist, would we
implement it?

Optimize:

Is the best qualified person doing the work?
Do employees have the proper tools?
Has sufficient training been given?
Could the work be made more challenging?
How could a team effort improve the process?
How could the work be done more efficiently?
Are the people most interested in the process involved with it?
What shortcuts have the workers learned?
Are they acceptable shortcuts?
If so, are they being universally employed?

Alter:

Can the process be improved by some addition?
Should there be a rearrangement of the steps or pattern?
Should a different person be doing it?
Should something be done more often?
Should any step be done for a longer period of time?
Should the process be duplicated?
Should it be done in a different place?
Should it be done at a different time?

Statistical Process Control

As far as Statistical Process Control (SPC) is concerned, Thor maintains that there are two necessary factors:

1. that there be a process; and

2. that there be statistical concepts in use.

In other words, he observes,

There are a lot of companies that go right out and train everybody on Statistical Process Control right away and yet there are a lot of people who are in barely repetitive processes. There are some but there are also a lot of others who are wild cards—they answer the phone; they are do-what-you-can kind of people.

Where you have a repetitive process and where you have sampling, then SPC ought to be known by everyone around. So, I think the only general tool that is needed is this "system sense," which I think best comes from flowcharting. Conceivably, the fishbone diagram as well, but that is essentially flowcharting.

While employees certainly need to be made aware of the tools they will need to perform their jobs in a TQM environment, Thor cautions against introducing change too quickly. Not all employees need all tools, he reminds us. And, not all employees need to be prepared for change.

He warns that we can be overzealous in getting employees to assume that there will be change. Clearly, he acknowledges, there is change over time, but not every employee's job will change continuously. Nor will change, when it is implemented, necessarily be a radical departure from the status quo. Again, he turns to his own personal and professional experiences for examples:

Our organization is a very flexible one, but I have found people sometimes so expecting change next week that they perhaps don't do as good a job as they should this week. In other words, you can overdo a change expectation in people. I would be a little suspicious about tenderizing people for change. They already have so much change in their lives.

Especially if you are talking about the high school level. Young people are quite change-adaptable. I think maybe it is harder to teach them a little constancy of purpose. I might go a little in the other direction. When you have a task, try to take away some of the change variables and try to develop a little constancy. I extrapolate from my own children.

They are constantly ready to do something else. The thing I have to work with them on is, "Sit yourself down when you are ready to do homework, get used to the idea of sitting in this chair, turning on your stereo if you wish, having your beverage." Get that into a routine and you will find that the routine, the system reinforces the learning. If there is no routine, then every time they do homework, it is a new adventure.

When I talk to people about getting used to systems, I talk about identifying the system, and also being personally comfortable as part of a system.

Small Changes

The small changes may not shake the earth on which the company is standing, but—as far as consultant Ford is concerned—"The whole point of TQM is looking for lots of little ways to improve, instead of waiting for the big breakthroughs." In time, he says, the little improvements add up, to finally constitute big breakthroughs for those organizations that have pledged fidelity to TQM principles over the long haul.

Often, companies look only to the end results of the production line and there assess commitment to Quality. At the end of the production line, there is an evaluation of the degree to which conformance has been achieved. Assuming the defect rate is higher than it should be, further determinations are then made about whether the non-conformance is due to special causes or common causes.

More and more companies, however, are going upstream to examine all of the processes that lead to the final product and are attempting to bring all processes into a stable state. Small measures are taken along the way. Means *and* ends must be inspected and changes made wherever necessary to bring all processes into control.

Flowcharts

When sufficient time and analyses have been applied to a process that seems to lack stability, flowcharts sometimes work to identify one aspect of the prospect that is troublesome. The systemization of work processes and the simplification of those processes often go hand in hand. When we simplify the work we do, we examine the process being used and break down that process into the basic components. This first step in work simplification is critical, because without it, the process is generalized and important components may be overlooked.

Defining the process may take some time, but the result—increased productivity and elimination of waste—will make the investment a worthwhile one. Each separate step in the process should be written as clearly and carefully as possible—one action for each step.

Following this breakdown of component actions, an analysis must be made of which steps are the most costly and/or the most time-consuming. The analysis may require further research or discussions with different individuals doing the same type of work to ensure that the time expenditures are solid averages and not a source of variation because of one individual's deficiency. For example, if processing a work order takes Clerk A ten minutes but Clerk B only two minutes, it is possible that Clerk A does not have computer skills or does not know how to type. When analyzing the time required for various steps, it is important to have averages based on commonalities and not on special cases.

On the other hand, if you were seeking to simplify the work of a single employee, then the analysis would identify what part of the process is problematic and would suggest an obvious remedy: send Clerk A to classes to help him acquire the necessary computer skills.

Armed with the knowledge of the most expensive steps, you can now determine ways to make the most costly steps more efficient. To enable us to undergo this work-simplification, we are dependent upon two important flowcharting tools.

FLOW-PROCESS CHARTS depict a computer process by way of numbers, symbols, and words. The symbols are used to identify important, productive operations and to separate those operations from others involving handling and storing operations.

FLOW DIAGRAMS can be compared to blueprints and can be used for any work process. Such diagrams track the actual physical route of the work as it moves through a work station.

As Dr. Deming states,

Every activity, every job is a part of a process. A flow diagram of any process will divide the work into stages. The stages as a whole form a process. The stages are not individual entities, each running at maximum profit. A flow diagram, simple or complex, is an example of a theory—an idea.

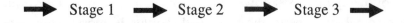

Work comes into any stage, changes state, and moves on into the next stage. Any stage has a customer, the next stage. The final stage will send product or service to the ultimate customer, he that buys the product or service. At every stage, there will be:

Production—change of state, input changes to output. Something happens to material or papers that come into any stage. They go out in a different state.

Continual improvement of methods and procedures, aimed at better satisfaction of the customer (user) at the next stage.

Each stage works with the next stage and with the preceding stage toward optimum accommodation, all stages working together toward quality that the ultimate customer will boast about.[3]

A sample flow diagram is depicted in Figure 2.

FIGURE 2

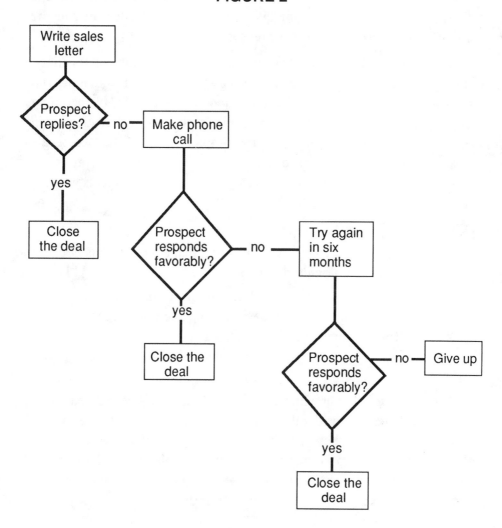

Employee Optimization

The optimization to which Dr. Deming alludes is vital for the workplace. In an effort to ensure such optimization is part of all systems, corporations are beginning to work with the educational system. Clearly, when incoming employees have difficulty with basic skills, their skills cannot be optimized. And it seems that such difficulty is not uncommon:

a poll of human resource officers in 1,200 major American corporations finds 64 percent of them saying that "high school graduates entering the work force cannot read, write, or reason well."[4]

According to William Kolberg of the National Alliance of Business, the organization that sponsored the survey, there is a widening gap between skills needed in the workplace and skills possessed by incoming employees. He says there are two reasons for that gap: (1) the decline in academic training and (2) the growing complexity of jobs. It is Kolberg's assertion that America needs to revamp the vocational training programs now in place so that apprentice training can be given to students who are not college-bound.

The survey also found that

- 75 percent of the officers polled feel that education has not kept up with technological advances.
- 72 percent believe math skills of incoming employees have deteriorated in the last five years; 65 percent believe the same is true for reading skills.
- only 48 percent find new employees can be retrained without much problem.

In the consideration of which areas retraining should be focused upon, companies have to consider the Quality movement and its future impact upon operations. If they assume that Quality practices will become standard operating procedures, if they assume that the tremendous investment being made in Quality is warranted, then the correlative question becomes, "What specific measurement tools do we expect employees to know how to use?"

Thor responded to the question this way:

I am a measurement specialist and so I could be expected to say "one of everything," but I am very much of the belief that there are different measurement tools for different purposes. The one exception is flowcharting. We can consider flowcharting, from the computer science domain, as being a measurement tool. I think it is something everybody can do.

It is not always the best educated who rise to the managerial ranks. In fact, there are those who believe that scholastic achievement cannot validly predict managerial capability. Granting that the decision-makers and innovators in organizations will not always have had the advantage of post-secondary educations, it is doubly important that the rudiments they obtain prior to workplace entry are solid. One of those rudiments is the logical thinking required for flowcharting.

One good example of an innovator who does not hold advanced degrees yet who made a substantial contribution to the American business scene is Edwin H. Land, who created the Polaroid camera. When asked if educational excellence accounted for discoveries, Land responded that advances are more often made by "some individual who has freed himself from a way of thinking that is held by friends and associates who may be more intelligent, better educated, better disciplined, but who have not mastered the art of the fresh, clean look at the old, old knowledge."

A willingness to consider new knowledge and/or to look at old knowledge in a new way is important then for discoveries, and "discoveries" is a word synonymous with "continuous improvement of processes."

In his study of American companies operating in Japan, Robert C. Christopher compares attitudes toward innovation held by American companies and Japanese companies.

> In a basic sense, of course, there is nothing uniquely Japanese about any of this: responsiveness to changing social and economic patterns is the hallmark of intelligent business management any-where. The difference is that in Japan—or so some U.S. executives with long experience there believe—the wave of the future tends to arrive sooner and to sweep away seemingly well-entrenched habits and preferences more easily than is the case in most other countries. "There's an enormous premium on innovation here," President Weldon Johnson of Coca-Cola Japan told me in the opening days of 1985. "Right now 25 percent of our sales in this company come from products and packages which were not even on the market three years ago.[5]

It would seem the ideal employee then would be lateralized in his thinking: able to integrate logical sequences and creative insights. Such an employee could rightfully be said to be functioning on the highest levels of Bloom's Taxonomy.[6]

Evaluation
Formulates unique ideas, judgments, opinions.

Synthesis
Combines divergent ideas to produce original expressions, solutions.

Analysis
Reaches conclusions, examines facts, specifies causes.

Application
Uses knowledge to select solution from limited number of possibilities.

Comprehension
Is able to explain, compare, paraphrase ideas.

Knowledge
Recalls learned facts and procedures.

In remarks to an audience of "Quality, Productivity and Competitive Position" seminar attendees,* Professor Kosaku Yoshida compared the analytical American culture to the holistic Japanese culture. He spoke of the American penchant for specifications, for clear delineations, for "telling it like it is." To illustrate, he used the diagram on the following page.

*Remarks delivered at Dr. Deming's Quality Seminar, July 26, 1990; reprinted with author's permission.

FIGURE 3

Japanese Concept of Desirability

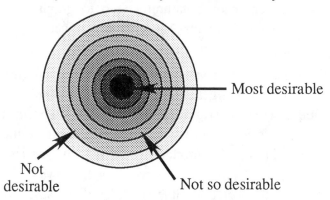

Most desirable

Not desirable

Not so desirable

American Concept of Acceptability

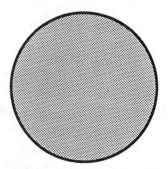

Everything inside is acceptable.

Everything outside is unacceptable.

While neither preceding illustration suggests a relaxation of standards, what they do suggest is that Americans are comfortable with black-and-white delineation. According to Yoshida, our range of acceptability is much wider than is the Japanese range, but—once an item falls outside the acceptable area bounded by rigid specification—it is clearly rejected.

By comparison, he notes,

The Japanese, because of their unified value system, tend to fill in the center first, establishing what is desirable. Americans, because of their wide variety of value systems, tend to first specify the perimeter or boundary for what is acceptable. It is relatively easy to define a center for a wide area, but it is considerably more difficult to define the area's exact perimeter. Furthermore, once rigid boundaries are fixed, people naturally tend to gravitate toward meeting the lower requirements of acceptability rather than striving to achieve the more exacting ones of desirability.[7]

The Japanese culture has a much narrower range of acceptability. Instead, there is a clear image or a target of the most desirable condition. However, if an item does not meet the rigid standard and narrow confines of the desirable sphere, it is not automatically rejected. Rather, the producer of that item would hope his product would fall into the less desirable range of acceptance, from which he would work toward the most desirable range. Even the worst possible label, "not desirable," is less definitive than the finality of the American term, "unacceptable." Japanese workers seek to achieve the more exacting requirements of desirability. In short, they strive to meet the target value, rather than merely striving to meet specifications.

You may be tempted to consider Dr. Yoshida's remarks as merely a question of semantics. Yet, his further illustrations of the Japanese mind-set toward holistic, comprehensive, overarching perspectives lend support to the ideal of evaluation and synthesis, as shown in the Bloom Taxonomy diagram. Rather than mere analysis, which focuses on specificity and detail and logic-orientation, the holistic approach synthesizes. It makes creative applications; it forges totally new pathways. It merges a thesis and an antithesis; it marries disparate and divergent elements to yield a holistic entity.

While analysis depends on singular, convergent responses, the holistic approach yields a synthesis, an entity that is ultimately evaluated. Judgments and risk-taking and intuition are often called for in the evaluation of the synthesized entity.

Yoshida cited the Japanese literary genre, the haiku, which takes only seventeen syllables to yield a poetic jewel of understatement. Deeply textured meanings and rich interior/exterior landscapes are conveyed by the way of this tiny linguistic gem, a perfect illustration of the holistic approach. The approach, like the haiku, shuns the overly analytical, excessively defined, too carefully drawn expression; it leaves much to the individual inference. There are grey areas of understanding, and multiple interpretations, and vision. It is Yoshida's opinion that managers should be trained in holistic thinking, so they can create and share visions, rather than tightly drawn five-year-plans.

Richard Foster, a McKinsey & Company director, substantiates this kind of creativity, which he describes as a metamorphosis, a way of "looking into the future a little more openly than American manufacturers [do]."[8]

Summary

If productivity is to be enhanced, there must be participation in Quality efforts on both management and worker levels, asserts C. Jackson Grayson, Jr., founder of the American Productivity and Quality Center. That participation is increased through Quality training, which must begin with a clear definition of Quality. Sufficient time and sufficient training must be provided if corporations are to realize results from their efforts to make Quality a way of life.

At Corning, employees are made cognizant of three emphases: the customer comes first, error-free work is expected, error-prevention is everyone's job. When work is error-free, it produces satisfaction on the part of the customer.

Carl Thor encourages recognition of both types of customer—internal and external—and the congruence of training and corporate aims. Many corporations, a Zenger-Miller survey found, espouse a customer-service philosophy but actually train front-line employees in behaviors not really designed to please the customer.

Flowcharts are a means of discovering what is wrong with systems, and a "system sense," Thor maintains, is critical if employees are to understand how their work station fits into the total system. Such knowledge, he feels, leads to a sense of empowerment. Flowchart techniques can easily be integrated into the high school curriculum. In fact, asserts

Thor, many high school students with part-time jobs at fast-food restaurants probably know more about satisfying customers and being part of a system than do their teachers.

Donald Ford lists the following activities as the essence of TQM: brainstorming problems; prioritizing them; analyzing and flowcharting; finding inefficiencies and opportunities to improve; brainstorming solutions; making action plans; trying out a course of action and finally evaluating. Part of the inefficiency-finding procedure is to consider ways to synthesize, minimize, optimize, and/or alter some stage of a process.

If processes are not conducted with frequency or if there is no sampling required, then SPC training is not necessary, Thor asserts. He also asserts that sometimes, in our eagerness to prepare employees for change, we do them more of a disservice than a service. Ford concurs, in his recommendation that small changes over a period of time can lead to big breakthroughs.

It is necessary to stabilize processes that are out of control, but we should be considering the microprocesses that constitute the macroprocess and not just the final product ensuing from the macroprocess. Such consideration will lead to optimization of the total process. Optimization can also be achieved by preparing employees to assume competent roles in the work force. Such training may be provided on the high school level, but often the corporation has to assume the further burden of retraining incoming employees.

For employees to innovate, they must be able to look at an "old" process from a "new" perspective. This ability, at least as far as Robert C. Christopher is concerned, accounts for Japan's ready embracing of change. The juxtaposition of the old with the new depends upon more than analytical skills; it depends upon synthesis and evaluation skills as well. And the melding of analytical and holistic skills (as Yoshida defines them) will lead to ultimate Quality successes.

For Further Consideration

1. How can we improve national productivity levels?

2. What percentage of your working hours are spent being trained?

3. To what extent does training in your company reflect corporate emphases?

4. Describe the system of which you are a part.

5. Explain Carl Thor's belief that "every work station is a control point."

6. How heavy a role does flowcharting play in your team's or department's problem-solving efforts?

7. Think of one thing you could do (or have recently done) to simplify your work.

8. Do you agree with Thor's statement that "not all employees need to be prepared for change"?

9. What big breakthroughs has your company had within the last five years? Describe the little improvements that preceded the breakthroughs.

10. How do you master "the art of the fresh, clean look at the old, old knowledge"?

11. Do you agree with Dr. Kosaku Yoshida in his delineation of American thinking as analytical and Japanese thinking as holistic?

12. How much cross-functional training have you received?

13. What advantages/disadvantages have you experienced with routines, in terms of productivity?

References

[1] "Quality Management Requires Heavy Training Investment," *Total Quality Newsletter,* Vol. 1, No. 3 (June 1990), pp. 3–4. Reprinted with permission from Lakewood Publications, 50 South Ninth St., Minneapolis, MN 55402. All rights reserved.

[2] *Ibid.,* p. 4.

[3] Deming, W. Edwards. *Out of the Crisis* (Cambridge: Massachusetts Institute of Technology, Center for Advanced Engineering Study, 1986), p. 87. Reprinted from *Out of the Crisis* by W. Edwards Deming by permission of MIT and W. Edwards Deming. Published by MIT, Center for Advanced Engineering Study, Cambridge, MA 02139. Copyright © 1986 by W. Edwards Deming.

[4] Briggs, Tracey Wong. "Firms Find Grads Lacking Basic Skills," *USA Today* (July 16, 1990), p. 1.

[5] Christopher, Robert C. *Second to None* (New York: Crown Publishing, Inc., 1986), p. 132.

[6] Bloom, Benjamin, ed. *Taxonomy of Educational Objectives, Handbook 1: Cognitive Domain* (New York: David McKay Publishers, 1956).

[7] Yoshida, Kosaku. "Deming Management Philosophy: Does It Work in the US as Well as In Japan?" *The Columbia Journal of World Business,* Vol. XXIV, No. 3 (Fall 1989), p. 12.

[8] Foster, Richard. *Innovation* (New York: Summit Books, 1986), p. 256.

Mark A. Apicella, Chairman, CEO
United Security Industries

"There are no free rides. You've got to
hustle. Sometimes the ideas are costly,
like getting into the electronic arena, but
we had to do it. The future is upon us,
after all."

Background

Mark Apicella, Chairman and Chief Executive Officer of United Security Industries (USI), has over 25 years' experience in the security field, having started his own contract security company at the age of 17. After the sale of that initial business venture, he worked with several security companies, including American Protection Industries and American Building Maintenance, where he served as vice president and chief operating officer before leaving to found USI.

Since 1983, when the firm was incorporated, USI has gown to become the fourth largest security firm in Los Angeles County, preceded only by three long-established, national firms: Pinkerton's, Wells-Fargo and Burns International. The first-ranked company, Pinkerton's, had $27.2 million in 1988 revenues in Los Angeles County; USI had $22 million.

USI works with both public institutions and private firms, and offers electronic alarm surveillance and concierge services in addition to its staple: security services. The corporate philosophy is defined as "personalized, responsive service to customers."

Apicella constantly seeks ways to improve the delivery of services to his clients. He designed the concierge division, Excelsior Corporate Concierge, to bring a traditional European concept to the American executive. It is the perpetual striving to better serve customers that makes innovation a reality at USI. Author Linda Lash commends such efforts.

> A company or organization with a commitment to service depends upon the continuous origination of ideas to get new customers, to satisfy existing customers and cause them to purchase again, and to cut costs. Somehow the ideas have to originate in all areas of the organization, and they have to pass through other areas of the organization to be effectively executed.[1]

Education of the Customer

In Search of Excellence described "service, quality, reliability" as operating policies that enhance both loyalty and revenues. These same three adjectives constitute the USI philosophy. Bringing about increased loyalty through service, quality and reliability, though, means ongoing dialogue with internal and external customers. Asked what specific steps he takes to ensure that loyalty, Apicella replies:

I think that one of the first steps we took was to educate the client on the difference between "ordinary" and "quality" service. It was a long, hard-fought battle because businesses are always under budget constraints. I attempted to inform the client that by paying a little more, he would get much more in return, versus the little or nothing he was getting at that time.

It was hard to do that but I would make a particular statement. For instance, I might tell him that if he would pay the security personnel "x" amount of dollars, he would get a more qualified security officer. But if he tried to cut corners [by going to a less expensive firm, for example], there would probably be negative consequences. I would make predictions and the predictions would inevitably come true. Then the clients would call me back and request my services.

Hoshin Planning

Customer requirements, of which the customer may not even be initially aware, are at the core of TQM. Those needs constitute the corporate goal, which is accomplished through daily control, cross-functional management and *hoshin* planning, the key aspects of which are as follows:

- A planning and implementation process that is continuously improved throughout the year (using the Shewhart Cycle of Plan-Do-Check-Act).
- Focus on key systems that need to be improved to achieve strategic objectives.
- Participation and coordination by all levels and departments as appropriate in the planning, development, and deployment of yearly objectives and means.
- Planning and execution based upon facts.

- Goals and action plans which cascade through the organization based upon the true capability of the organization.[2]

Graphically, the TQM system, incorporating hoshin planning, would look like this:

FIGURE 1

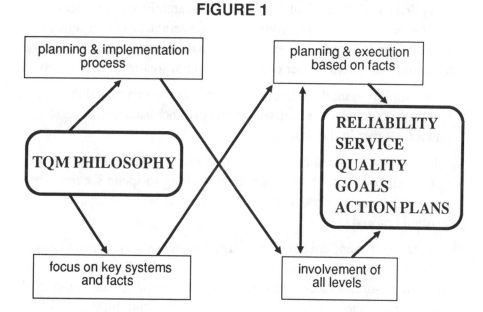

Satisfying the Customer

It is this same careful attention that Apicella provides his clients, in an equally well-structured manner. Such attention is the prelude to customer satisfaction. By understanding a client's monetary concerns and juxtaposing those with the consequences of bargaining for security services, Apicella demonstrates his thorough understanding of client concerns and their subsequent demand for high-quality services.

In view of all that has been written and spoken about how to satisfy customers, one wonders why more firms have not undergone the kind of customer-education process in which Apicella believes. Such customer-attending goes beyond altruism: it ensures customer loyalty.

In a study of advertising strategies, the Coca-Cola Company found that customers tell twice as many people about a negative experience as they tell about a positive experience. Further, 30 percent of consumers with a complaint that was not answered *never* return to the firm that was the source of that complaint.

Additional eye-opening data about consumer reactions have been compiled by the Technical Assistance Research Programs, Inc. (TARP) of Washington, D.C. They found that the average customer tells nine to sixteen friends about a bad experience he had. In some cases, customers tell more than twenty other people about poor treatment they received.

In a similar vein, the Direct Sales Association concluded that it costs five times as much to get a dissatisfied customer back as it costs to make him a customer in the first place.

How can so many companies routinely fail to pay attention to the needs of their customers? And why are firms willing to spend six times more to attract new customers than to retain old ones? Why are loyal customers so often ignored?

As we have mentioned, USI is a firm that makes it a practice to convert customer needs and expectations into standards of service. One way Apicella ensures a close conformance between the requirements of the customer and the realities he is providing is to send out a survey to all accounts, four times a year. The survey's specific, pertinent questions deal with these issues, among others:

1. Clients' perceptions of the importance of security in the successful operation of a building.

2. A rank ordering of factors involved in selection of a contract security firm. (Not surprisingly, price was not the determining factor; it actually placed third in the survey conducted by Lewis and Associates. Quality of the personnel and reputation of the firm were the two most important factors in selecting a contractor.)

3. A rank ordering of the top five security companies in the Los Angeles area from the viewpoint of quality. (USI was ranked first

by 50 percent of the respondents. The next most highly regarded company received 20 percent.)

4. Clients' perception of the security firm that provides services for the majority of commercial buildings in the Los Angeles area. (Again, the majority of respondents—56 percent—believed USI was providing security services for the majority of area commercial properties.)

5. A determination of one factor that would cause clients to review their current services. (The quality of personnel was the factor that the majority—54 percent—cited as a reason for switching from their current to a new provider of services.)

6. Suggestions for improved service. (The words "service," "quality," and "reliability," were cited repeatedly in the respondents' comments.)

Such surveys give clients an opportunity to express their satisfaction or dissatisfaction with the service they receive. And this expression-opportunity has proved to be a crucial factor in customer loyalty. Lash cites TARP research to substantiate this point.

> One of TARP's most significant findings is that customers are more likely to purchase a product or service again if they have been asked their opinion or given an easy way to express a complaint, even if their opinion is never acknowledged or their complaint is not answered or not answered satisfactorily. This means that companies can immediately take a step toward improving customer perception by asking customers for their opinions and comments and by encouraging complaints and questions from customers. Following this, of course, companies will want to take further steps to correct problems experienced and to answer complaints and questions in such a way that a higher and higher percentage of customers will want to purchase the product or service again.[3]

Commitment to Quality

USI takes the validated data supplied by the Lewis survey and incorporates those data into the design and development of new services or processes that are subsequently offered to clients. Such a client-driven approach to the introduction of improvements also minimizes the time and effort associated with implementing the changes, since the groundwork has already been laid. Continuing with the theme of working cooperatively with clients, Apicella recalls,

It took many years to accomplish this [making the client aware that the least expensive price could mean a poorer quality of security officer]. So I think that in conjunction with consistency and Quality, patience on the side of the provider is essential because the educational process takes time.

"Patience" is an especially revealing word here. In view of USI's position as a relatively new entrant in the security services field, and in view of the concomitant hunger new enterprises usually experience, Apicella has had to resist the temptation to provide less quality and thereby hope to attract more customers through lower prices. Increased quality, in a manufacturing company, can bring about reduced prices. The same is not always true in a service company.

What *is* true is that a credo-integration—a merging of fundamental aims on which a business enterprise is based—will increase quality. The aims can be considered equally important legs of the three-legged stool of business success. In this case, the legs are quality, service, and reliability, as identified by Waterman and Peters.

For USI, the credo-integration has paid off. Apicella attributes his financial success to his company's delivery of quality, service and reliability:

Now the community has a perception of us as being a quality firm, and one that stands behind its statements. We have been successful because of it.

FIGURE 2

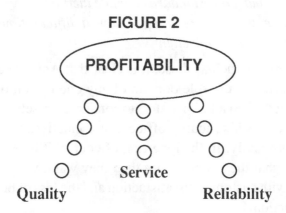

Again, that success might have resulted in laurels-setting in another company. But Apicella remains committed to projecting an image based on the three words listed above. He is adamant about keeping USI elevated above the level of mediocrity that typifies some of his competitors. As he observes, "Growth, of course, always causes control problems. But our philosophy must stay intact at any cost."

When a business does experience growth as rapid as USI's, there is often an intensified focus on expanding facilities and production. Accordingly, profits are plowed back into the expansions. It is not uncommon for this new growth focus to overshadow the Quality endeavors. Apicella, however, has made a conscious effort not to let this happen. He has created occasions for himself and his staff to deliver superior service. Standards not only remain high; they get higher as the result of greater attention to the root causes of breakdowns. In Apicella's words:

Quality control problems start with our product. Security officers, even with USI, are not the highest paid individuals in the world. We recruit from the ranks of the unemployed. In the Los Angeles area, unemployment typically runs around 5 percent.

USI's policy is to be extremely selective in our recruitment process. We hire 1 in 14 people we interview. It stands to reason that if the unemployment rate is 5 percent and if we only hire 1 in 14, and if we insist they be both U.S. citizens and high school graduates, and if our standards include their being articulate and presentable, then we are going to have a difficult time in getting the right product to the client.

With statements such as these, it is clear that Apicella does not view customer service as the sole domain of any one person or department. Just as he expects USI administrators to conduct themselves professionally, he also expects his security officer representatives to conduct themselves professionally. In the long run, of course, it is less expensive to give clients what they want (*more* than they want, whenever possible) than to deal with customer dissatisfaction and the loss of business caused by dissatisfaction.

The Cost of Lost Accounts

The cost of losing customers can be exorbitant. The Customer Service Institute calculated that if a retail operation loses each day a customer who spends $100 a week, the annual revenue loss is over $1 million. It is an awareness of such figures that makes Apicella determined to maintain and continually expand his client bases. This determination is reflected in his hiring philosophy:

Due to the fact that our product is service, we make a concentrated effort to put the money in attracting desirable personnel. Once you have the desirable personnel and they are trained properly, your problems usually are minimal because the client is happy. You are happy because you do not have a lot of turnover. The employee is happy.

His words echo those of J.W. Marriott, Jr., chairman and president of the Marriott Corporation, who has been quoted as saying, "Motivate them, train them, care about them, and make winners out of them.... If we treat our employees correctly, they'll treat the customers right. And if customers are treated right, they'll come back." A graphic representation of this philosophy is shown on the next page.

FIGURE 3

The Success Loop

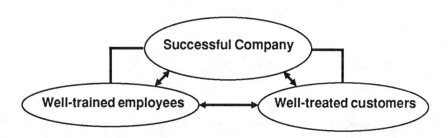

Linking Customer and Employee Needs

Like all companies on the cutting edge of Quality, USI employs key strategies in linking personnel needs and customer needs. Apicella's business plans demonstrate this integration of human resources and client priorities. He continues,

These are some of the things we do differently to keep our employees happy: we have a tremendous benefit package. We do not take on a new client unless we ourselves [the managers of the company] would not mind working there. Because we do not want to exploit our people, we want them to be happy. It's hard to keep people happy all the time, but we do not want to start off on the wrong foot.

We want to make sure that the account is a nice place to work. We want to make sure our client has empathy for both the company and the personnel. We want to make sure it's a joint venture between us and the client to achieve success.

This kind of bottom-line attention to the front-line employees explains, in part, why USI has maintained the Quality culture Apicella established when he formed the company. Attitudes at USI are typified by

- a cooperative mindset not uncommon to a burgeoning firm

- the recognition that delivery of Quality costs less, not more, in the long run

- pride

- concern for employee well-being.

There is depth, as opposed to superficiality, in the recruitment and subsequent training of USI employees, with a service-oriented culture the result. Such a culture rejects the traditional view of workers as resources whose feelings are not important. Instead, workers are regarded as employees who can make significant contributions to the company's operations.

Sole-Source Suppliers

In speaking of client relationships, Apicella identifies another element of Quality interactions: the sole-source supplier. In a seeming paradox, he speaks of buyers trying to keep the seller happy:

Many of our large institutional clients, because of our philosophy, actually won't even go out to bid year after year because they know they want to keep us happy. They want us to be happy because if we are happy, our employees are going to be happy and in turn they [the clients] are going to be happy.

These institutional clients to whom Apicella alludes are typical of the kinds of firms engaging in single-source and long-term relationships described as necessary by Dr. Deming.

Purchase of commodities and services should also move to the single supplier. The same commodity may be obtainable from several sources at different prices. However, consideration of inventory and ability to deliver the goods within a reasonable time, and with certainty of date, are important to the customer.[4]

In *Kaizen,* Masaaki Imai asserts that "service quality downstream is best assured by maintaining quality upstream."[5] It is clear that Apicella concentrates on upstream quality through selecting the best guards he can find and training them to represent the USI philosophy so that upstream quality will be assured. In the short run, such care taken at the beginning of the client-service process will require considerable expenditures of time and money. However, in the long term, time and money are saved because clients are more satisfied with the personnel assigned to them and the personnel are less likely to leave.

Such practices seem to be working at USI, for the firm is a designated supplier for a number of properties in the Los Angeles area. (Although few managers would admit it, the three-competitive bid process is often used only to satisfy corporate directives. The final selection is often the one that would have been made, even if there had not been two other bids.)

Historically, organizations viewed themselves and their relationships with customers as a pyramidal structure with management on top, employees in the middle and clients forming the base.

The Quality movement has caused organizations to rethink that structure. Today, firms like USI put clients on top and encourage employees

FIGURE 4
TRADITIONAL STRUCTURE

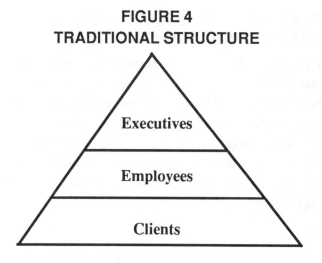

to understand the clear message: without clients, there would be no company. It is the client who, in the final analysis, foots the bill for all the work that is done, all the purchases that are made, all the profits that are realized.

The Corporate Ethic

FIGURE 5

QUALITY STRUCTURE

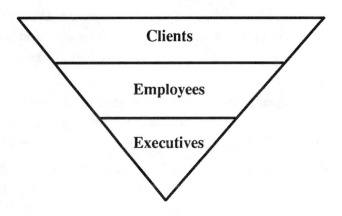

Not only does Apicella foster a familial ambience among his staff, he strives to achieve that same sense with his clients.

Some people lose sight of the common-sense aspect of business because of the balance sheet. I tell my customers to choose a regionally owned and operated company like ours, one which will do them justice. We live in this community. We want our children to carry on the business. We want to create not only the dollars but also the long-term reputation and the provision of a Quality service. Our children will then have more than a business to carry on; they will have an obligation.

In my years in the business—I have been in this business now over 25 years—I could tell you some scary stories about the industry. When I started my company, I wanted to professionalize the business and provide a high-quality service.

Quality experts agree that defining and then continually repeating a firm's Quality commitment is imperative if Quality is to permeate the organization. As painful as it sometimes is, management must terminate individuals who are unwilling to conform to the Quality requirements that have been established. For example, Apicella recounts,

I've had people work for me as long as 20 years and because of their not adhering to the program for whatever reason, a separation had to occur. It hurts sometimes but you make a commitment to the client and you keep it. If you see something that is not working, you have to make sure a change takes place so it does work.

A clearly defined corporate ethic must penetrate every level of the organization if Quality is to become actual service and not just lip service. In Fortune 500 companies, an executive officer is more and more often appointed to be responsible for Quality. This does not mean that the president can forget about Quality after such an appointment. Rather, it is a way of declaring the importance of Quality in the organizational structure. Having the Quality officer report directly to the top executive is another way of emphasizing the Quality commitment.

In smaller organizations, such as Apicella's, it is the top executive who must symbolize the organizational emphasis. It is he who must make a statement and manifest the statement that the customer is indeed at the top of the inverted pyramid. It is he who must champion both the recruitment and retention of customers, by continuously searching for improvements. The task is a demanding, typically difficult one.

The organization itself can perhaps be regarded as a child and its president the caring but decisive parent. As in child-rearing, decisions— sometimes unpleasant ones—must be executed toward the goal of having the company grow and flourish. Apicella observes,

I think it is important to make changes, if needed, to ensure our commitment to the client is fulfilled. You cannot just sit back and rest on your laurels and not grow. The company has to grow internally the way it grows externally. You have to have a strong foundation and that starts from within. What we try to do is educate our employees, making sure they understand what is expected of them. We want them to grow with the company.

Taking Responsibility for Quality

The Quality-oriented company is one that has Quality specifications in its overall business plan. It is one that translates those specifications into corporate practices and processes. Such translation cannot occur unless the leader makes all employees aware of company and client expectations.

FIGURE 6

Symbolizes the Quality aim.	Supplies necessary tools, resources, training.
Continually assesses effectiveness of strategies, changing them if need be.	Emphasizes Quality until it is part of daily conver-sations.

Apicella's words echo the leader's obligations shown in Figure 6.

All my managers are extensions of me. I am the person who started the company and developed the philosophy. When people come into the organization, they have to agree that their philosophy is similar to ours so there will not be a conflict of interest.

If all these things are the philosophy and policies of our company, then I think the profits will automatically come. But profit should not be the primary motive for being in business, nor the primary motive behind all business actions.

In reflecting on recent events in the business community, Apicella notes,

We have gone through a terrible period over the years, with takeovers and all. I know a lot of companies were concerned. Some of these companies that were making too much money had too much cash and were targets. Subsequently, they were taken over. I think a fair profit should be made, but we are here for the long term, and so other considerations must become part of the picture.

Customer Feedback

Apicella's service philosophy includes periodic assessments of the company (through a quarterly survey), a feedback system to ensure that client concerns receive prompt attention, and a fidelity to the service standards that are pledged to clients.

Apicella notes with pride that word-of-mouth business has resulted from this system.

We have been in business for over seven years and we did not hire our first salesperson until a year ago. And, we only did that because we needed someone to make the presentations and to keep the paperwork in order. Every single bit of business we have on the books is a result of referrals from our existing clients.

Clearly, when clients are satisfied with the return they receive for investments in security, they tell others. Research shows that when customers are *not* satisfied,

- The situation seems to get worse. Irate customers who are ignored or treated poorly wind up costing a company a great deal, for the situation worsens in their minds. Therefore, they make greater demands when they are finally dealt with.

- Opportunities for return business are lost. Customers with serious complaints tell twice as many other people about the negative experience as satisfied customers tell about a positive experience. So, not only does the firm stand to lose the business of the disgruntled customer, it also stands to lose the business of many others who have been exposed to damning information (some of it no doubt exaggerated in the telling) from the client who is upset.

- Advertising dollars are wasted. Marketing students know the most effective advertising is word-of-mouth advertising. And when this oral advertising impugns a company, it also diminishes the effect of money spent trying to project a positive image.

Expanding the Client Base

The entwining of customer expectations with corporate philosophy is evident in Apicella's next comments:

Our clients have been our salespeople. They are, in a sense, our partners. They help us advertise our company. They help us sell our business. We are a full-service company now and so we are reaching a broader base of clients.

We will go in to the architectural stage and design a security system for you. We will sell you the equipment. We will provide the maintenance program for that requirement. We will install the equipment. We will man the equipment and supervise it.

As Apicella reveals, the extending of that client base has been facilitated because of USI's reputation.

Because we have done such a good job with our first line of business, which is physical security, our clients automatically use us for the other lines of service. They know they can trust us. They know we provide them good service.

What else can organizations do to ensure the business community recognizes a company's name and understands its Quality-dedication? The task need not be a formidable one, although it should be an ongoing one. An effective yet inexpensive way to promote the company image is to have each employee an unofficial spokesperson for the firm. As E.J. Thomas notes, "A well-informed employee is the best salesperson a company can have." Other means of advertising without hiring an advertising firm would include strategies such as the following:

- Write articles for local newspapers or trade journals on a relevant topic.
- Appear on local radio and talk shows with an interesting slant on the business.
- If your firm is cited for an award, make mention of that award in the promotional literature that is sent out.
- Ask your current customers to recommend you.
- Do an inexpensive mailing or an informational newsletter.
- Offer an Open House for prospective clients to learn about your firm.

USI prides itself on specific certitudes in which clients can take assurance. States Apicella:

Our clients know three things about us.

1. They know we are honest.

2. They know we work very hard, as hard as we possibly can, to provide the best service possible.

3. They know we will endeavor to consistently be responsible.

Because we have the best company, our clients can truly say they have met their fiduciary responsibility to seek and retain the best qualified company in the industry. Our record speaks for itself.

Precisely because USI is known to deliver what clients expect, Apicella usually finds clients' most pressing questions deal with his meeting their expectations, their needs.

Anytime there is a major problem and we get called in, people don't even ask us about the price. They just want to get us in there because they are afraid. The problem is that if clients start to cut corners in this area, they can have serious problems develop.

Security is not like ordering paper clips. Certain services cannot just be a clerical ordering process. Paper clips are pretty much all the same. But then even in those areas, other considerations come into play, such as how quickly can you get this delivery.

Quality control is associated with areas of production. All these things are important in making the customer happy.

But in my business where the product is people, you really have to concentrate on delivering a feeling of security.

Joint Planning

Security from both a physical and a psychological perspective is what clients expect. And to meet that expectation, careful planning must be done for both the short and the long term. Apicella has a detailed plan that integrates indicators of Quality into the company's strategic plan. Feedback from both clients and employees is used to develop the plan. Monitoring is periodically embedded in the control process to ensure conformance to established requirements. USI's chairman describes that process:

The Quality Assurance program that we have initiated has our people constantly asking clients about their needs. We want to ascertain their feelings about our service. We actually burrow in, to try to find out what, if anything, is wrong. Our managers will actually go out and work in the field to learn what is wrong.

Apicella is clearly not a proponent of the "if-it-ain't-broke,-don't-fix-it" management style. "Everyone's top priority," he asserts, "is to make our clients satisfied." And if that satisfaction requires change in the operations or a change in personnel, so be it. In fact, USI engages in change-anticipation; they have instituted a managerial practice, described as follows, that accounts in part for their dominant position in the security field.

We have a level of management that some of our competitors think is superfluous: our Customer Service Managers. In the structure of these other companies—I am not criticizing our competitors, but in their structure—maybe it is superfluous because it is money that could be dropped to the bottom line if the Service Manager positions were eliminated.

These managers are required to physically visit each site once every two weeks and call them a minimum of once every week. That is done religiously unless the customer does not need to have a face-to-face meeting. Then our Customer Service Manager will still go to that location but will simply check with a secretary and leave a business card.

With such a policy, problems can be identified and rectified before they reach the point of customer dissatisfaction.

Intelligence-Gathering

Another hallmark of the Quality-oriented service firm is one that engages tirelessly in intelligence-gathering. Certainly much of the data can be acquired through questionnaires or on-site visits. The most competitive firms, however, have in place a systematic approach to learning more about the marketplace. This marketplace knowledge is then brought to clients. Says Apicella,

We constantly look for new security measures, programs, equipment services, systems to recommend to our clients. For instance, we say in the community [Santa Monica, California] that with all the new buildings being put up, there is going to be a lot of unleased space. So, I suggested to some of my clients that they have in the building an individual modeled after a hotel concierge.

It's a tremendous selling tool because so many executives waste their secretaries' time on planning parties, setting up luncheons, making reservations, arranging travel plans—time that could be put to much better use.

Known as the Excelsior Corporate Concierge, this division of USI is a feature that building owners and developers mention in their advertising to attract clients. Geared to the busy executive, the service lends an air of sophistication as well as efficiency to the normal operation of a building.

Quality experts are alike in asserting that the best way to attend to customer needs is to consistently ask them what they want. Sometimes, however, they don't know what they want or, quite simply, don't know what they are missing by not having a particular service. Such was the case with Apicella's idea for the concierge services, an uncommon feature of building tenancy.

When we first started the Concierge division two years ago, every single tenant in the building was given a profile card, which asked about likes, dislikes, birthdays, anniversaries, travel plans they could project, favorite airlines, etc. Then, anytime a tenant requires specific services, he can call down to the concierge, who will handle the transaction.

Actually, we will go up to the individual a week before a special event and remind the person of that event and even offer to purchase a gift if he wishes. It really works out well.

The building owner pays us strictly for the labor. We make our money through the commission from a particular vendor. With the high-volume relationship we have with our vendors, we will get a better deal for the client than he could get himself. It stands to reason: if we provide 100 air trips a week, we are going to get a better rate than you can get simply by arranging one.

We make our money from the vendors and not from the clients. We get the service cheaper than they could get it for themselves and it's handled better. Everyone wins.

Future Considerations

Even an overarching emphasis on Quality will not solve all other problems. For example, financial constraints may delay the implementation of innovations. In Apicella's case, some plans simply had to be postponed, relegated to a back burner, despite their money-making potential. He speculates about the future:

My problem has been capital. I would like to expand things a lot. Instead of owning 70 percent of a $30 million company, maybe it's best for me to own 35 percent of a $200 million company.

Apicella concludes with some general tips for succeeding in today's business environment:

First, you have to be willing to work very hard. At the same time, you have to work very smart. I tell my secretary that if all she has to do is sit there and do her nails, she should take the day off.

I have to plan my day with a good organizer. The successful business person must plan his time. When you feel you are exhausted, take the day off. Don't burn yourself out. The hours you put in should represent focused, productive, hard-working time.

His down-to-earth philosophy is evident in his self-assessment and in his realistic approach to keeping pace with technology.

The only reason a person like me could achieve the measure of success I have is that if somebody worked eight hours, I worked twelve. If they worked twelve, I worked sixteen. If they worked six days a week, I worked seven days and I just kept working hard.

Don't kid yourself. You cannot cram in business. Take advantage of the opportunities but make sure you know what direction you are headed in. Don't make the assumption that you are doing a good job. You have to weigh the production value and if you are not producing results, then you are doing something wrong. Once you get the right formula, implement the controls to monitor that success and never veer off. It's really simple.

There are no free rides. You've got to hustle. Sometimes the ideas are costly, like getting into the electronic arena but we had to do it. The future is upon us, after all.

Summary

Quality, service and reliability have been identified as the ingredients necessary to promote customer loyalty and to increase revenues. These are three of the cornerstones of the USI foundation. Another is the education of the client and the kind of planning, hoshin planning, that is comprehensive and reflective of the corporate goal. The Plan-Do-Check-

Act cycle is an additional feature of hoshin planning, as are attention to cross-functional activities, a study of systems, and the measurement of results.

Poor service not only costs a company in terms of losing a given customer, but also in terms of losing other potential customers with whom negative experiences have been shared. It is six times more expensive to get a customer back into the buying fold than it was to include him in that fold in the first place.

Apicella is determined to provide the best possible service to customers, a service characterized by the integration of the principles on which USI is founded—quality, service, reliability, client-education, joint planning—and the integration of employee needs and client needs.

Although he has refused to let growth lessen his fierce application of Quality principles, Apicella admits that finding qualified personnel is a difficult process. Without such personnel, however, his clients will become dissatisfied and may eventually turn to other providers of security services. USI's continued inclusion in the success-loop means remaining as the sole-supplier and repeated supplier for both current and future clients.

To do this, Apicella operates from an inverted-pyramid structure, making all within his organization cognizant of their constant need to keep customers' priorities ahead of their own. Growing internally (i.e., through the education and training of staff members) is just as important as growing externally (i.e., through expanding the client base).

Apicella speaks of a oneness, a collective manifestation of the principles on which the company was founded. His employees are reflections of him and of the customer-service attitudes he espouses. As a result, employees become spokespersons for the company, and clients become salespeople.

There are numerous other ways to make the public aware of what a company stands for, thereby attracting the business of those who seek Quality service. Corporate leaders can write articles for newspapers or trade journals, appear on radio or television shows, make potential clients aware of awards the company may have received by mentioning such awards in the company's promotional literature, hold an Open House for the public, etc.

Charting a client-responsive course of action means acquiring information—through surveys or other means—in order to build client concerns into strategic plans. It also means making clients aware of the latest technology available, so as to prevent future-shock.

For Further Consideration

1. What has been done in your company to develop customer loyalty?

2. What steps do you take to make an idea an effective execution?

3. What education have you given to your customers—internal and external?

4. Do you survey your customers? If so, what sorts of questions are asked? If not, what sorts of questions could be asked?

5. Describe the bottom-line attention given in your organization to front-line employees.

6. Identify the attitudes that typify your company.

7. What beliefs are part of your corporate credo?

8. Do you agree with J.W. Marriott, Jr.'s observation that employees who are treated correctly will treat customers correctly? How are employees treated in your company?

9. Is quality maintained upstream as well as downstream in your company? Explain.

10. Why do you think some people do not adhere to Quality requirements that have been established?

11. Are customers given an opportunity to periodically assess your company? Discuss.

12. Are your customers salespeople for your company? Why or why not?

13. What do your customers know about your company?

14. To what extent does your company incorporate feedback from both customers and employees into its strategic planning?

15. In what intelligence-gathering measures does your firm engage?

16. What is your company doing to prevent future-shock?

References

[1] Lash, Linda M. *A Complete Guide to Customer Service* (New York: John Wiley & Sons, Inc., 1989), p. 51.

[2] GOAL/QPC Research Committee, *Hoshin Planning: A Planning System for Implementing Total Quality Management (TQM)*, *1989 Research Report, No. 89-10-03* (GOAL/QPC, 13 Branch Street, Methuen, Maine 01844, 1990), p. 1.

[3] Lash, *Ibid.*, p. 92.

[4] Deming, E. Edwards. *Out of the Crisis* (Cambridge: Massachusetss Institute of Technology, Center for Advanced Engineering Study, 1986), p. 38. Reprinted from *Out of the Crisis* by W. Edwards Deming by permission of MIT and W. Edwards Deming. Published by MIT, Center for Advanced Engineering Study, Cambridge, MA 02138. Copyright © 1986 by W. Edwards Deming.

[5] Imai, Masaaki. *Kaizen: The Key to Japan's Competitive Success* (New York: Random House, 1986), p. 211.

Dr. David Nadler, President
Delta Consulting Group

"The commitment to Quality needs to run deep, and the fulfillment of the promise requires vision, leadership, and tenacity.

The challenges are great, but so are the rewards."

Background

Dr. David Nadler is president of the Delta Consulting Group in New York City. His firm aids organizations undergo substantive change by working with senior managers who are expected to make transitions between present and future conditions. He began his firm in 1981, after serving on the faculty of Columbia University, where he taught organizational behavior and management to MBA and doctoral students in the Graduate School of Business. While at Columbia, he was also involved in consulting and research for companies such as Citicorp and AT&T. Long interested in the process by which change transforms a corporate culture, Nadler decided to leave Columbia to build a private practice. He defines the work of the Delta Consulting Group this way:

Our work basically is defined around the notion of managing change. We usually work with CEO's or heads of major operating units or subsidiaries on the task of implementing changes that have some sort of organizational content, maybe strategic changes, changes in structure, operating style, new technology, acquisitions. There are a lot of different things that we are engaged in.

Our relationships with clients are long-term. Our approach is collaborative. That is, we are helping them develop and implement change, not doing it for them. Since 1981, we have worked with about 40 major companies on their issues of change; we probably work with 18 companies on an ongoing basis. Currently, one of our practice areas is Quality, but it is only one of the issues on which we work. It is an important part of what we do, but it is not the only thing we do. Quality issues represent about a quarter of our work.

The Change Process

Change, whether in the form of Quality initiatives or any other social, technological, political, legislative or economic thrust, offers opportunities for increased profit and productivity. But change also represents possible sources of frustration, fear, subversion, and even rebellion if the corporate culture is not conducive to change or willing to sustain it.

While those who are comfortable with change recognize its inevitability and perhaps even find the change process an exhilarating one, there are others whose sense of security seems tied to the immutability of the status quo. The leader's job is to transition from the old to the new and to explain—to those who will be affected by it—the nature of, and the rationale for, the change. Whether the change is foisted upon an organization by external forces, or introduced less drastically by internal forces, the leader is charged with minimizing the negative impacts of the change and extending its positive potential.

Management is more than a catalyst for change, for catalyst agents initiate change but do not participate in it. Instead, management must be both catalyst and active advocate of change. Management must have long-range vision and tolerance and "constancy of purpose." Management must, to the greatest extent possible, keep those who will be part of the change informed and involved.

Psychologist Kurt Lewin has defined the process of planned change as involving three separate steps or phases.[1] In the first stage, it is important to communicate the need for change and to illustrate the ameliorative effects of the change upon the organization. The leader implants the seed of change in this first stage and does all in his power to nurture and guide that seed's growth, despite resistance from both internal and external forces inimical to any alteration of the current environment.

All impacted aspects of the organization are dealt with during the second stage, which has the actual change taking place. Not only employees, vendors, and customers are involved in a different way of doing things. Also undergoing change would be organizational structures, machinery, processes, strategies, practices, aims, systems, etc.

Once the seed of change has become a fully grown organism, with roots reaching into the deepest parts of the organizational soil, then management continues with a maintenance program. This third stage is important in making employees feel the change will have far-reaching benefits and that management will continue to support the change and measure its effectiveness, making moderate alterations where necessary.

Challenges

Leaders contemplate the future and embrace, or at least accept, the changes that accompany it. To reject the inevitable or to lack the vision to see what is possible, is foolhardy behavior on the part of leaders. History is replete with examples such as the following, which have made laughable the shortsightedness of certain noteworthy figures:

- Lord Kelvin, president of the Royal Society, 1895
  "Heavier-than-air flying machines are impossible."
- Grover Cleveland, 22nd and 24th American President, 1905
  "Sensible women do not want to vote."
- Robert Milikan, physicist and Nobel prize winner, 1923
  "Man can never tap the power of the atom."

In its anniversary issue, *Business Month* asked a number of American business leaders what they felt the most significant challenge was facing American business.[2] These challenges, most likely, will translate into changes in the American way of doing things. The answers clustered around these points:

- being able to compete globally
- applying intellectual assets
- raising our productivity
- being responsible to the needs of shareholders and work force
- having a motivated, well-prepared work force
- coping with the regulatory environment
- using telecommunications to give consumers information
- balancing shareholders' expectations and public/government expectations
- protecting home markets

- encouraging long-term investment/focus
- balancing currency values
- satisfying customers
- learning to do business on an international level
- adjusting to the impact of other-country dominance on our standard of living
- creating better value, quality, service for our consumers
- taking pride in our products
- deficit-spending by Congress
- dealing with a litigious society
- continuing to restructure, in response to changes
- maintaining flexibility
- developing our capital base
- providing flexible financing
- determining market needs
- acting responsibly
- managing ideas
- investing in research and development, expansion, etc.
- making our facilities more efficient
- seeking commonalities among financial institutions
- financing our investments
- dealing with change
- lowering production costs

These are but a few of the issues with which today's managers are faced as they prepare themselves, their staffs, and their organizations for the challenges and inevitable—but manageable—chaos which a new decade, new century, and new millennium will force upon us. In the opinion of many, that chaos, as Tom Peters consistently advises, will enable us to thrive.

Changing Behavior

Nadler's organization is less concerned with preparing the incoming work force to deal with the changes a new environment will require of them, than with changing the behavior of large numbers of people already working inside a given organization. The Delta Consulting Group's work begins, as a rule, with a diagnosis of the realities of a company's culture. Whether an executive has specified the problem in advance, or whether Delta has been asked to define the problem, Nadler's group still focuses on behavioral change:

We are concerned with the bigger problem, which is how do you change the behavior? Once you have done that, you can then socialize people. Obviously, the big issue these days is that people can't read or do basic arithmetic and so its hard for them to contribute to improving Quality.

Yes, there are big issues there and other issues on how you socialize people. But I don't think that's the most problematic issue. Our concern is bringing about change in the people who are already part of the culture.

Nadler's group began working with the Xerox organization in 1979 to design a Quality process and to implement a strategy for employee involvement. Three years later, Xerox unveiled its "Leadership through Quality" program, one result of which was the award of the 1989 Malcolm Baldrige National Quality Award.

No matter who or what initiates the change, however, if employees regard it as unwanted or uncontrollable, their anxieties and fears will be unloosed and they will resist. Some of the manifestations of that resistance may be poor morale, increased absenteeism, small acts of sabotage, declining performance, and ultimately, perhaps, turnover.

One of the biggest mistakes management makes, as far as the introduction of change is concerned, is a failure to sufficiently prime employees for the change and its impact upon their lives. With extensive change, organizations have to commit extensive resources and must be prepared to invest heavily in change so that it can become an iterative expectation for employees. Nadler projects a five-to-seven year plan in order to fully integrate a specific change upon an organization's culture, especially the culture of large companies. As far as implementing Quality is concerned, Nadler reveals,

We tell companies, "If you are not going to do it right, it probably is not worth committing yourself to doing it publicly." Because it takes a lot of time and effort and it's not something that the top can delegate to the middle to do to the bottom. Quality is a major change, and a significant one. It's tough but we have evidence that it's doable for all kinds of companies."

The initial putty of employee thought can be sculpted into solidified commitment, but only if employees are given an opportunity to be informed and to give input into the ultimate result the changes will cause. Education is a vital part of the commitment process. One way to educate employees, to encourage them to attempt the change with an open mind, is to let them hear from counterparts who have not only survived the change, but who are thriving because of it. Peer feedback is often more convincing than management prognosticating.

Overcoming Resistance

To overcome resistance, management has to identify and then allay fears. Resistance to quality, or to any other cultural reformation, is predicated on a reluctance to give up the benefits of the known present for the dubious advantages of the unknown future. Managers can demonstrate what the end result of efforts will be. Since more people learn through the visual modality than through any other, employees can be literally shown (through photographs, films, or even the final product itself) what the changed behaviors can lead to.

Nadler is critical of companies that rush into change for the wrong reason or that go about change in the wrong ways. He censures "cosmetic" efforts. Instead, he encourages companies to pursue Quality improvement in a systematic fashion. Quality management is here to stay, he avows, and demands for quality will continue to grow. Companies that fail to recognize the inevitability of Quality changes will probably not be in existence as we enter the new millennium.

American consumers are becoming more vocal in their demands for quality, and are even willing to pay more to obtain it. If we are to win back our market share from foreign competitors, then, indeed, we must prove the worth of our products. The cost of poor quality (recalls, rejects, scrap, rework, warranty work, customer service, etc.) adds up. Doing it right the first time is far less expensive than having to do it a second time. To quote Philip Crosby, "You can get rich by preventing defects."

Nadler admits the difficulty in bringing about company-wide Quality changes:

We think quality involves a large-scale organizational change. It has both social and technical elements to it. It takes a fair amount of time and it is not the answer to everything. It's not a substitute for effective strategies, for the appropriate structure, for hiring the right people.

On the other hand, we believe that in many industries, it's becoming a core competitive issue and also an issue for survival. So, it's something that we urge managers to look at, to consider.

Meeting Customer Requirements

Crosby has defined quality as conformance to requirements and in a similar view, Delta Consulting defines quality as "meeting customer requirements." That customer, of course, may be internal (the person who receives the result of our work) or external (that person who purchases the product or service our organization creates). Knowing what the customer wants means being close to the customer. It means communicating and listening and responding and surveying and checking.

Not only must customer requirements be clearly specified, the overall mission of the company must also be made clear to each and every worker. Unfortunately, that kind of communication is all too rare. A recent *Wall Street Journal*[3] article explained how a failure to make goals explicit can actually lessen worker loyalty. Nearly 70 percent of 400 executives surveyed by Robert Kelley, a professor at Carnegie Mellon University, cited the lack of vision at their firms. The leaders of these executives were simply not making clear the direction in which the firm was headed. In a separate Hay Group survey of more than a million subjects, a mere 34 percent of the employees interviewed expressed satisfaction with the way their complaints were listened to and dealt with by their companies.

Feedback is the operative word, in both internal and external circumstances. We find Lee Iacocca using consumer response in his ads: "GM is bigger. Ford is richer. But neither of them beats Chrysler when it comes to satisfying the customer. Who says? You do. For three years in a row, Chrysler had the highest customer satisfaction of any American car company. Not GM. Not Ford. Chrysler."

Lesser known figures like Barry Fribush, president of Bubbling Bath Spa and Tub Works, Inc., one of *Inc.* magazine's 500 fastest-growing small private companies, regards listening to customers as a "competitive edge" for his company. His story[4] is validation of the Crosbian assertion that quality really is free—it's non-quality that is expensive.

Fribush begins with a quality product, refusing to stock or sell spas that are not known for their reliability. He also tests every spa before it is sold to a customer. After the sale, he uses installation materials of the highest quality, claiming that "if you try to scrimp, you end up having to spend more time supporting it."

Another requirement to which he insists on conforming is having a staff member available to deal with customer service calls. No matter when a problem arises, Fribush will have a service person at the customer's home within four hours. He has adjusted his crew schedule to meet customer's schedules. Few customers use their spas during the day. And so, Fribush keeps a minimal staff working during the day and then uses part-time help for the rush hours—the after-work hours when people are most likely to use their spas.

Such an arrangement, according to Fribush, benefits him as well: he has lower labor costs and his part-timers are highly qualified people who work during the day at technical jobs. Service crew members must own a spa if they wish to work for Fribush. This way, he maintains, they will fully understand what may malfunction. What truly sets Fribush apart, however, is his refusal to pay an employee who has not done a repair job right the first time. Prior to establishing this policy, Fribush was getting three customer complaints that the repair was done wrong for every ten repairs that were made. Since the do-it-right-the-first-time-or-don't-get-paid-policy was instituted, Fribush only has six callbacks a year. His insistence on listening to customers and conforming to their requirements pays off: Fribush's growth rate over the last five years is 844 percent.

From the Fribush story, we can extrapolate several elements that constitute customer service of the highest order, as depicted in Figure 1.

FIGURE 1

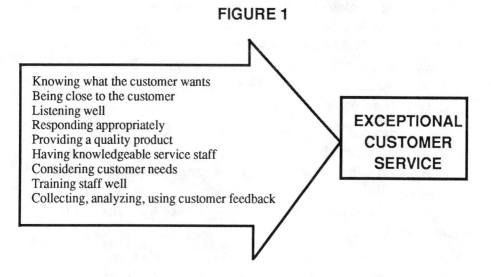

Knowing what the customer wants
Being close to the customer
Listening well
Responding appropriately
Providing a quality product
Having knowledgeable service staff
Considering customer needs
Training staff well
Collecting, analyzing, using customer feedback

EXCEPTIONAL CUSTOMER SERVICE

Measurement

Continuously trying to improve the process of servicing the customer demands constant consideration and measurement of methods designed to improve Quality. Like many other Quality advocates, the Delta Consulting Group places prevention over detection in working to produce a Quality product. Inspection assumes that errors will be made; prevention assumes they will not. Continuous improvement means continuous measurement so that we will have quantitative evidence to tell us if processes need to be maintained, altered, or replaced.

Feigenbaum defines total quality control, control needed for prevention, as

> An effective system for integrating the quality-development, quality-maintenance, and quality-improvement efforts of the various groups in an organization so as to enable production and service at the most economical levels which allow for full customer satisfaction.[5]

Nadler, too, recognizes the importance of the customer in the Quality equation:

> *The quality of output—that is, whether or not it meets customer requirements—is determined by the work processes. This is a central concept. There are two notions here: whether the process is capable of meeting customer requirements and whether it can do that consistently over time. This is what we call process control or the process being controlled.*
>
> *We get involved with training senior teams, helping them to get an understanding of the measurement concept. We teach them about control and variation and how to create control charts, how to determine whether a process is under control or not, process capacity, the seven statistical tools—all the standard Quality analytics.*

One of the seven statistical tools is a histogram or bar chart. It has two continuous variables, which are shown as contrasts. The variables will be depicted as increasing or decreasing. The mean or average of the distribution is shown on the histogram with the symbol "$\bar{x}$." Skewing in the distribution is sometimes caused by a few outstanding bars. These bars may cause inflation of the mean and so must be carefully considered: what may have caused the bars to be skewed?

In a normal distribution, the bars will represent the bell-shaped curve rather than a lopsided distribution with more than one peak. Again, attention must be paid to the range or dispersion of values. If there are isolated bars at the end, they must be studied to learn the cause of the variation.

Typically, a histogram will look like this.

FIGURE 2

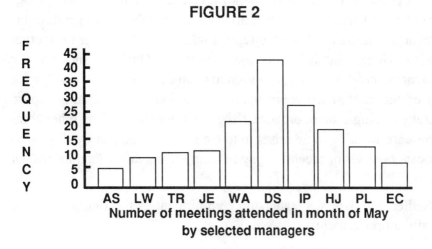

Number of meetings attended in month of May
by selected managers

Decisions about what is to be measured and how, how often and by whom, where and when, and what will be done with the data acquired, can be made by both management and employees. (In keeping with Dr. Deming's figures, Delta feels that in the company-wide establishment of a Quality culture, management's role requires 85 percent of the total activity and employees' roles constitute the remaining 15 percent.)

The data should be taken from several different sources: functional areas, costs, processes, vendors, etc. Ultimately, those data should be fed back to individuals in a position to make changes based on it. And, corporate leadership should use the data in formulating trends or changes so that the process is truly being continuously appraised and altered.

Strategic planning, as well as quotidian activities and steps for mission deployment, should also have quantitative information at its core. The data-collection process need not necessarily be long or expensive, and it need not necessarily deal only with "hard" statistics.

Leadership

What leadership does with the Quality data is critical. Messages will be sent, either directly or inadvertently, throughout the company as a result of how top executives manage the measured indices. At Motorola,[6] for example, Chairman Robert Galvin has altered the basic agenda of his meetings. Ordinarily, financial reports take precedence over most other reports. Under Galvin's direction, reports on Quality issues are not presented ahead of the financial reports. On occasion, Galvin will walk out of the conference room upon completion of the Quality report, thereby issuing a silent broadcast about his priorities. Many other companies are working to tie raises in to the improvements in Quality, or to allocate bonuses or incentive pay to team efforts rather than individual effort.

Nadler, too, stresses leadership commitment as the *sine qua non* of Quality improvement.

Leadership is critical because large-scale changes in organizational functioning involve values and culture as well as technical systems. We have seen no real examples of total Quality transitions where the leadership wasn't very heavily involved and committed in a very active way. Sometimes the leadership must counter opposing conceptions of how the company operates and what dictates success.

Leaders help their companies make that transition to Total Quality by making personal statements, often using the company newsletter as a forum for their views. They involve themselves with goal-setting and planning and revisions of mission statements. They keep abreast of progress others are making toward quality goals and provide opportunities for themselves and others to either receive or provide training on Quality concepts.

Additionally, leaders make visible and audible the extent of their commitment to Quality. There is continuous communication about the company's values and manifestations of the leader's allegiance to those values. Programs are in place to ensure continued dialogue about quality values, and leaders will often go beyond the company to write a news-paper column or journal article about their firm's aims. Too, leaders will speak before groups that have a direct, or even a peripheral, interest in the topic.

IBM, which evinced Quality concepts long before it was considered necessary to do so, had the motto, "THINK," emblazoned on posters and publications throughout the company. When banners are put up with a great flurry, Dr. Deming tells us, and then forgotten three weeks later, they have no importance whatsoever (except possibly confusion) for the work force. But when a given phrase becomes synonymous with the corporate way of doing things, we do not have an exhortation but rather a deeply ingrained behavioral pattern in the corporeal entity. Such was the case with founder Thomas Watson's favorite phrase. "THINK," in a precursorial way, captures the spirit of the Quality movement: finding ways to continuously analyze and improve the process, using both the head and the hands of the employees.

Continuous Process Improvement

The process must be viewed as a journey, not as a destination. Con-tinual calibration dictates the way employees work with the process. In this never-ending effort to make what we do the best we can do, we must know the process so well that we can explain it without hesitation to others. The process should also be clearly defined and documented so that someone new to the department could refer to that delineation of steps in the process and be able to follow them correctly. Ideally, the documentation will require ongoing revisions as evaluations are carefully and deliberatively made, and as adjustments—simplifications even—are instituted.

Lew Chatham of General Dynamics in Pomona, California; Victor Peters of the Naval Supply Center in Pearl Harbor, Hawaii; Jim Beirne of the Wharton School in Philadelphia; and Loginn Kapitan at the Uni-versity of Southern California in Los Angeles, (participants in Dr. Deming's *Quality, Productivity, and Competitive Position* seminar), worked with Dr. John Whitney of Columbia University to issue the following statement concerning the psychology of change.

A Theory of Change encompasses various workstyles and attitudes toward change. Both the long-term and short-term impacts of the change must be considered, as well as the purpose and rationale behind the change. The mechanics of the change, the implementation strategy, must be attended to, and the following questions must be addressed.

- How can change be measured?
- How can we control change?
- Where are we not?
- Where are we departing from?
- Where are we going to go?
- What is our aim?
- What is the scope/magnitude of the desired change?
- What will make people want to change?
- Who should initiate change?
- What will successful change look like?
- What do we currently do well?
- What do we currently do poorly?*

Calibrations of the Process

These questions can be applied to both major changes of a process and mere calibrations to that process. Since the calibrations do not usually involve a major overhaul, employees do not experience undue stress. The simplification of the process may be as minor as determining if a given report or form or regularly scheduled meeting truly is necessary, and deciding—if it is not—to eliminate it. The value-added question often helps employees or teams make their assessment more readily. At several points during the day or during the process, employees should ask

*Used by permission of authors.

themselves, "If the customer could see what I was doing right now, would he be willing to pay for it?"

If the answer is yes, the employee is no doubt adding value to the process. And if the answer is no, it probably means that that particular step in the process could be simplified or perhaps even omitted. By continually assessing and then being able to justify each microcosmic step of the final macrocosmic product or service, individuals can make significant contributions to their organizations and ultimately to their customers. And, the simplicity of this question ensures that anyone in the organization, from entry-level to executive level, can assess the work done and enhance the way it is done.

Quality Receptive Environments

Such willingness to contribute will come about only if the working environment is one that is truly conducive to Quality implementation. The commitment must go beyond lip service. Nadler refers to the anti-thesis of such an environment in Figure 3 on the following page.

The chart was part of

an article by Jeffry Heilpern, who is managing director in our firm. He wrote an article that talks about the elements of the culture of an organization and the operating style. Some views may be deeply held but the environment may actually be hostile to Quality.

I gave a talk on this at the National Quality Forum last October. We have identified a number of key assumptions that we see present in organizations, such as, "We know better than our customers do about what they want." We think those assumptions could be significant blockages to what we view as Quality.

The Quality-receptive environment, then, would require the uppermost echelons of power and authority within the organizations to do more than establish the parameters of the new ambience in which Quality is expected to flourish. Management cannot merely define the new environment; it must live in the new environment. Rather than merely telling

FIGURE 3
Quality Hostile Assumptions

Cluster	Illustrative Assumptions
Corporate Purpose	• Our primary and overriding purpose is to make money—to produce near-term shareholder return. • Our key audience is the financial markets, and in particular the analysts.
Customers	• We're smarter than our customers—we know what they really need. • Quality is not a major factor in customer decisions—they can't tell the difference.
Performance	• The way to influence corporate performance is portfolio management and creative accounting. • It costs more to provide a quality product or service—and we won't recover the added cost. • Strategic success comes from large, one-time innovative leaps, rather than from continuous improvement. • We will never be able to manufacture competitively at the low end.
People	• Managers are paid to make decisions—workers are paid to do, not to think. • The job of senior management is strategy, not operations or implementation. • The key disciplines from which to draw senior management are finance or marketing.
Problem Solving and Improvement	• To err is human—perfection is an unattainable and unrealistic goal. • Quality improvement can be delegated—it is something the top can tell the middle to do to the bottom. • Celebrate success and shun failure; there is not much to learn by dwelling on our mistakes. • If it ain't broke, don't fix it.

Used by permission of Dr. David Nadler, Delta Consulting Group, Inc.

"how," management must become the "what." Management must become both the techniques and the technology, the content and the context. In short, those who establish strategic policy must not only determine the medium through which the message will be delivered, they must become the message itself.

Management does this by making known its commitment to the quality process, by stressing the obligation of each employee to strive toward error-free work, to supply the necessary tools or resources that will enable employees to indeed work without error.

What else should management do to create an environment that is Quality-receptive? Ensure that everyone is trained on Quality principles so that everyone can be totally involved. "Universal participation" is only a phrase unless everyone speaks a common language and performs with a common purpose in mindsetting ever higher standards because clarity of, and constancy to, purpose have been made manifest.

Rewards must be tied in to the execution of Quality. Those who challenge the way things are done should be acknowledged and not penalized. The small successes must be discovered and applauded, for they will ultimately lead to the grand successes. When Quality is the dominant theme in a company, it is considered first among equals. Cost, schedule, and volume—the traditional emphases of Quality Assurance departments—are still important, of course, as are profit, productivity, innovation, and becoming or remaining competitive. But quality becomes as familiar a concept as the nature of the company's business.

In a culture driven by Quality, prevention of errors is the goal, rather than detection of errors, which has long been the thrust. Quality must move from Control and Assurance departments and so become the responsibility of every person in the Quality organization. While failure is certainly not encouraged, in a Quality environment, it is permitted, for it reflects an individual's or a group's willingness to move from a static situation to one in which things are happening.

A Quality-fostering setting can be characterized by the "Four C's," depicted in Figure 4. With iterative attention to these factors, a drive

FIGURE 4

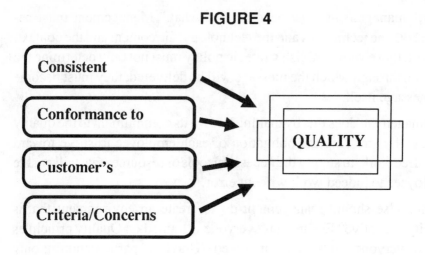

toward excellence should be unleashed and a measurable increase in both customer satisfaction and rising sales should be realized.

Nadler describes Delta's efforts to bring about what they call a Quality-friendly organization:

We work with companies to develop their plans. It isn't ever a question of their program colliding with ours. We are usually involved with working together to build what it is that they will be doing. Xerox is clearly a case where we worked with them on the design of their training, the follow-up training, the workshops, and things of that nature.

If you talk with David Kearns (former CEO of the Xerox Corporation), you realize that from the point at which he decided to make the major implementation policy strategy in October 1982, there was close to a year, through September 1983, that was just focused on getting the senior management involved in testing where they were, educating them, creating awareness, and helping them to build a long-term strategy for Xerox.

Minimizing Errors

One of the dangers of implementing a Quality plan is that too much may be expected by some contingents too soon. All changes require learning-curve time and when employees are allowed to incorporate the new knowledge of change into their own pace (ideally, at a slightly-faster-than-comfortable pace), the transition from what used to be to what should be will occur more easily. The results will be more deeply ingrained.

One way to lessen the expense of errors associated with the innovation might be to appoint an unofficial Quality leader for each small unit of the organization. (The appointment might be rotated periodically.) The leader's purpose should be to provide intensive and extensive follow-up to the quality training that has been given. Individuals in a classroom setting may feel foolish asking questions in a public setting. But having a leader with whom they might talk privately about their concerns, questions, or ideas should help Quality to be so tightly woven into the company's fabric that it becomes indistinguishable from the other threads that constitute the organization's mantle.

Quality environments take time to develop and the process of refining them never stops. Periodically, technology, training programs, supplier relations, strategic plans, benchmarking data, economic factors, etc. must be reviewed and recalibrated. With the nearly incredible pace of change in today's global economy, various forces need to be assessed frequently to determine their impact upon Quality efforts.

The changes being introduced must be handled in progressive stages, as Nadler illustrates:

> We tend to think of Quality on three levels. We define Quality as creating an offering. That offering could be a product or a service. It could be any number of things the customer chooses to purchase. But the offering, in the final analysis, must meet or exceed customer requirements.
>
> The second concept is Quality Management, which is designing and developing, creating, building, maintaining work processes

that can consistently produce a Quality offering. Statistical Quality Control comes into this phase.

The third term is Total Quality Management, which is developing an organizational architecture, a structure. Processes, people, strategies are all involved. This structure will essentially lead to the promoting and maintaining of processes to develop, design, build, see or service high-Quality offerings.

So it is those three phases—Quality, Quality Management, and Total Quality Management that are the things we talk about in terms of defining Quality.

Summary

Delta Consulting Group, Inc. manages change within corporations. They recognize the opportunities inherent in the change process, but also recognize the problems that can arise when change is introduced without sufficient planning. Whether the force behind the change is external or internal, the change process must be explained to those who will be affected by it. It is incumbent upon the leader to minimize the negative aspects of the change and to maximize the positive aspects. The leader is not only a catalyst for change but an agent of that change as well.

Attention to Lewin's model for change—unlocking old attitudes, introducing the change, setting new attitudes in place—will facilitate the process. But deploying the model requires planning and a long-range vision. It means anticipating change by looking at current trends and forecasting the likely eventualities they portend.

Delta encourages the involvement of employees in change, insisting that change should not be cosmetic but rather intensive and extensive. It must be company-wide and must address the various facets of the corporate essence. Quality-induced change will yield positive results but cannot mend every serious lesion in the corporate entity. Quality cannot make poor hiring practices disappear, for example, nor can it necessarily replace antiquated structures or systemically poor practices.

Quality moves can restore corporate wellness, however, if communication is open on all levels of the organization. Barry Fribush is cited as an example of a small business owner who regards listening to the customer as his competitive advantage. He implements what he has learned and takes care to prevent defects rather than correct them after they have been detected.

In a manufacturing environment, especially, it is important to have a basic understanding of process control and of variation. Delta uses standard Quality analytics to learn if a given process is meeting customer requirements and meeting them consistently. Leaders in all environments take data from multiple sources and use them to improve the processes in which their organizations are engaged. One consideration that is useful in providing a surface analysis is the question, "If the customer could see what I was doing right now, would he be willing to pay for it?"

Delta examines a number of assumptions that create hostility in environments. They encourage management to transform hostility into receptivity by making quality first among a number of important equals, by making quality everyone's responsibility. The Four C's: Consistent Conformance to Customer's Criteria/Concerns, is an easy mnemonic to use in fostering a Quality setting. In that setting should be an unofficial Quality leader who can extend the Quality training that has been provided.

For Further Consideration

1. What do you think is the most significant challenge facing American business?

2. How do we as a nation become more globally competitive?

3. How do you know that the purpose in/of your organization has constancy?

4. Define your company's culture.

5. What is the possibility of your company being awarded the Baldrige Quality Award within the next five years?

6. How does your company deal with complaints?

7. What data-collection process(es) is your team or department involved with?

8. What messages is the leadership of your organization sending?

9. If you could have a one-word motto (other than "Think") for your company, what would it be?

10. What questions do you ask before undertaking the change process?

11. Is your culture Quality-receptive or Quality-hostile? Explain via specific examples.

12. What is your company's long-term strategy?

References

[1] Lewin, Kurt. "Group Decision and Social Change," in G.E. Swanson *et al.* (eds.), *Readings in Social Psychology* (New York: Holt, Rinehart, 1952), pp. 459–473.

[2] "View from the Top: What is the Most Significant Challenge American Business Faces?" *Business Month,* Vol. 132, No. 1 (July–August, 1988), pp. 66–70.

[3] "Labor Letter," *Wall Street Journal* (January 30, 1990), p. 1.

[4] Brown, Paul B. "For You, Our Valued Customer," *Inc.* magazine, Vol. 12, No. 1, pp. 108–109. Reprinted with permission, *Inc.* magazine (January 1990). Copyright © 1990 by Goldhirsh Group, Inc., 38 Commercial Wharf, Boston, MA 02110.

[5] Feigenbaum, A.V. *Total Quality Control* (New York: McGraw-Hill Book Company, 1961), p. 1. Reproduced with permission of McGraw-Hill, Inc.

[6] "Message From on High," *Total Quality Newsletter,* Vol. 1, No. 2 (May, 1990), p. 8. Reprinted with permission from Lakewood Publications, 50 South Ninth St., Minneapolis, MN 55402. All rights reserved.

[7] Chathman, Lew, *et al.*, "Report to the Working Group on the Psychology of Change." Paper presented at Dr. Deming's *Quality, Productivity, and Competitive Position Seminar*, Newport Beach, California, July 23–27, 1990. Used by permission of authors.

Index

About the Author

Dr. Marlene Caroselli is a nationally recognized author and consult-ant in communication and leadership growth. In 1984, she founded the Center for Professional Development, an organization dedicated to helping professionals enhance their communication skills. She has served as a consultant to many Fortune 500 companies and educational institutions. Among her clients are the Xerox Corporation, Mobil Chemical, Magnavox, Allied Signal, the New York State Education Department, and the United States Office of Personnel Management.

Dr. Caroselli has previously published seven books, entitled *PowerWriting, Communicate with Quality, The New Manager, Hiring and Firing, Think on Your Feet, Meetings that Work,* and *The Language of Leadership.* Lee Iacocca had this to say regarding his contribution to *The Language of Leadership*: "I have to confess that I've never stopped to analyze my speaking style as methodically as Dr. Caroselli has. I'm glad that it seems to stand up to such highly professional scrutiny."

Dr. Caroselli maintains a lifelong interest in enhancing the quality of worklife in the areas of communication, management, and corporate creativity. She is listed in *Who's Who in America, International Leaders* and *Who's Who of American Women.*

Other Titles From HRD Press

◆ **The Language of Leadership** *by Dr. Marlene Caroselli*
   274 pages (Hardcover)   ***$24.95***

The Language of Leadership offers a comprehensive analysis of the leadership language of ten successful American leaders – Lee Iacocca, Governor Mario Cuomo, Ronald Reagan, Tom Peters, Judith Bardwick, Peter Drucker, Judy Columbus, Barbara Henry, Pat Russell, and Kitty Carlisle Hart, individuals who have made an impact in business, politics, psychology, journalism, and entertainment.

The Language of Leadership is unlike other leadership titles in that it uses direct examples from the language of influential leaders. The speaking and writing styles of leading communicators are carefully critiqued and analyzed to help the reader strengthen and improve communication skills. References to historically famous speeches are highlighted as reinforcement to help the reader better understand the elements of leadership language.

In a carefully formatted, easy-to-follow style, each chapter guides the reader through exercises and an organized analysis, with diagrams and checklists for practical help in bringing the elements of leadership language into his or her own speaking and writing styles.

What People Are Saying...

"I have to confess that I've never stopped to analyze my speaking style as methodically as Dr. Caroselli has. I'm glad that it seems to stand up to such highly professional scrutiny."   ***Lee Iacocca***
                                        Chairman, Chrysler Corporation
"...Dr. Marlene Caroselli has whittled down voluminous and varying advice into savory morsels of wisdom. Her analysis of words and presentation styles help break down the mysticism surrounding leaders and the secrets of becoming one."   ***Training & Development Journal***
                                        published by The American Society
                                        for Training and Development

HRD Press offers a 30-day exam on all our books. To help you address your training needs, we offer special quantity discounts. For ordering or to request a free HRD Press catalog, call 1-800-822-2801 (outside the U.S. call (413) 253-3488). Our FAX number is (413) 253-3490, or write to us at 22 Amherst Road, Amherst, MA 01002.

Other Titles From HRD Press

◆ **Learning From Conflict** *by Lois B. Hart*
200 pages (3-Ring Binder) $49.95

Learning From Conflict A Handbook For Trainer's and Group Leaders is a highly effective book that offers ready to use, fully reproducible activities for in-house training on recognizing and resolving the major causes of conflict in the workplace. Participants will reduce their stress level and increase their productivity.

◆ **Talk It Out! 4 Steps to Managing People Problems in Your Organization** *by Dr. Daniel Dana*
246 pages (Paperback) $13.95

Talk It Out! offers refreshing solutions for resolving employee communication problems. Poor interpersonal communication in the workplace is a leading cause of poor morale, low motivation, and high job stress. Conflict and ineffective discussion between workers and managers is a major contributor to low productivity in workgroups and throughout organizations.

Daniel Dana's book, **Talk It Out! 4 Steps to Managing People Problems in Your Organization,** introduces a highly effective, easy technique for improving person to person communication in your firm. His easily learned 4-step approach helps us to understand and resolve conflicts before they become unproductive stress-producing crises.

The ideal of a conflict-free workplace becomes a distinct possibility after reading **Talk It Out!**

HRD Press offers a 30-day exam on all our books. To help you address your training needs, we offer special quantity discounts. For ordering or to request a free HRD Press catalog, call 1-800-822-2801 (outside the U.S. call (413) 253-3488). Our FAX number is (413) 253-3490, or write to us at 22 Amherst Road, Amherst, MA 01002.

Other Titles From HRD Press

◆ **Is Coffee Break the Best Part of Your Day?** *by Dick Leatherman*
   252 pages (Hardcover)   *$24.95*   *(Paperback)*   *$12.95*

Is Coffee Break the Best Part of Your Day? is a very special "how-to" manual for employees in any type of organization,. The book provides practical, tested suggestions and techniques for the employee who wishes to become more productive. It is written in simple, clear language, and is illustrated with many real-life examples.

This book is specifically designed (1) to encourage the employee to take responsibility for his or her job performance, and (2) to provide clearly stated practical suggestions for improving performance in thirteen critical areas, including: attitude assessment, receiving work assignments, benefiting from criticism, working effectively with others, improving communication, problem solving, decision making, the importance of planning, managing time, taking charge of one's performance appraisal, career development, accepting change, and managing one's boss.

◆ **The Workplace Literacy Primer**
   by Dr. William J. Rothwell and Dr. Dale C. Brandenburg
   444 pages (Hardcover)   *$49.95*

The Workplace Literacy Primer is a carefully constructed manual that gives straightforward and practical advice on how to tackle employees' basic skills problems. The authors describe how to identify the "basic skills" expected of employees, analyze employee performance problems, determine their cause(s), and identify the appropriate performance improvement strategies for addressing them.

Business professionals and educators alike will find **The Workplace Literacy Primer** a useful and readable book with the necessary materials for establishing, operating, and evaluating an in-house basic skills training program. The material includes activities, worksheets, and a comprehensive directory of workplace literacy resources.

HRD Press offers a 30-day exam on all our books. To help you address your training needs, we offer special quantity discounts. For ordering or to request a free HRD Press catalog, call 1-800-822-2801 (outside the U.S. call (413) 253-3488). Our FAX number is (413) 253-3490, or write to us at 22 Amherst Road, Amherst, MA 01002.